IMAGES
of America

ATASCADERO

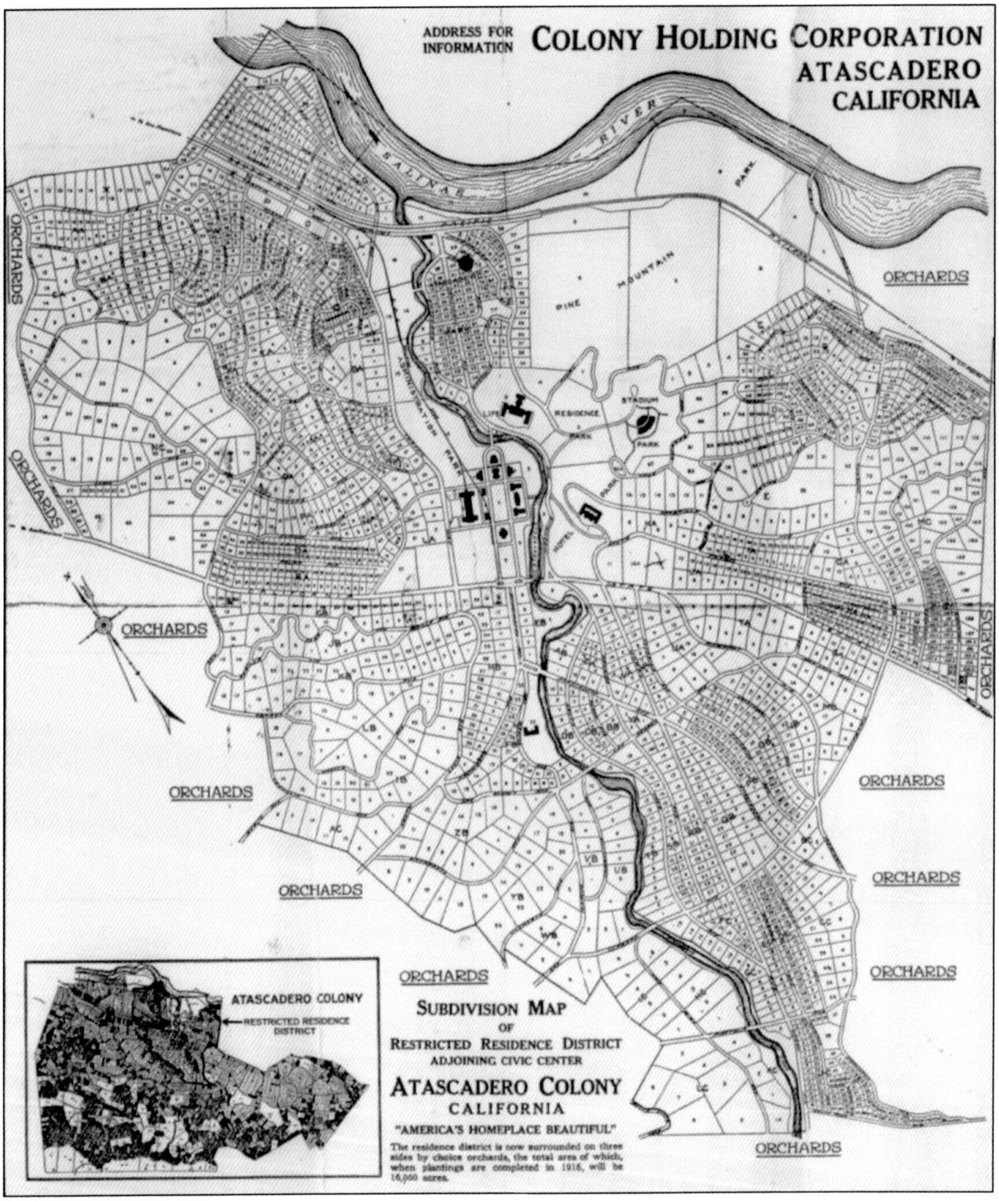

This is a subdivision map of the restricted residence district adjoining Atascadero Civic Center of Atascadero Colony, California—"America's Homeplace Beautiful." "The residence district is now surrounded on three sides by choice orchards, the total area of which, when plantings are completed in 1916, will be 16,000 acres." (Courtesy of Atascadero Historical Society.)

On the Cover: Welcome home! Tent City residents greet newcomers to the colony of Atascadero. (Courtesy of Kent Kenney Archives.)

IMAGES
of America

ATASCADERO

S.W. Martin

ARCADIA
PUBLISHING

ISBN 978-0-7385-8916-9

Published by Arcadia Publishing
Charleston, South Carolina

Printed in the United States of America

Library of Congress Control Number: 2011933261

For all general information, please contact Arcadia Publishing:
Telephone 843-853-2070
Fax 843-853-0044
E-mail sales@arcadiapublishing.com
For customer service and orders:
Toll-Free 1-888-313-2665

Visit us on the Internet at www.arcadiapublishing.com

To the family of E.G. Lewis, the city of Atascadero where I grew up, and to all who recognize and appreciate its unique genesis and history

Contents

ACKNOWLEDGMENTS

It is with a deep sense of gratitude that I acknowledge all of the people who have supported the effort to make this book a reality by encouraging me and providing source material, photographs, anecdotes, and other resources. Kent Kenney Archives, the Atascadero Historical Society, and Lon Allan provided the early historical photographs for this book. Joyce Rabellino graciously shared her collection of photographs of the Atascadero Speedway. Other miscellaneous photographic contributors are noted in the book. Source materials included *E.G. Lewis—Fraud or Friend* by E.G. Lewis (Wilkins Creative Printing, 1967); *The Birth of Atascadero* by Marguerite A. Travis (Wilkins, 2006); *The Siege of University City* by Sidney Morse (University City Publishing Company, 1912); and *Atascadero: The Vision of One, the Work of Many* (The Miracle Book Company, 2008) and *Atascadero's Historic Business District* (self-published, 2010) by L.W. Allan. L.W. Allan also contributed to this work by reviewing it for accuracy. Finally, I would like to thank my wife, Jennifer, who says she was first drawn to me because I wanted to be a writer.

INTRODUCTION

It was supposed to have been utopia. Atascadero, California—located almost exactly halfway between Los Angeles and San Francisco—is the brainchild of a man thought by some to have been a visionary and a con artist by others, but what con artist has left in his wake a collection of unique architecture in a city that is the first planned community in the state of California? What con artist establishes roads, water mains, power grids, agricultural cooperatives, even a 17-mile road to the Pacific Ocean? What con artist builds the nation's first enclosed shopping mall?

Atascadero, California, founded by mega-entrepreneur E.G. Lewis in 1913, attracted hundreds of colonists to a "Tent City" where they resided while reviewing the real estate and plans for the city. They came, they saw, and they staked their futures on Lewis's dreams, schemes, and plans. Those plans included the concept of providing a rural lifestyle with the amenities of an urban center, incorporating art, agriculture, and commerce into the canvas of the community. Lewis wrote of his vision in one of his many bulletins:

> In publishing this Bulletin, or Digest of the Atascadero Estates and Plan, the originator and those who have been and are helping to carry it to completion, are as proud of the MENTAL concept that gives it life and momentum, and continues to inspire it as the project progresses, as they are the tangible and PHYSICAL work that has already been accomplished. The BIG IDEA and central thought back of the Plan is the combining of an effective, businesslike, scientific, coordinated production, conservation and direct-to-the-consumer marketing of the products of the soil, with the business of providing the highest beauty and desirability of a place in which to live a complete and well-rounded life. Recognizing that the highest state of organized society is predicated upon individual freedom and voluntary co-operation, the Atascadero Plan is not based upon any common religious or political conviction, but leaves questions wholly to the individual initiative.

E.G. Lewis also founded University City, Missouri, and Palos Verdes, California. His vision knew no bounds and, for a time, it seemed he was destined to become another William Randolph Hearst. Indeed, he had accumulated a far greater fortune than Hearst's long before that name became a national household word.

E.G. Lewis established publications geared toward rural women. He was perceived by authorities to be preparing women for a major role in national politics, even before women won the right to vote. Many credit this endeavor for Lewis's downfall. In conflict with the US Postal Service, he exhausted his fortune successfully defending his name. He tried to start again but ultimately died in Atascadero in 1950, a broken man.

Today, Lewis's dream lives on in the city of Atascadero. It is one of the largest cities in San Luis Obispo County. Although bisected by Highway 101 in the 1950s, the community has retained traces of the Lewis dream. The stately civic center/administration building still stands behind a large, green, sunken garden in the center of town, with the ornate fountain still flowing. Many other historical structures stand also: the great brick building that housed Lewis's printing presses, the buildings that housed his fruit and vegetable drying plant, portions of the first high school, several commercial buildings, and many of the first homes built in the colony. Through narrative and photographs, this book provides a sampling of the history, triumphs, and challenges experienced in the colony of Atascadero.

Unfortunately, many of the historical structures no longer exist. The great Mercantile (or La Plaza), which was home to the first indoor shopping center, has burned down, as have various other structures in the historic downtown. E.G. Lewis's home, the colony's "Headquarters House," was destroyed in the early 1960s to make way for a supermarket.

Still, other historic structures have been shifted or rebuilt. The original pavilion building at Atascadero Lake has been replaced with a modern meeting/wedding center. The stately Carlton Hotel in the center of the historic downtown Colony District has been carefully rebuilt to resemble the original building.

The entrepreneurial spirit lives on in Atascadero. City officials encourage economic development and tourism promotion. The community presents impressive special events and festivals, an accredited zoo, the county's inspiring Veterans Memorial Complex, a high quality of life, and its rich heritage and unique genesis as enticements to visitors from all over the country.

Atascadero, California—it was supposed to have been utopia. Perhaps such a place cannot exist in reality, but it did in the mind and spirit of E.G. Lewis. Today, amidst all the hustle and bustle of the 21st century, his vision of a rural community offering urban amenities persists. The visionaries of this new era still borrow from his energies and leadership as they carry the city of Atascadero into the future.

One

E.G. Lewis

Edward Gardner Lewis's entrepreneurial interests were unique and colorful. He marketed a product called Anti-Tobac, an alleged remedy for the negative effects of smoking. The business was successful briefly but eventually failed, leaving Lewis broke. Undeterred, he developed new products, including Anti-Skeet mosquito repellent, Bug Chalk cockroach deterrent, and Anti-Fly to disperse flies. Other products included a cold remedy, foot powder, and a toothache medicine.

According to L.W. Allan in *Atascadero: The Vision of One, the Work of Many*, Lewis acquired *The Winner* magazine in 1901 in St. Louis, Missouri, and renamed it the *Woman's Magazine*. Between 1906 and 1907, he started the *Woman's National Weekly*, which quickly achieved a circulation of 1.6 million. Lewis intuited that magazine subscriptions were purchased primarily by women, not men. One of his motivations for forming the American Woman's League was to create a sales force of women to market magazine subscriptions. The members of the Woman's League sold subscriptions, and about half of the money was returned to the league to be spent as it saw fit. In 1904, he created a bank-by-mail operation, which he believed to be the first such banking business of its kind. After founding University City, Missouri, he served as mayor for more than seven years.

Caught up in a controversy over postal rates, Lewis was accused of fraud by postmaster general George B. Cortelyou. Some claim the postal service was concerned about his progress in the development of his bank-by-mail operation. Some claim the fraud charge was a smoke screen to cloak concerns of the male-dominated political machines of the time that Lewis was preparing a huge block of women voters in anticipation of passage of the 19th Amendment, which would grant women the right to vote. The American Women's League later became the Woman's Republic. The Woman's Republic generated organizations that paralleled state and national government.

Lewis prevailed, and his rights were reinstated, but by that time, the damage was done. US Congress censured postal authorities for their war on E.G. Lewis, going so far as to suggest he be given $1.5 million in restitution. Lewis did not pursue restitution.

Lewis then borrowed $2,000, set his eyes westward, and announced he was going to California to found a new utopia. Thousands followed him to a place called Atascadero.

Later in life, Lewis would again be hounded in court by postal authorities for what he described as "largely technical charges" and eventually would serve time in prison. While in prison, Lewis befriended the warden, teaching him to paint. He designed a sewer system for the prison and published a prison newspaper. After his release, he returned to Atascadero, where he died in 1950 at the age of 81.

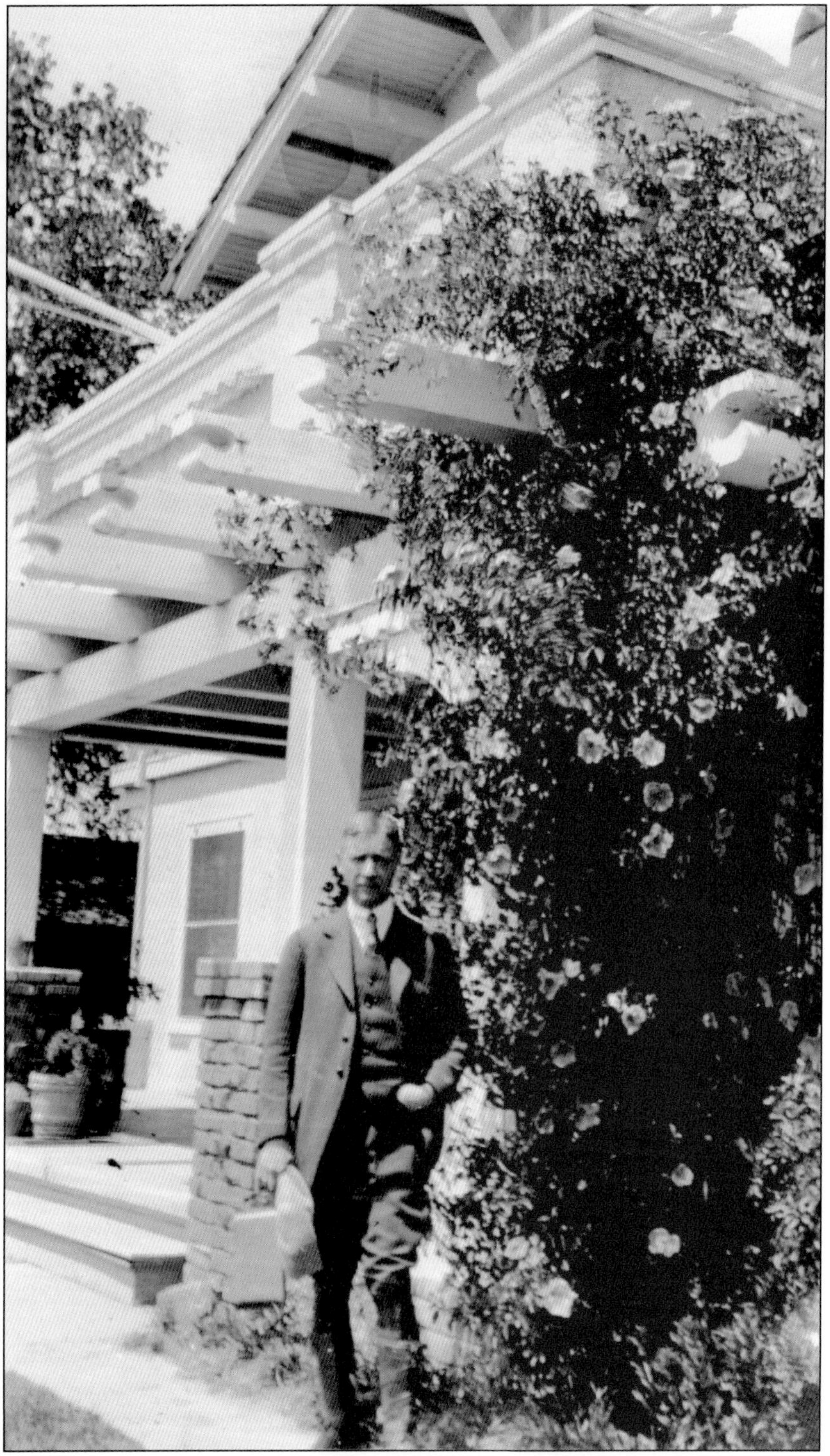

Atascadero founder E.G. Lewis is pictured outside his home, Headquarters House. The house was the only structure purchased as part of the land that would later become the city of Atascadero. (Courtesy of Kent Kenney Archives.)

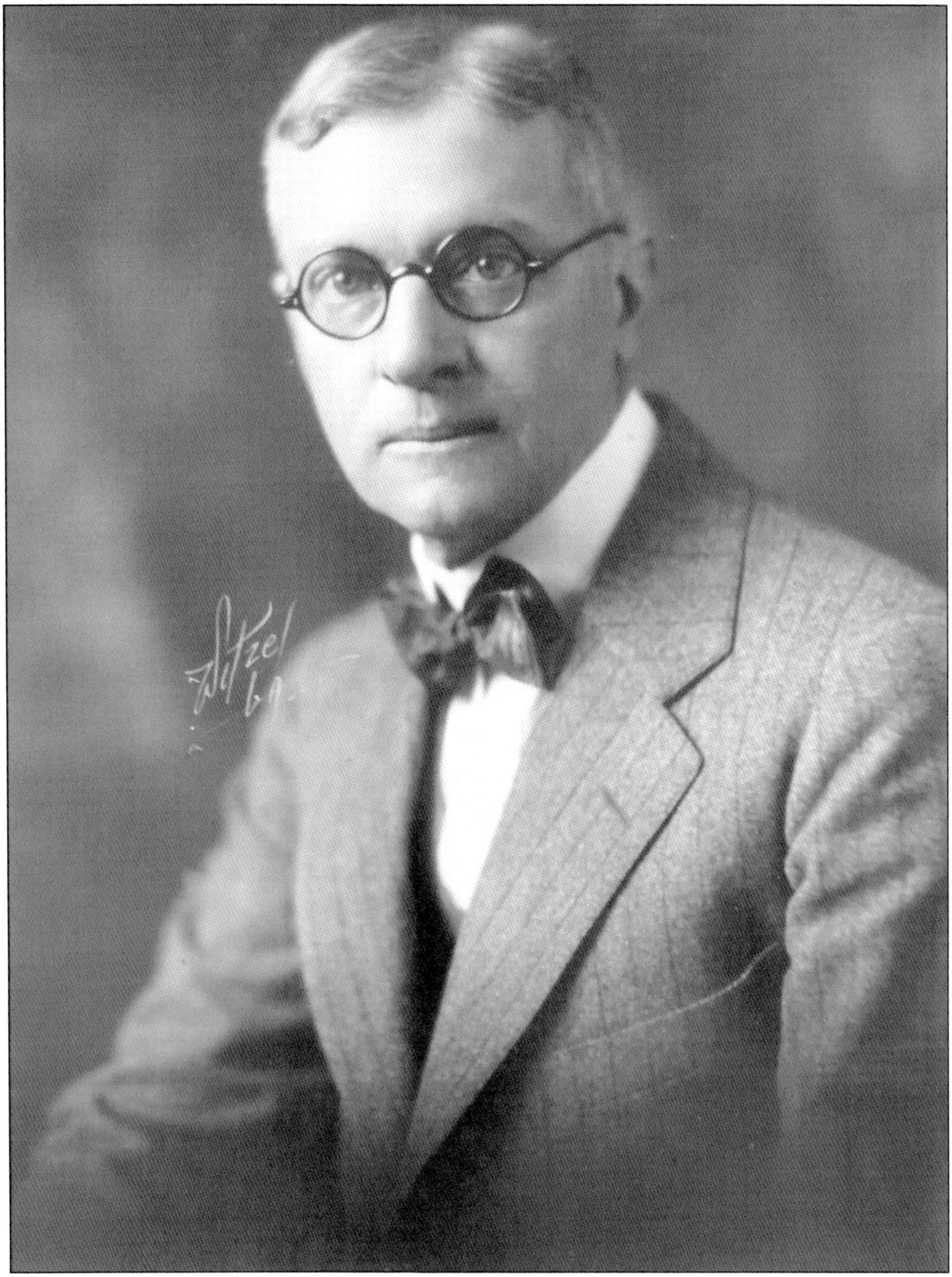

Pictured is E.G. Lewis, founder of University City, Missouri; Atascadero, California; and Palos Verdes, California. (Courtesy of Kent Kenney Archives.)

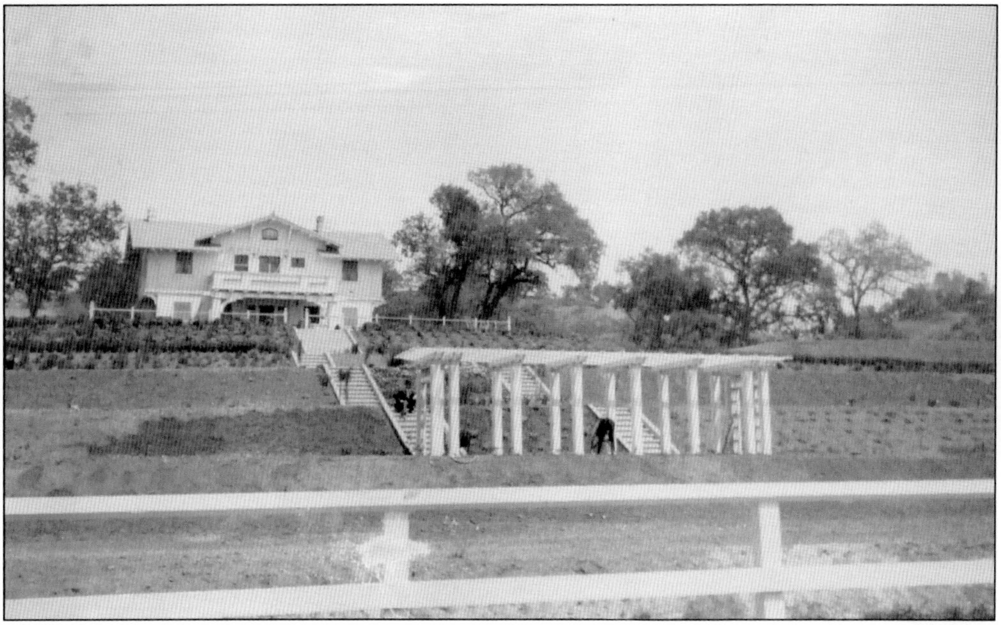

Headquarters House was the one structure purchased as part of Atascadero Rancho, which was 23,000 acres of land destined to become the home for Atascadero. The house was used previously by the property's prior owner, J.H. Henry. (Courtesy of Kent Kenney Archives.)

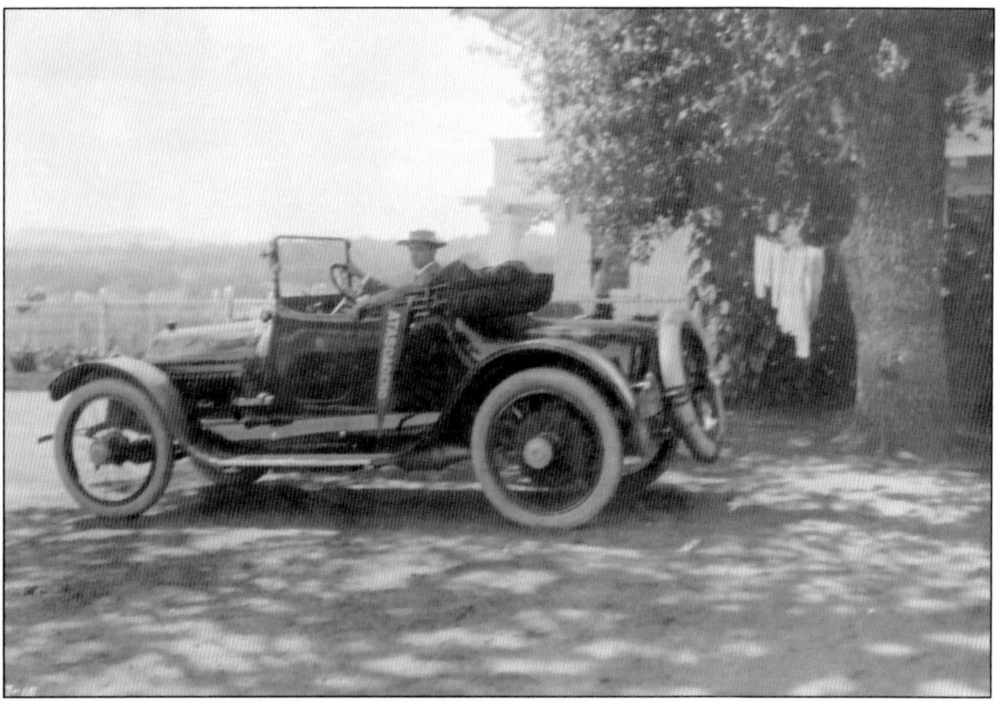

The irrepressible E.G. Lewis is pictured in a car adorned with an Atascadero pendant. The automobile could be emblematic of the city since it was designed to accommodate cars. (Courtesy of Kent Kenney Archives.)

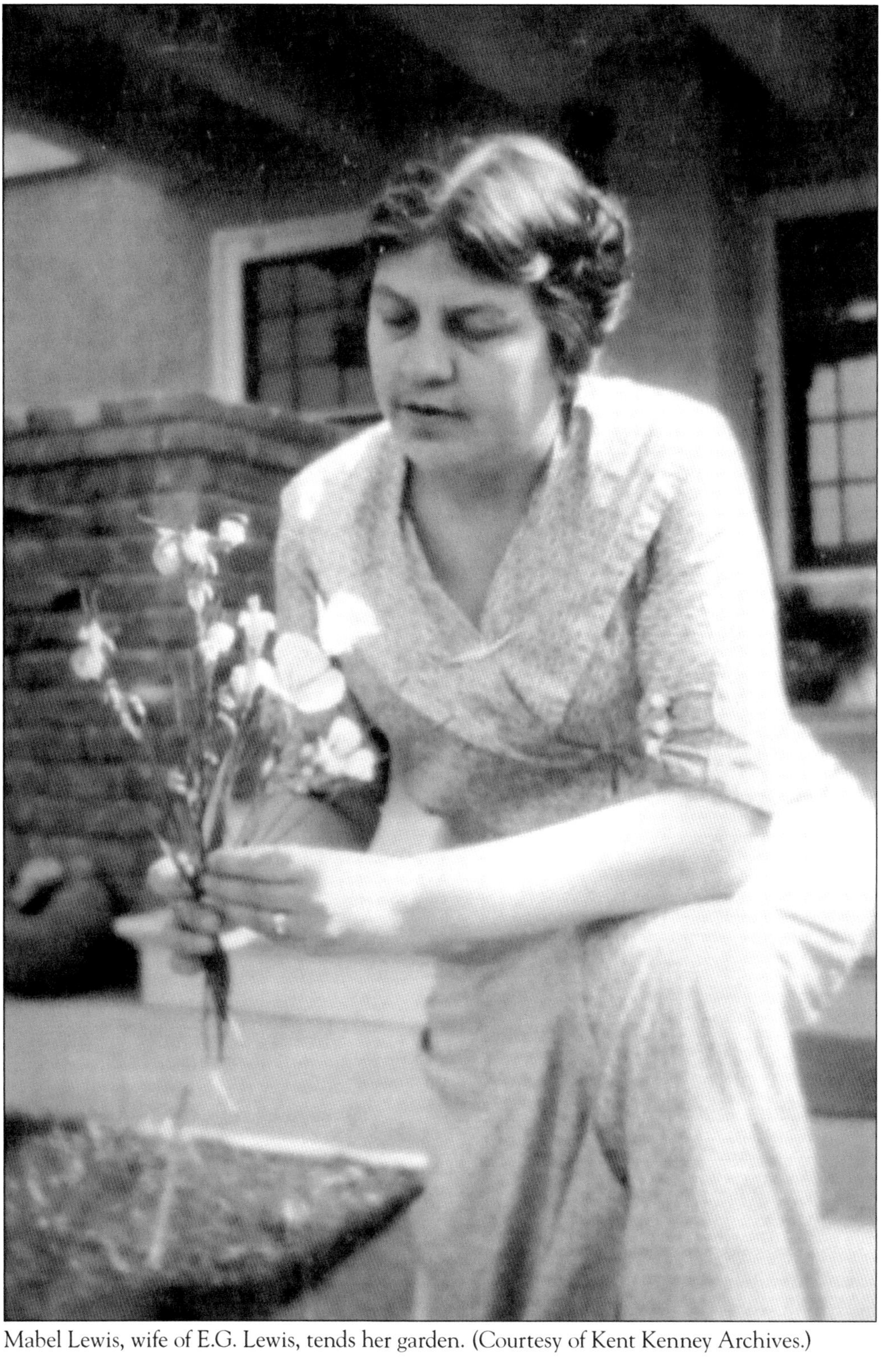

Mabel Lewis, wife of E.G. Lewis, tends her garden. (Courtesy of Kent Kenney Archives.)

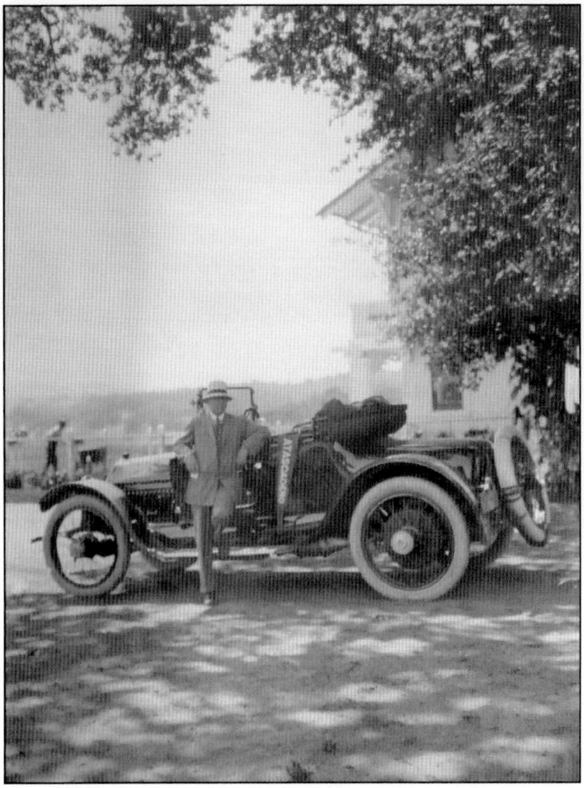

Here is another view of Lewis in his favored mode of travel. (Courtesy of Kent Kenney Archives.)

Another view of Headquarters House is shown. The structure was burned down in the early 1960s to make way for a supermarket. (Courtesy of Atascadero Historical Society.)

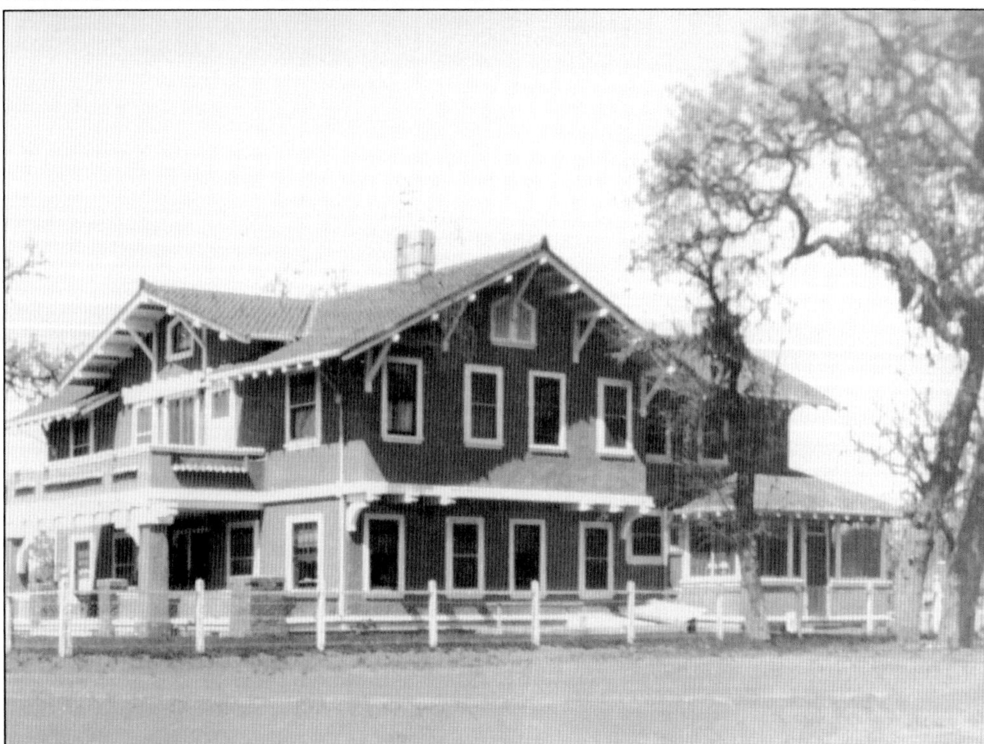

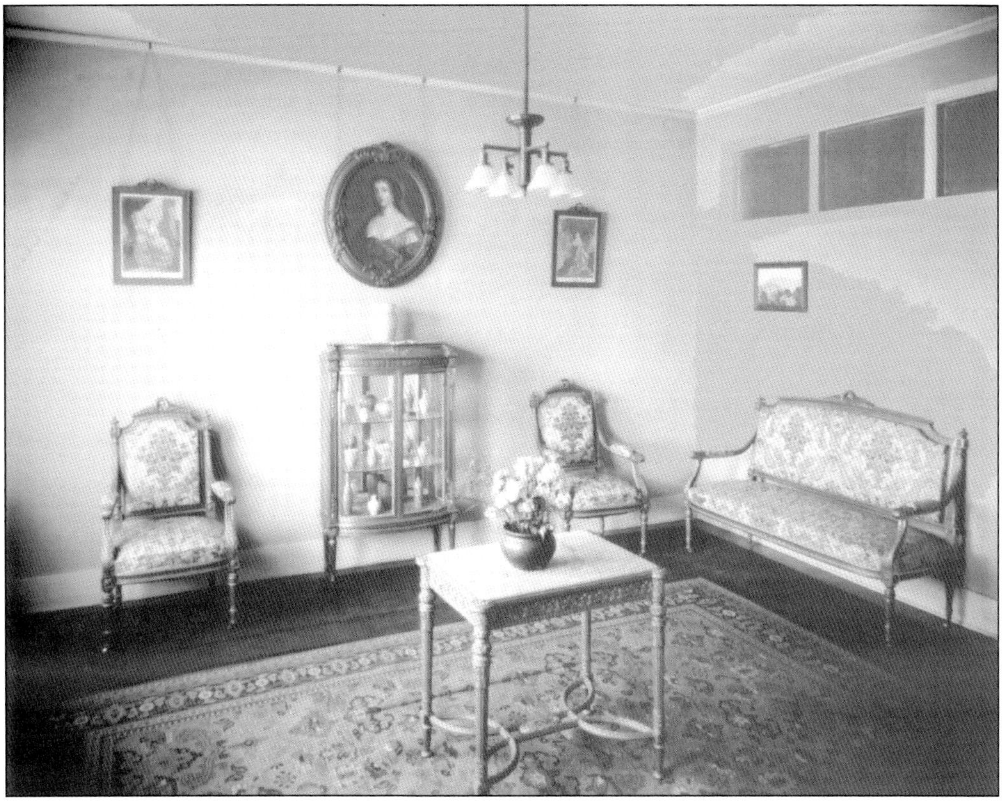

Pictured is a sitting room in Headquarters House. (Courtesy of Kent Kenney Archives.)

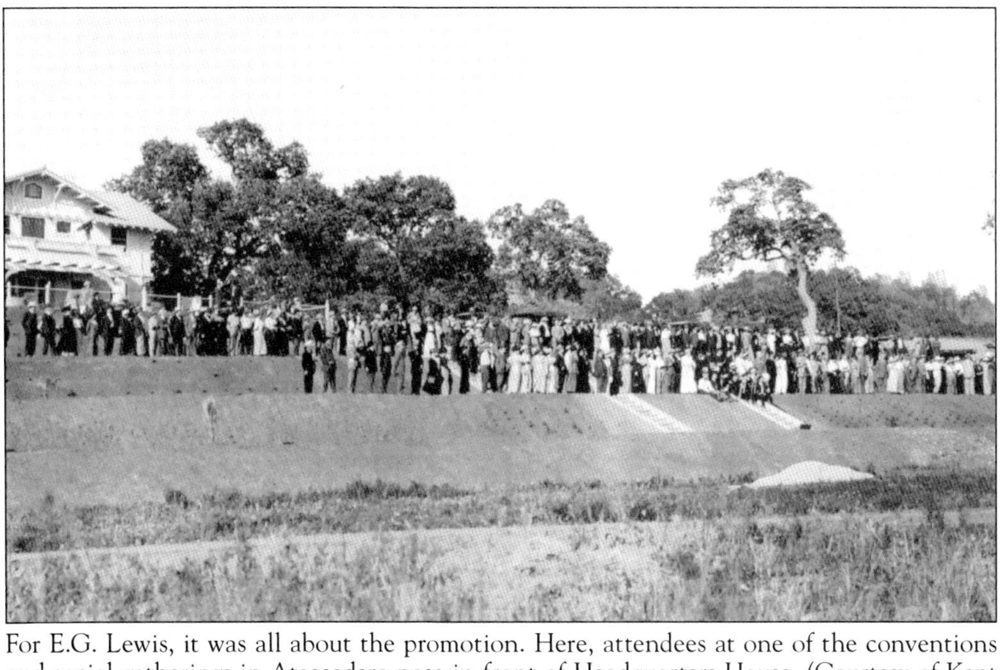

For E.G. Lewis, it was all about the promotion. Here, attendees at one of the conventions and social gatherings in Atascadero pose in front of Headquarters House. (Courtesy of Kent Kenney Archives.)

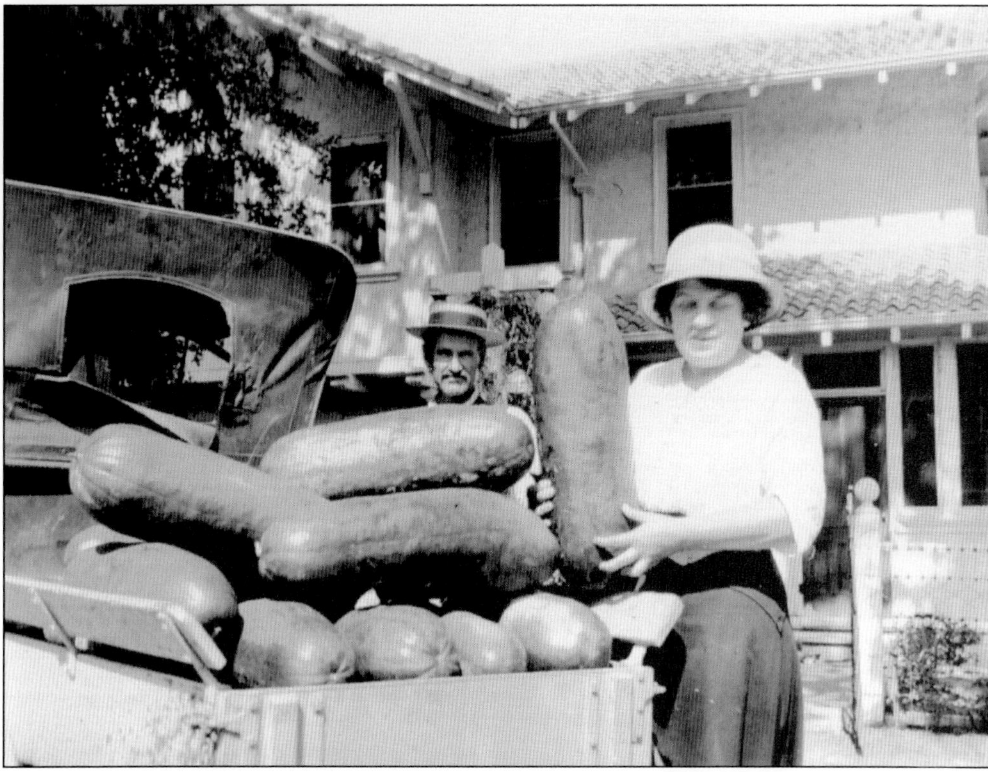

In a theme to be repeated time and time again, agricultural produce is featured in early promotional photography, displaying bountiful harvests to be reaped from the soil of the new colony. (Courtesy of Atascadero Historical Society.)

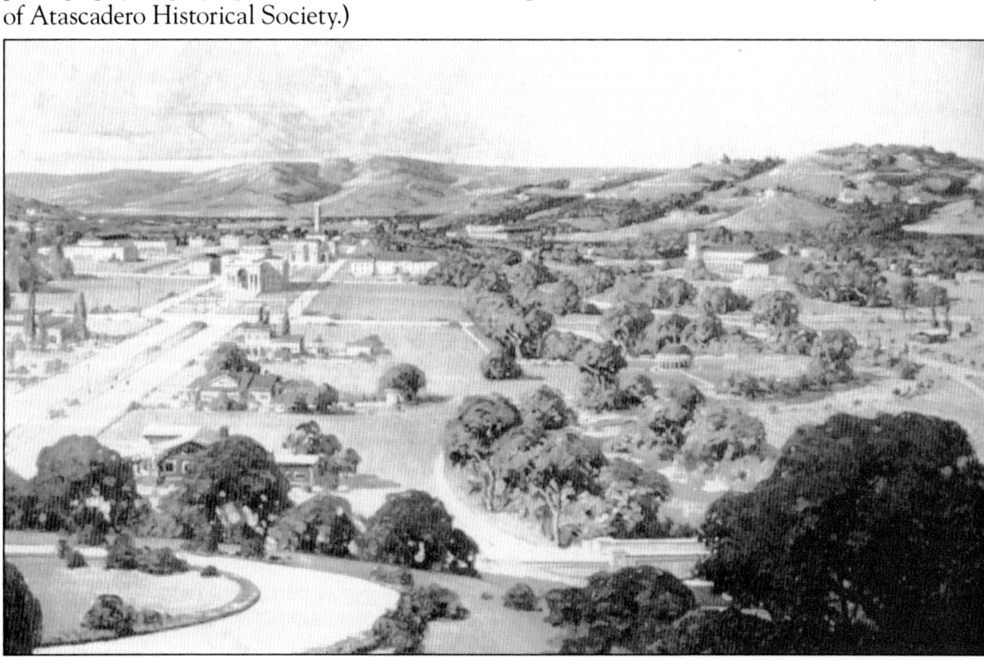

This is an artist rendition of the civic center in downtown Atascadero. A reproduction of the full panel is on display in the modern Atascadero City Hall. (Courtesy of the City of Atascadero.)

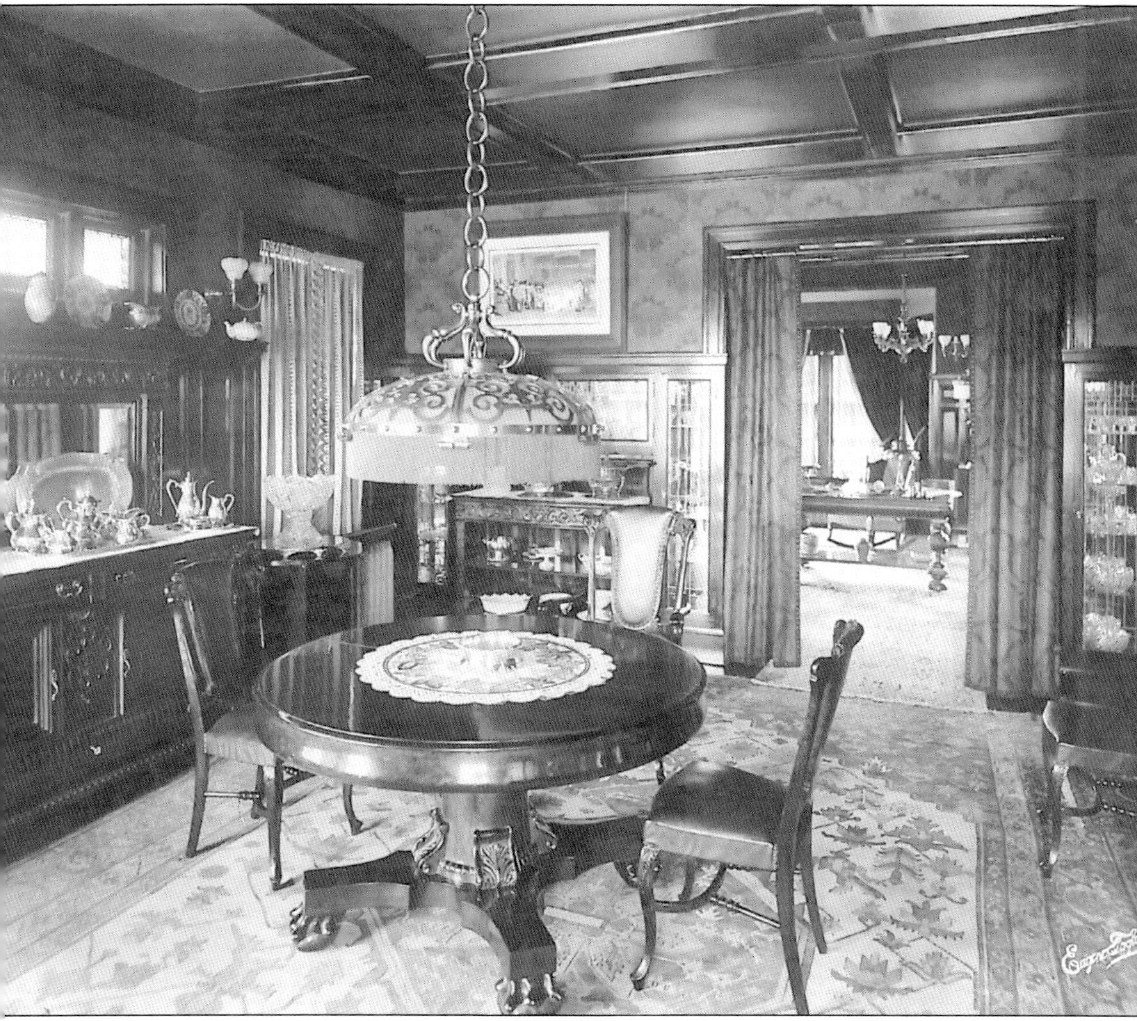

Pictured is the ornate dining room in Headquarters House. (Courtesy of Atascadero Historical Society.)

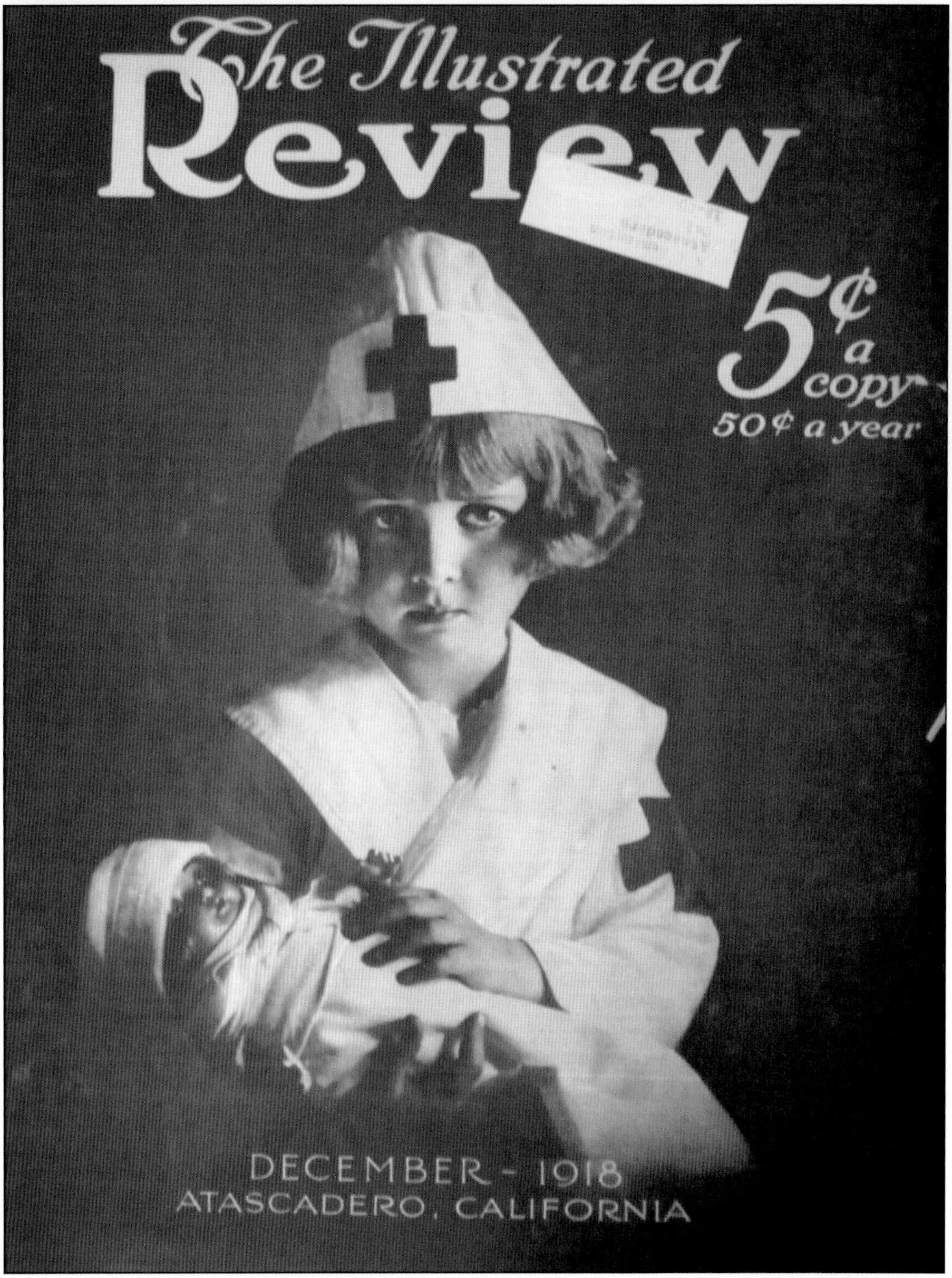

This is a cover from Lewis's *Illustrated Review* in December 1918. (Courtesy of Lon Allan.)

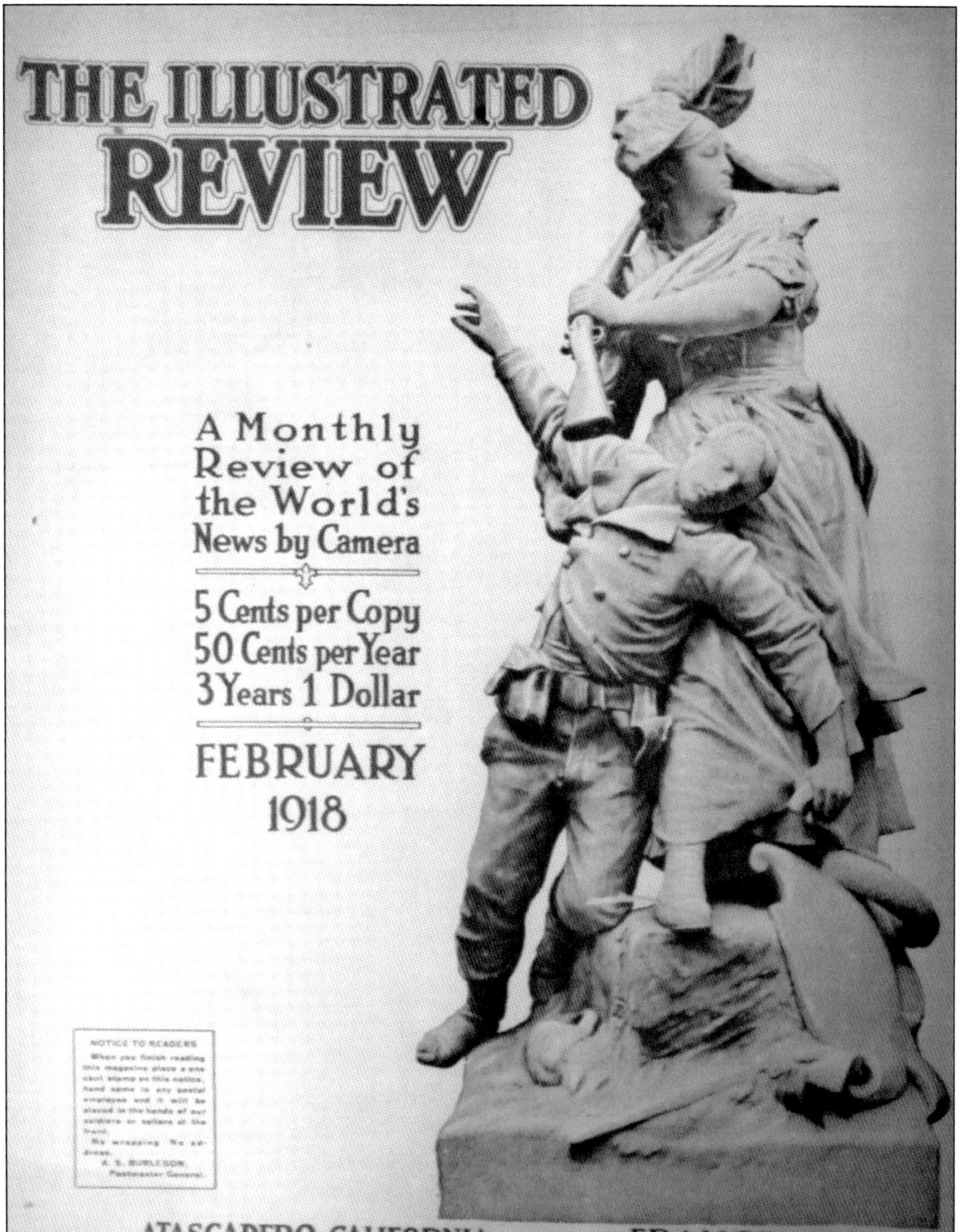

This is another cover from Lewis's *Illustrated Review* in February 1918. Although published in Atascadero, the magazine included news items from around the world. (Courtesy of Lon Allan.)

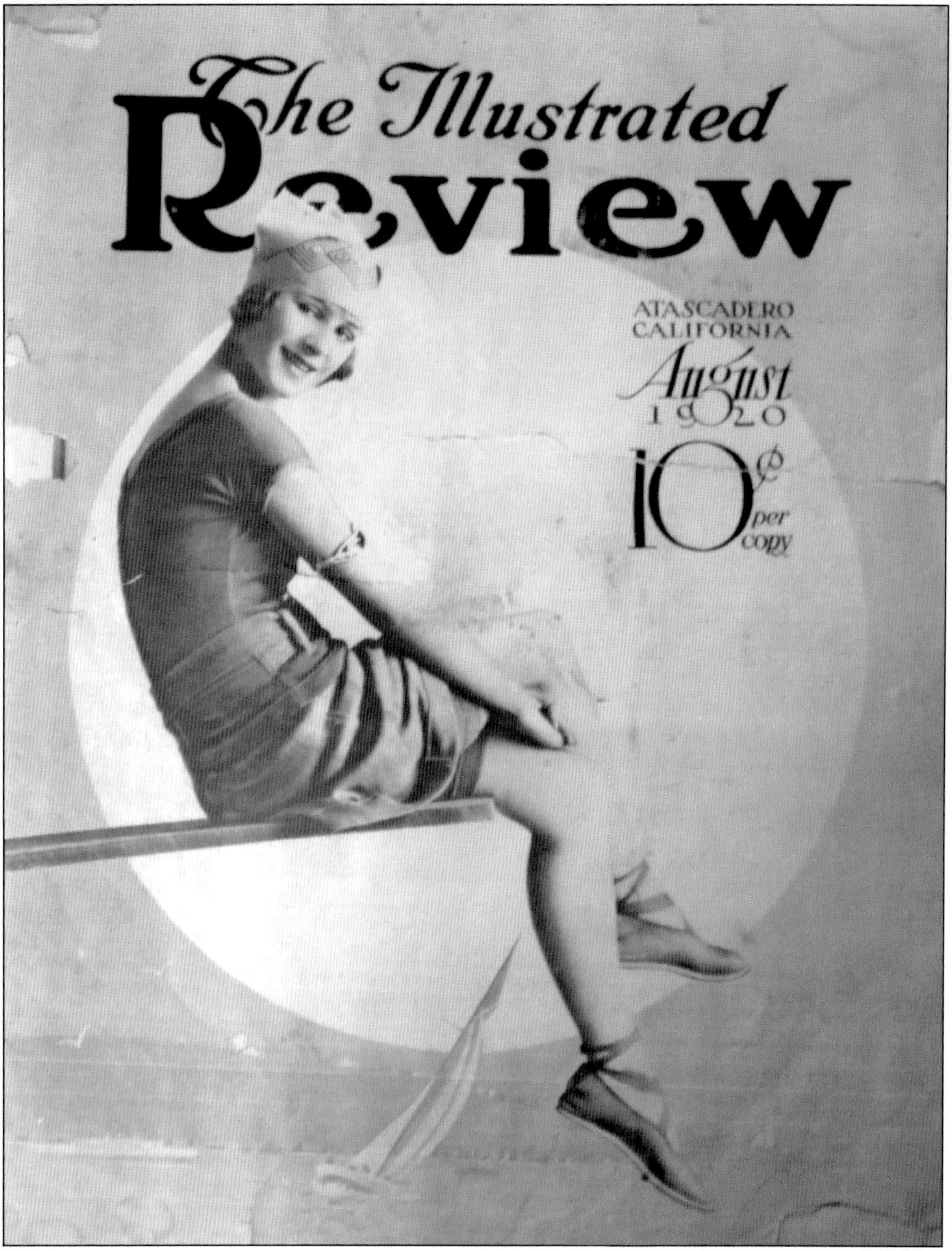

This is a cover from *Illustrated Review* in August 1920. Perhaps this idyllic coastal illustration was designed to lure people to the central California coast and Lewis's beachfront resort, the Cloisters. (Courtesy of Lon Allan.)

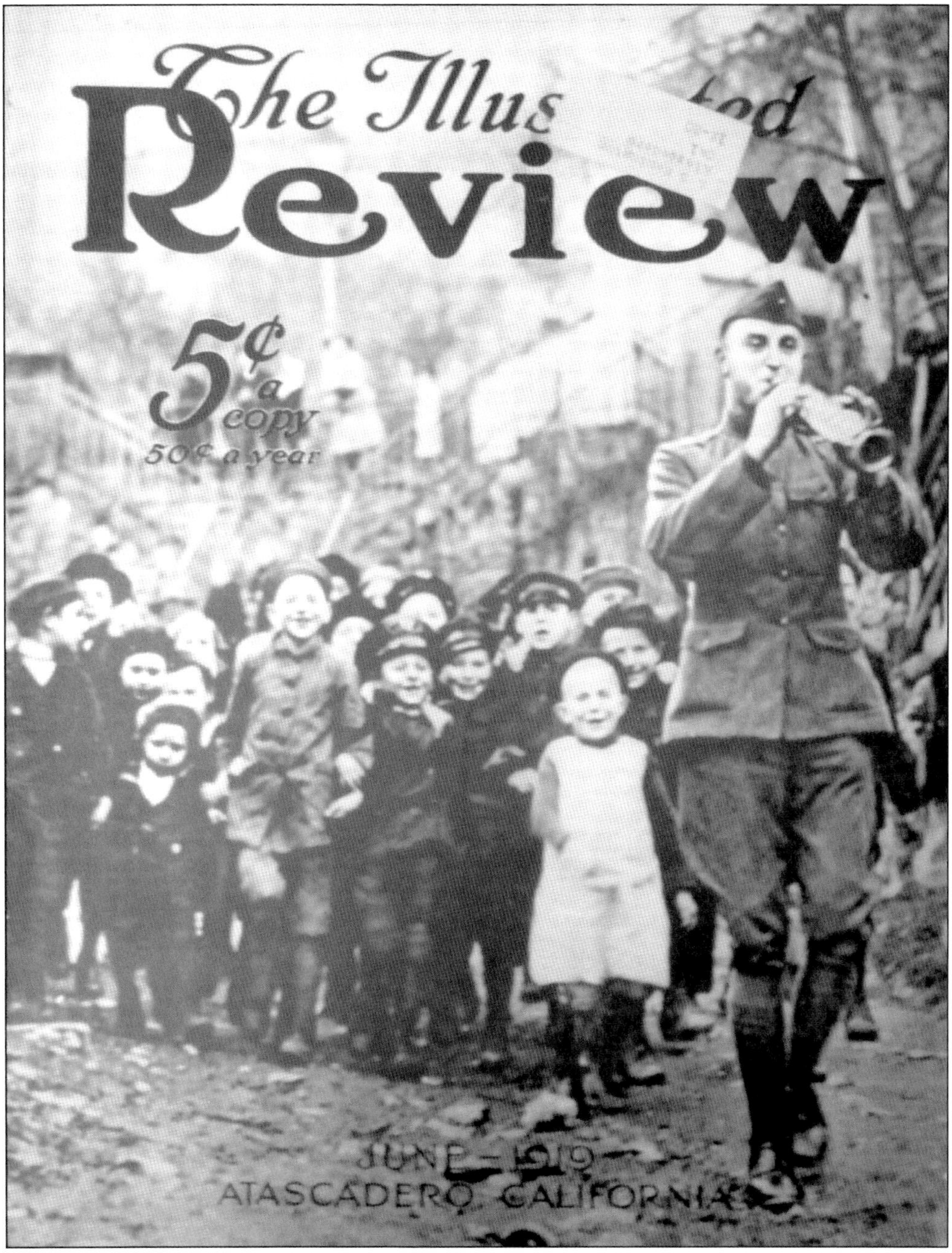

This cover is from *Illustrated Review* in June 1919. Many of Lewis's covers included images of Europe and the Great War. One of the Lewis's business ventures was to provide dehydrated fruits and vegetables to the US Army. (Courtesy of Lon Allan.)

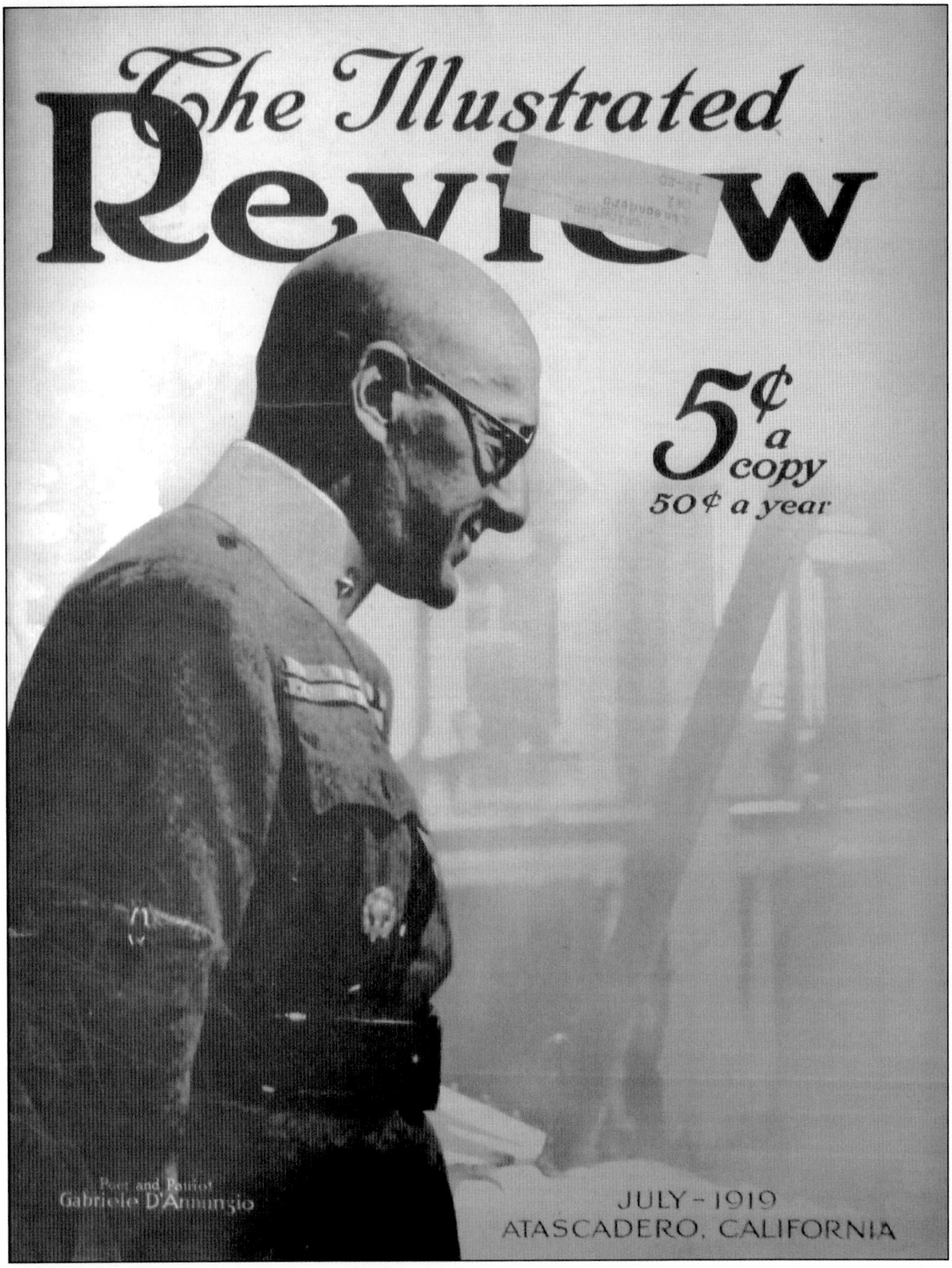

This is a July 1919 cover from Lewis's *Illustrated Review.* The magazine had an immense subscriber base for a publication of this era. (Courtesy of Lon Allan.)

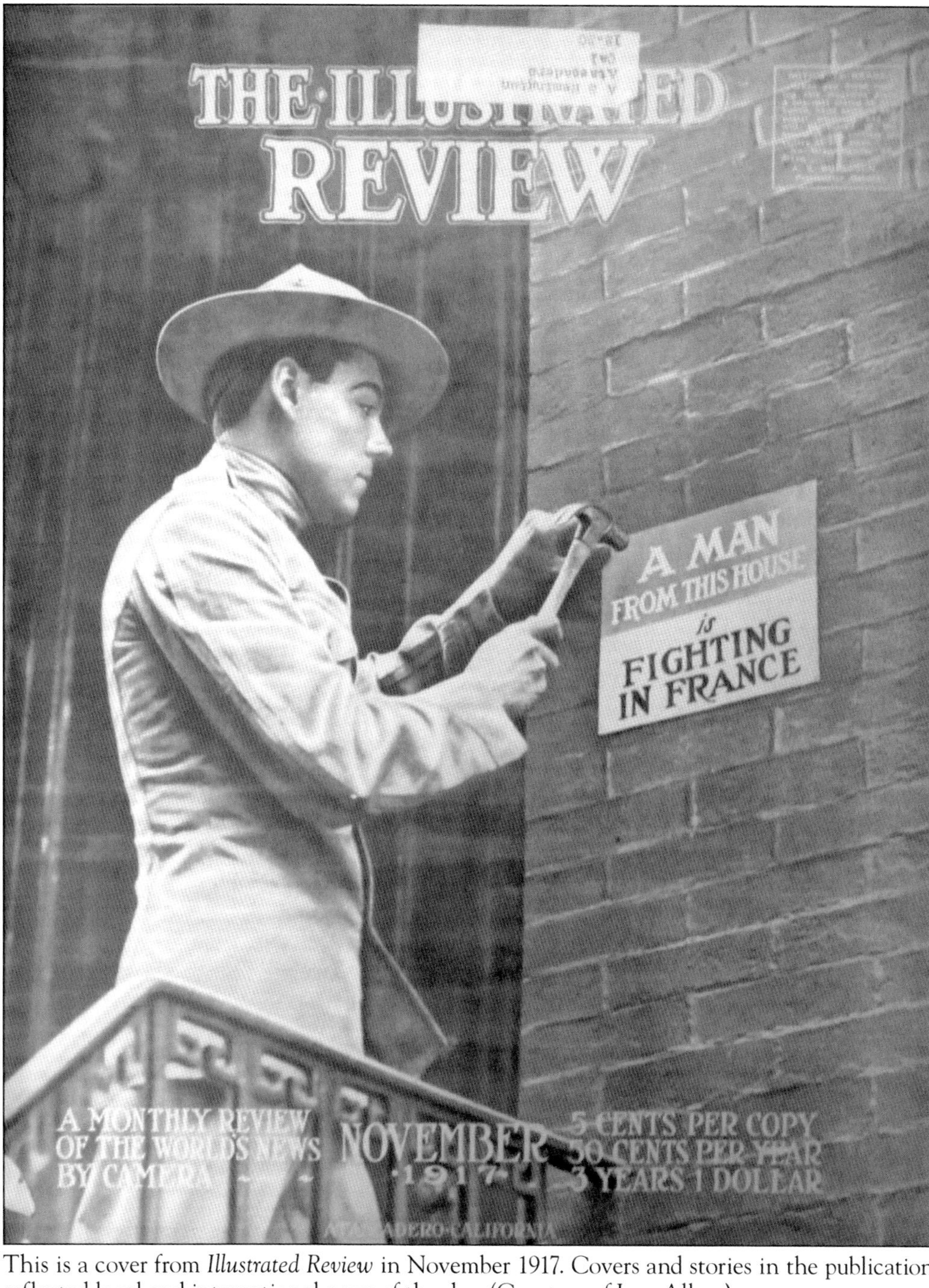

This is a cover from *Illustrated Review* in November 1917. Covers and stories in the publication reflected local and international news of the day. (Courtesy of Lon Allan.)

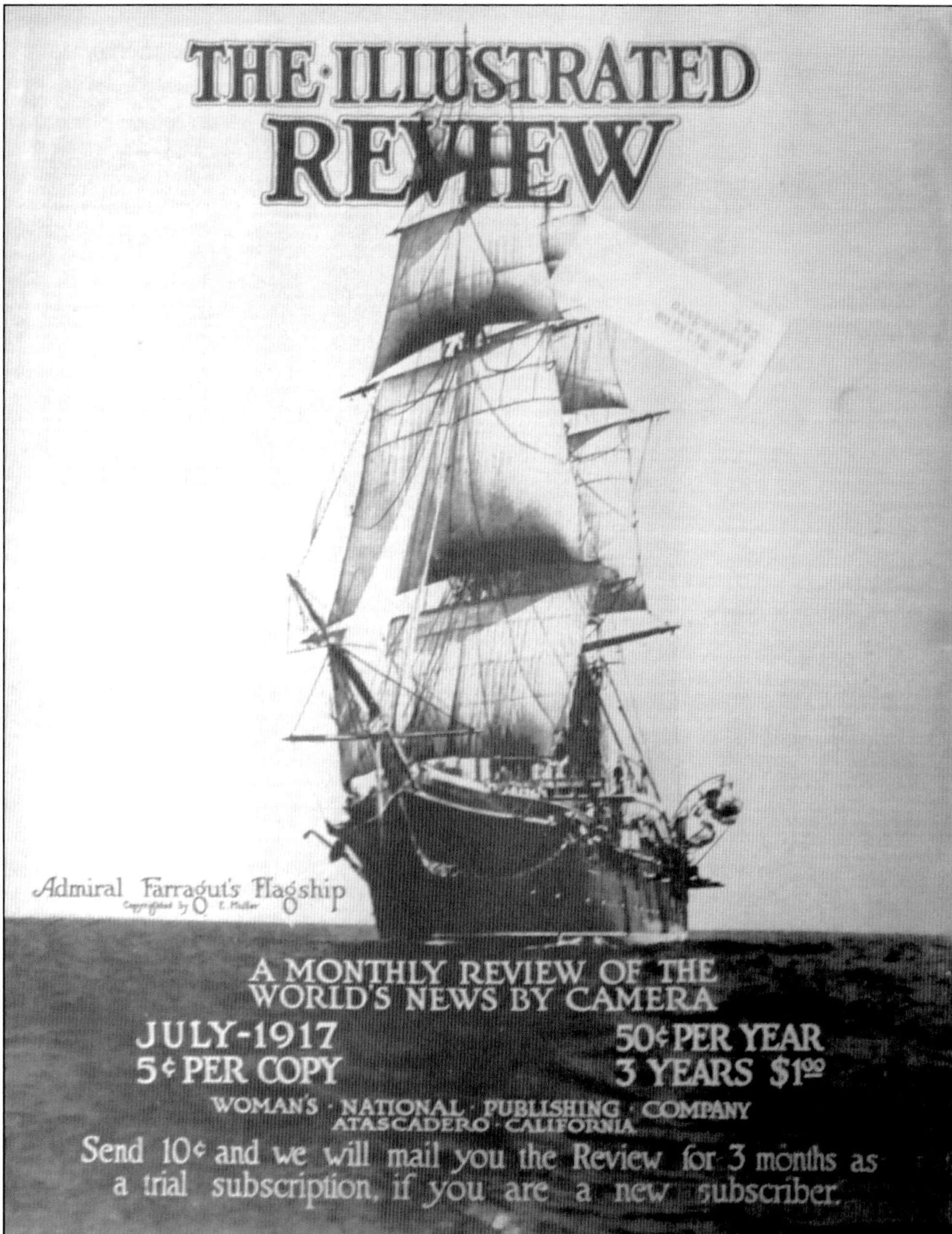

This is a July 1917 cover. From one era to another, a survey of covers reveals an eclectic and sometimes unrelated series of images. (Courtesy of Lon Allan.)

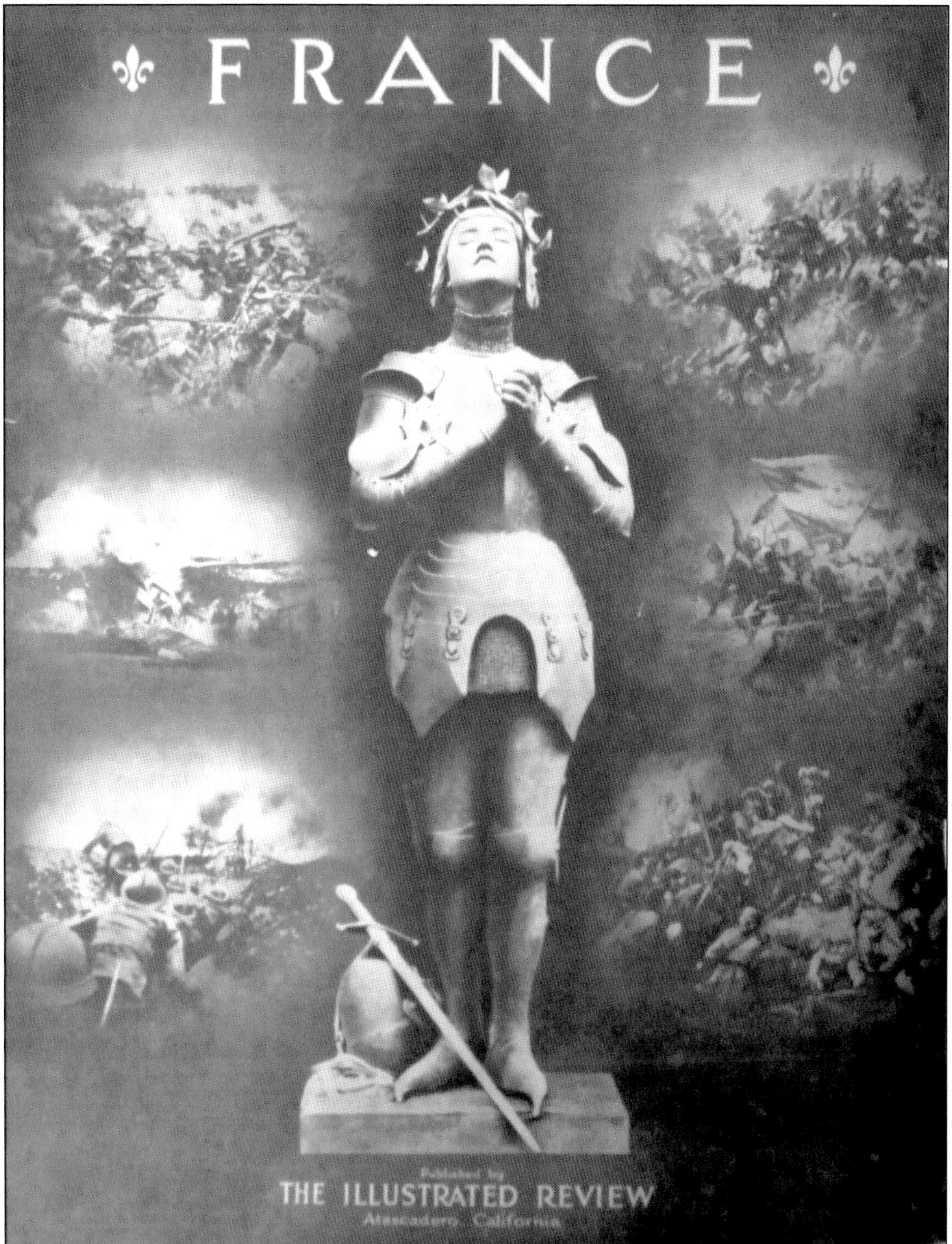

This issue of the *Illustrated Review* featured France. The many references to France and the European conflict revealed either an interest in history or a great availability of copy and photographs in this area. (Courtesy of Lon Allan.)

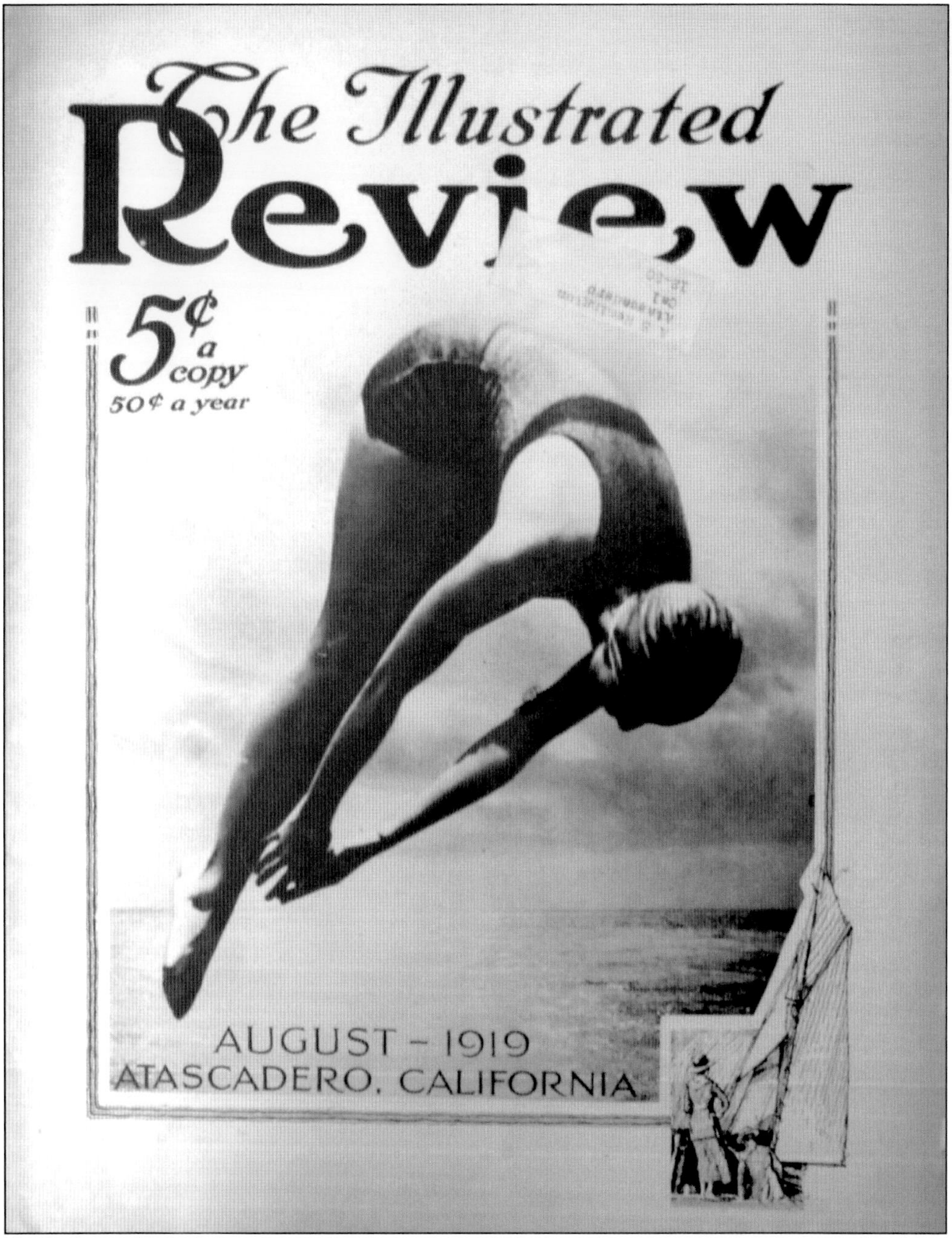

This is a cover from Lewis's *Illustrated Review* in August 1919. This photograph-within-a-photograph cover again piques the curiosity of Middle Western Americans who made their way to Lewis's utopia in California. (Courtesy of Lon Allan.)

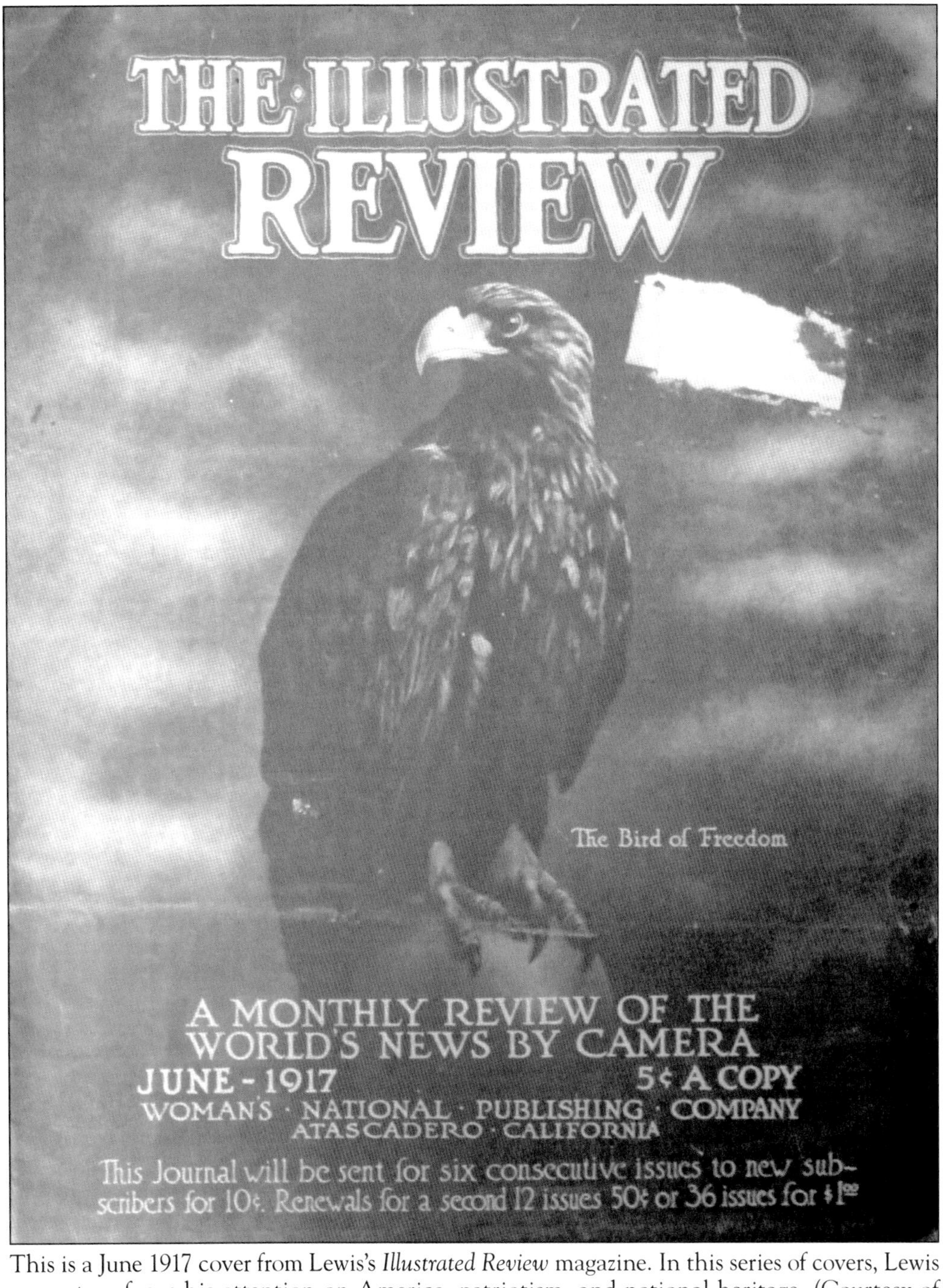

This is a June 1917 cover from Lewis's *Illustrated Review* magazine. In this series of covers, Lewis seems to refocus his attention on America, patriotism, and national heritage. (Courtesy of Lon Allan.)

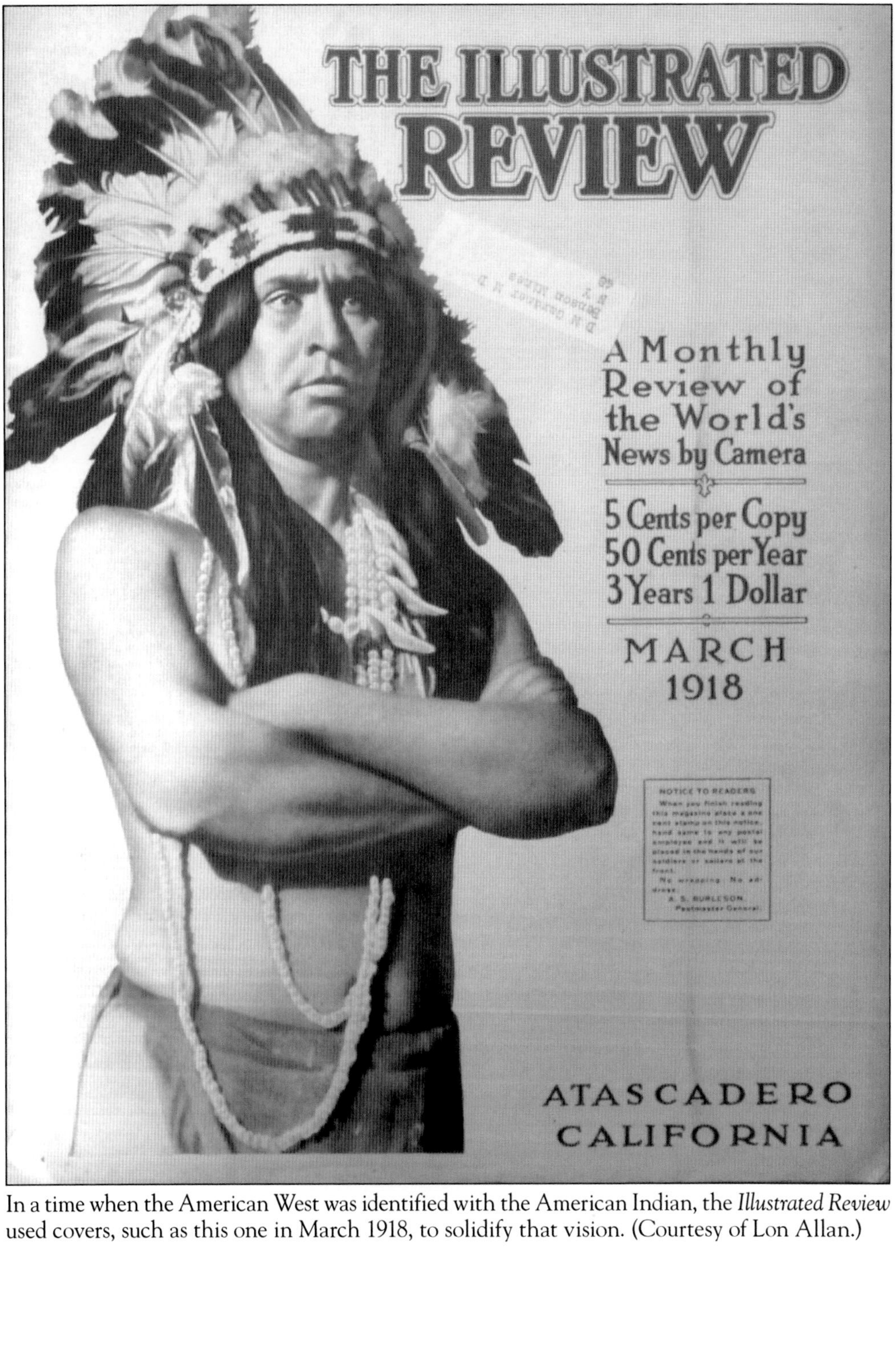

In a time when the American West was identified with the American Indian, the *Illustrated Review* used covers, such as this one in March 1918, to solidify that vision. (Courtesy of Lon Allan.)

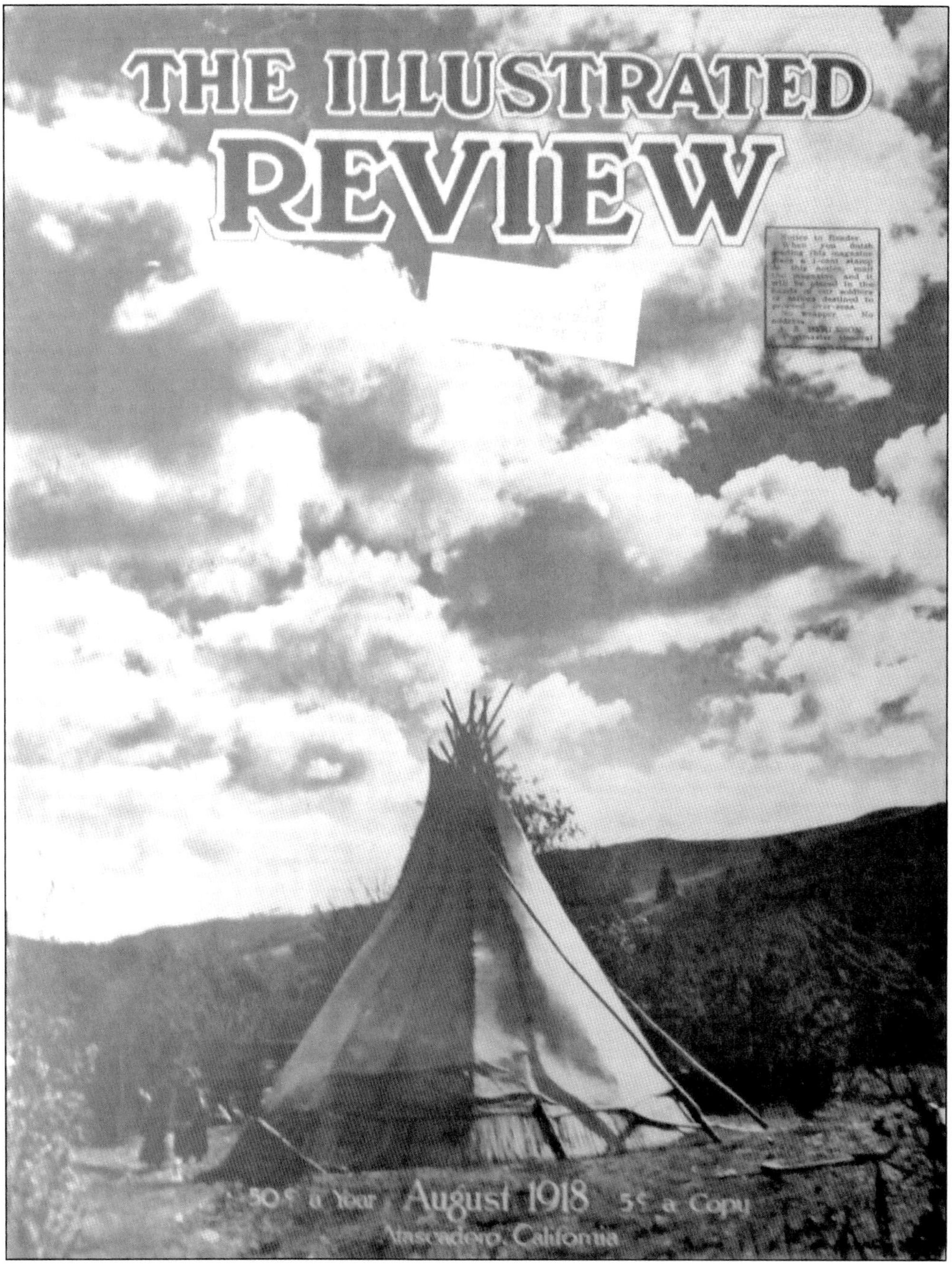

This is a cover from Lewis's *Illustrated Review* in August 1918. It is unlikely that authentic tepees like this ever existed within view of Lewis's own Tent City. (Courtesy of Lon Allan.)

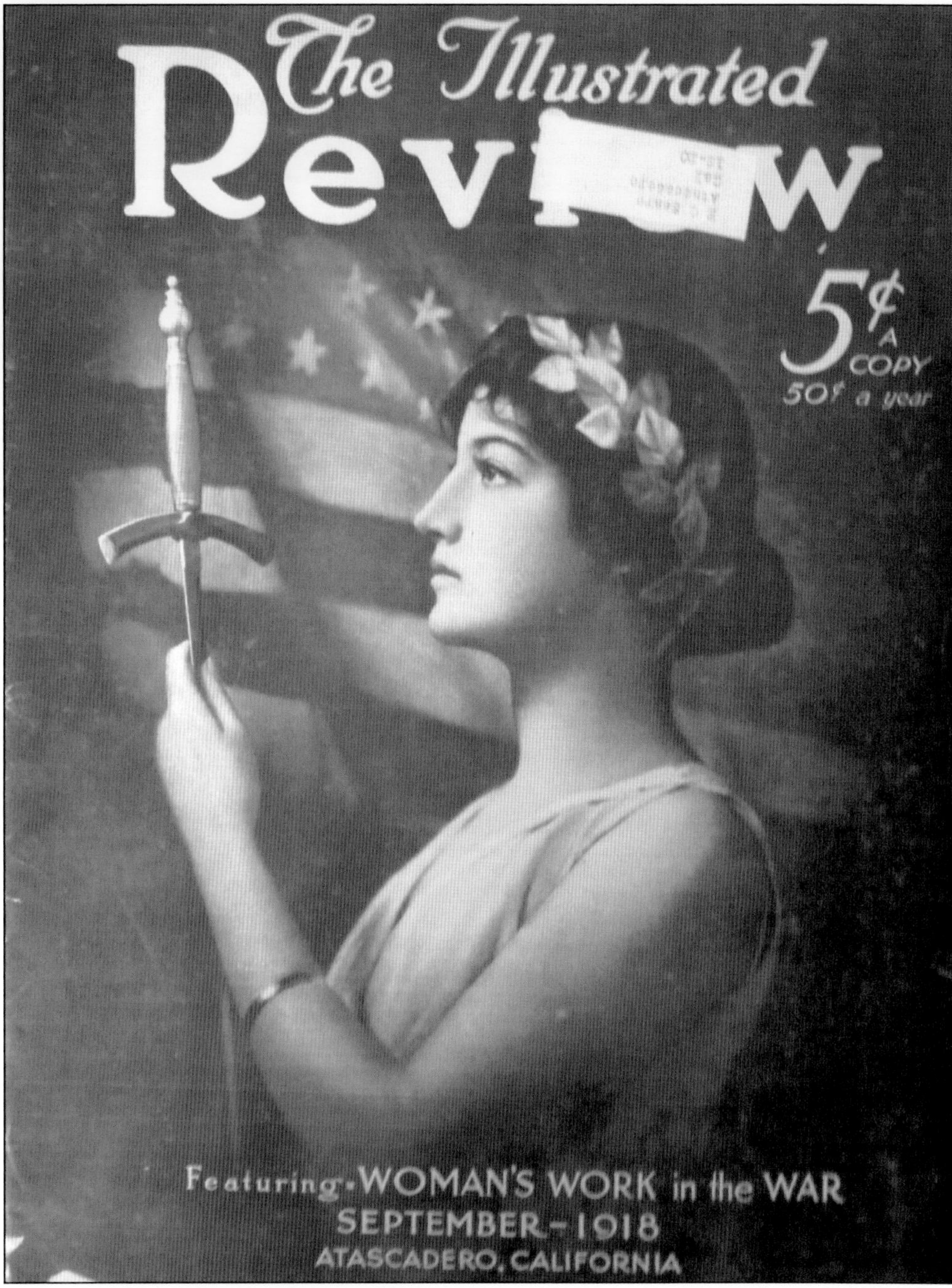

The September 1918 issue of *Illustrated Review* featured women's work in the war. Lewis was a strong proponent of woman suffrage. This philosophy was often espoused in his publications. This cover uses classic images to honor women's contributions to the war effort. (Courtesy of Lon Allan.)

Two

Tent City

Tent City was neither a campground nor a new idea. Lewis had employed tents to house early residents of University City. One early Atascadero resident, Marguerite A. Travis, recounted those first days of Tent City in *The Birth of Atascadero*.

> The tents were placed at regular intervals in long rows with streets between the lines, nearly a thousand tents in all, of various sizes according to their uses. The dwelling tents each held twin beds, kitchen table, four chairs, a screened door cabinet for food and dishes, an airtight, wood heating stove, gasoline range, and hooks on the wall for clothes hangers. Wood, cut in stove lengths, was placed on the door steps every morning early. The tents were all lighted with electricity.

According to Travis, nonresidential tents housed grocery stores and a laundry with hot and cold running water, and there was a clothes-drying tent open at the top. There was also a large assembly tent where residents could meet or view motion pictures.

The colony was to have been a place where residents could enjoy the best of rural and urban lifestyles. Lewis used his investors' money to plan and prepare the place where they would eventually live. He had used $850,000 borrowed from former investors in St. Louis, Missouri, to purchase the land for $37.50 per acre on February 6, 1913. On July 4, 1913, Lewis's wife, Mabel, representing the American Woman's Republic's Atascadero chapter, accepted the deed from J.H. Henry.

Social life soon evolved around a unique geographic feature: Stadium Park, a natural amphitheater tucked into the hillside near Tent City. Stadium Park was host to many conventions from 1918 to 1921. Lewis capitalized on these events to promote Atascadero. He would provide a fleet of cars to drive conventioneers to specific points of interest in the hope he would inspire them to report the desirability of the community far and wide.

Atascadero's first church, the Federated Church of Atascadero, was created by Tent City dwellers around July 1915. It was the aim of settlers to create a nondenominational congregation "open to Christian people without regard to creed or sect." In 1929, the Federated Church split into the Community Church of Atascadero (which is still operating at 5850 Rosario Street) and the Atascadero Bible Church (which is still operating at 6225 Atascadero Mall Street).

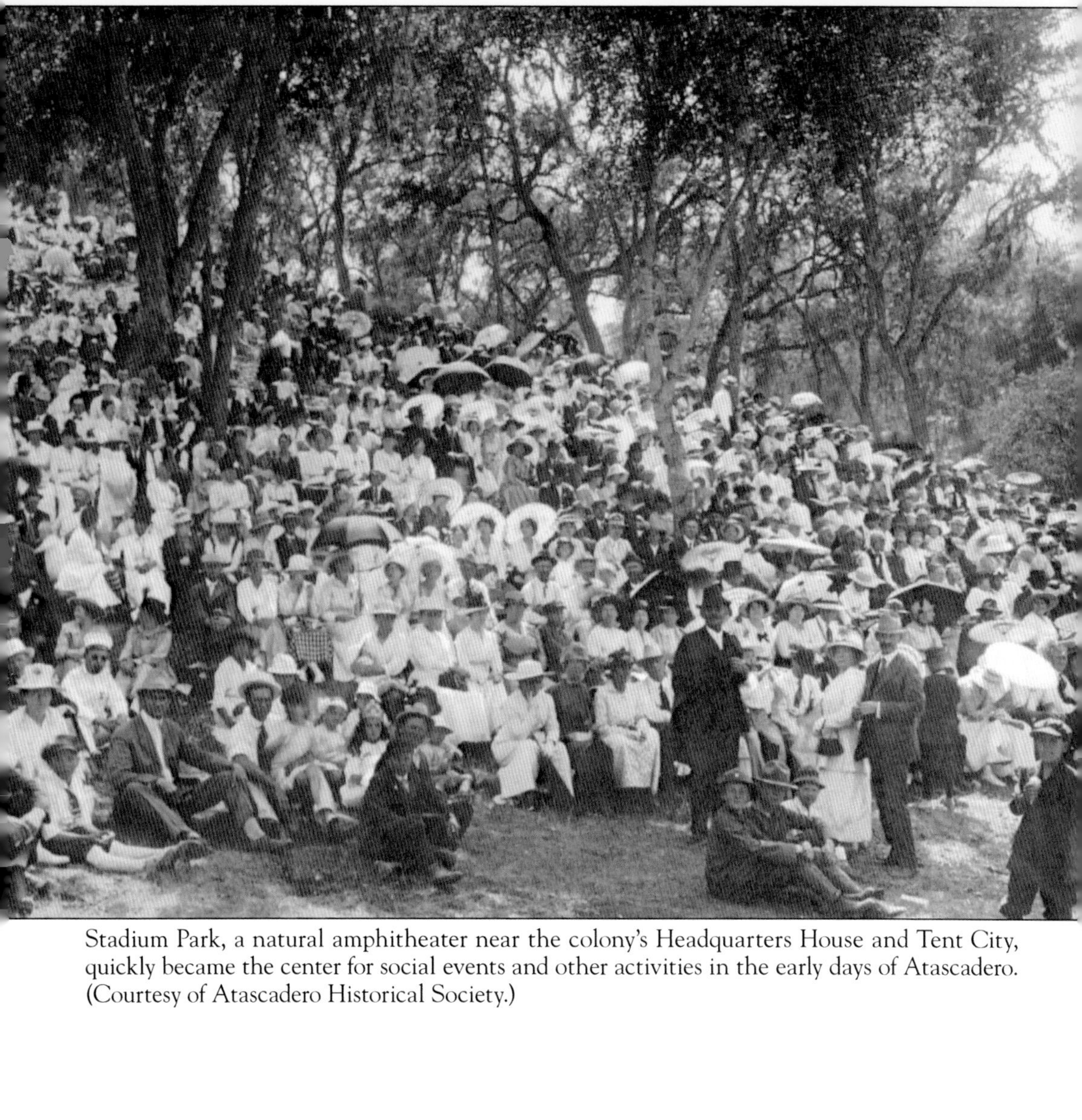

Stadium Park, a natural amphitheater near the colony's Headquarters House and Tent City, quickly became the center for social events and other activities in the early days of Atascadero. (Courtesy of Atascadero Historical Society.)

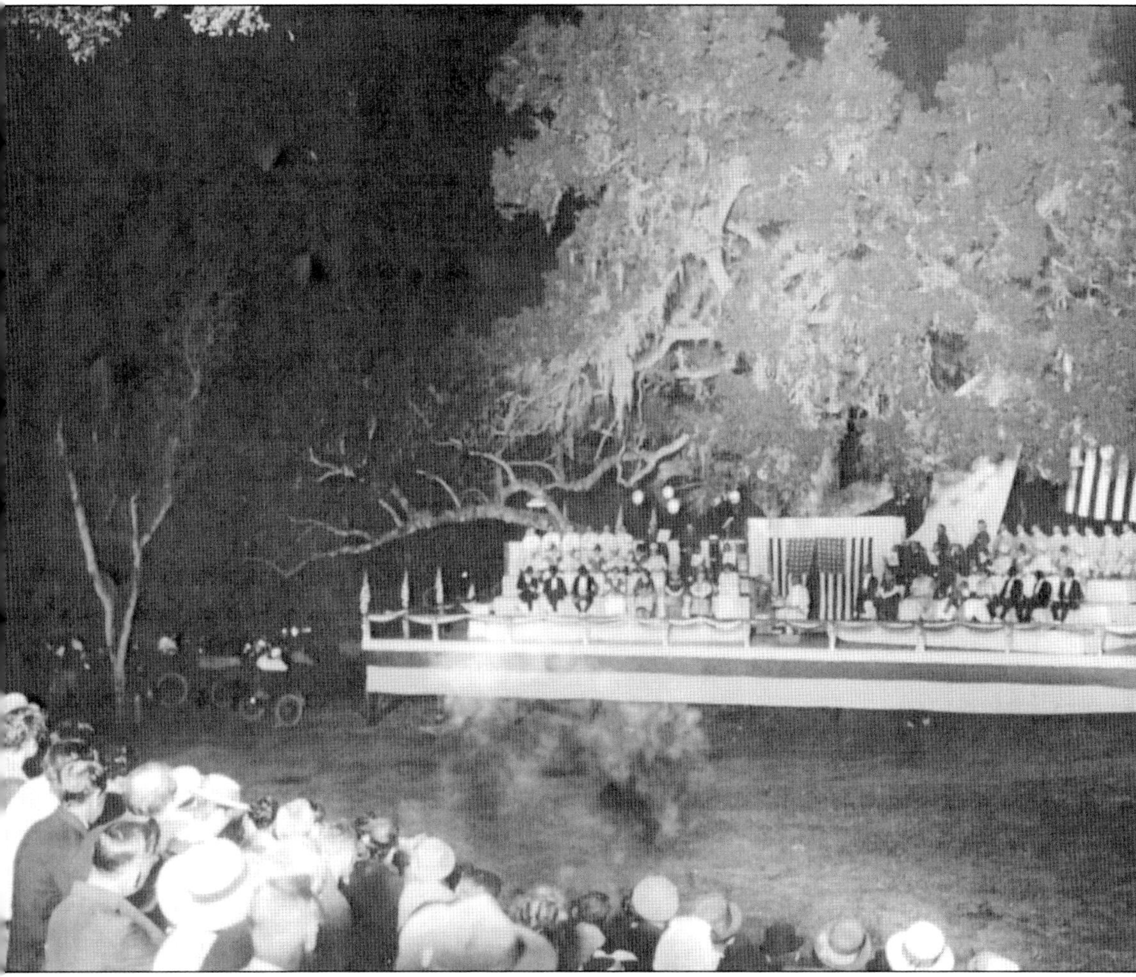

Evening hours were no detriment for local revelers. Part of the preparation of Stadium Park was the installation of electric lights in the trees, making nighttime activities possible. (Courtesy of Atascadero Historical Society.)

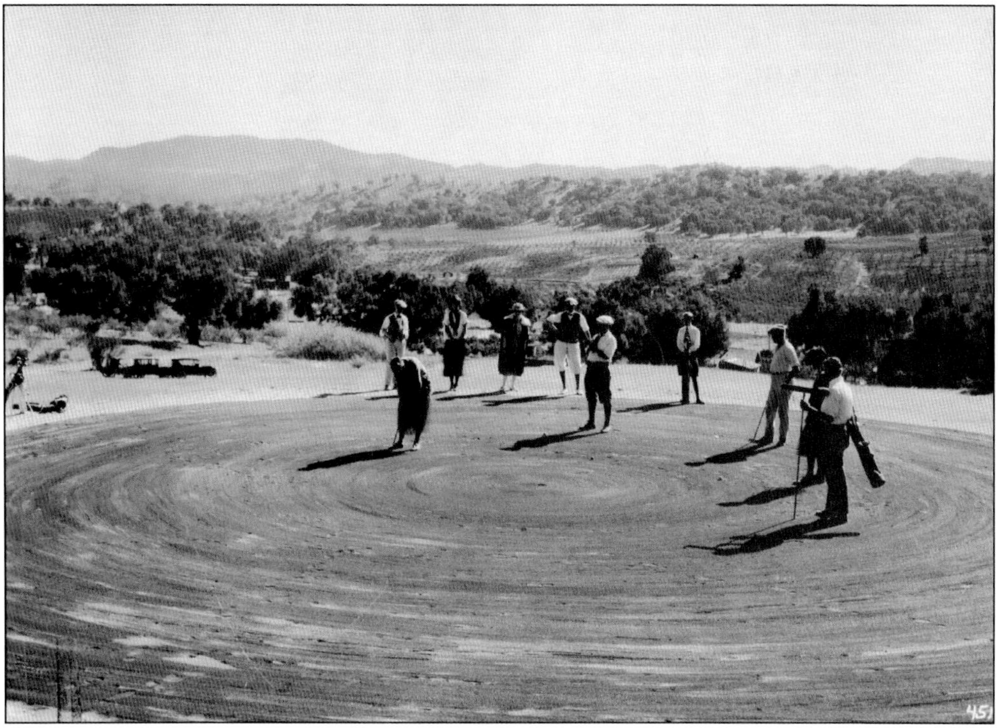

Early golfers made their needs known. There was no grass yet, so the game was played on sand. (Courtesy of Atascadero Historical Society.)

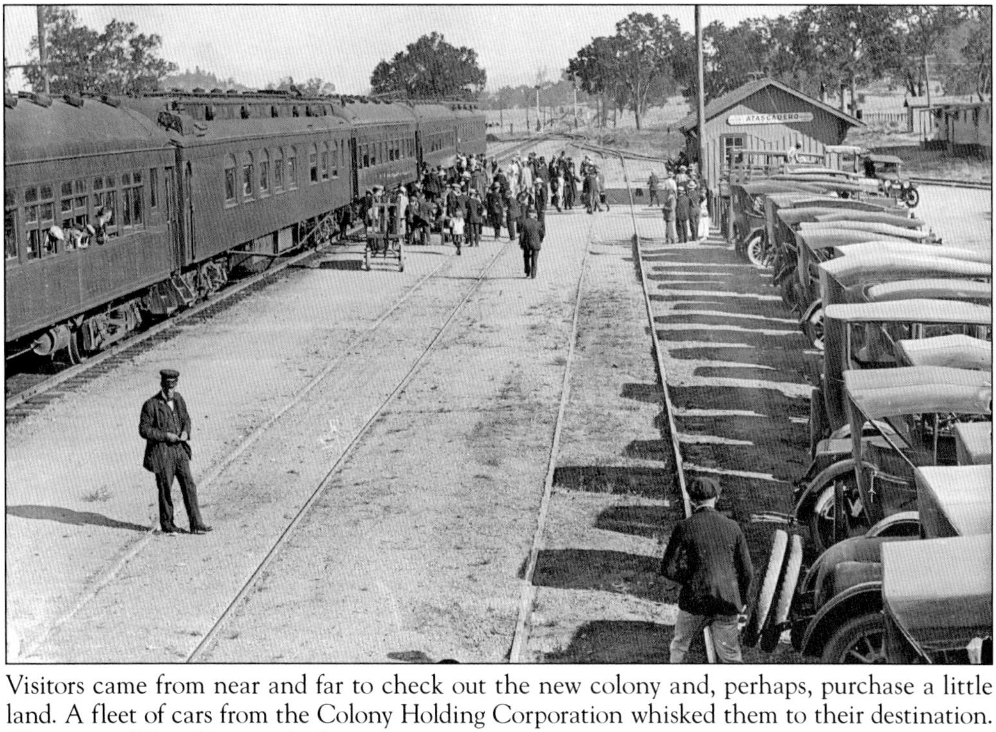

Visitors came from near and far to check out the new colony and, perhaps, purchase a little land. A fleet of cars from the Colony Holding Corporation whisked them to their destination. (Courtesy of Kent Kenney Archives.)

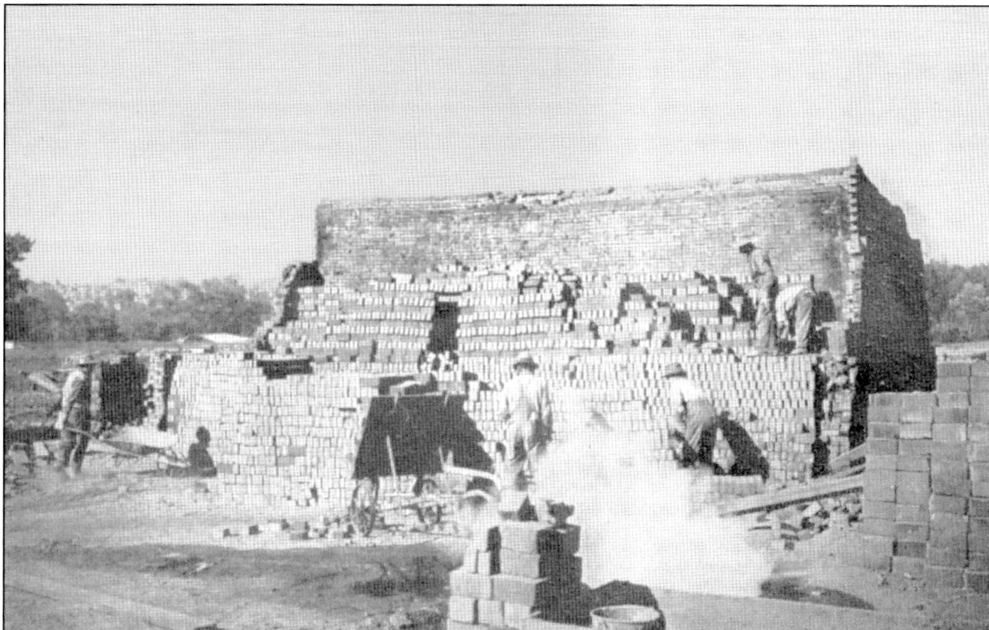

Taking down a burnt kiln of quarter-million bricks.

A brick plant was constructed very early in the history of the colony to supply building materials for the city's ornate municipal structures. This plant turned out 50,000 bricks per day. (Courtesy of Kent Kenney Archives.)

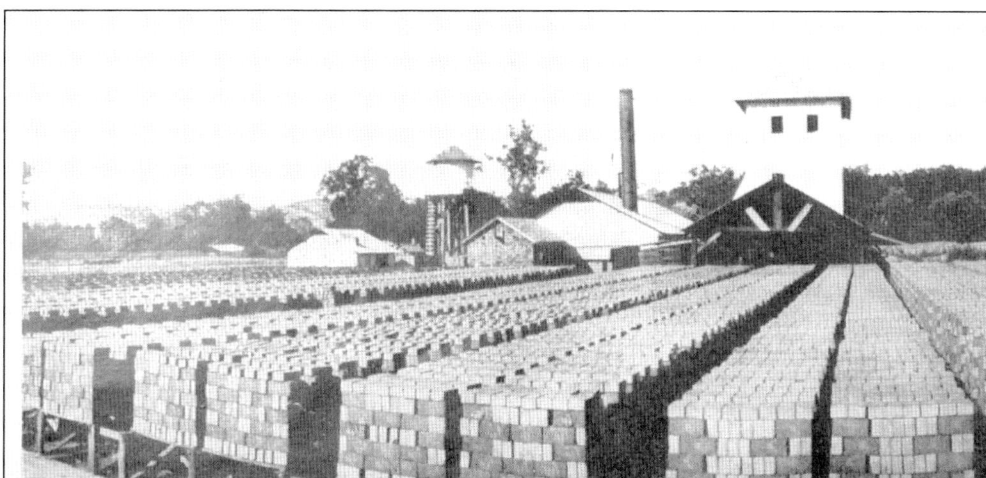

The Brick and Terra Cotta plant has millions of bricks to supply for the

Row upon row of bricks rest in the sun, waiting to be used in the construction of Atascadero's earliest municipal structures. (Courtesy of Kent Kenney Archives.)

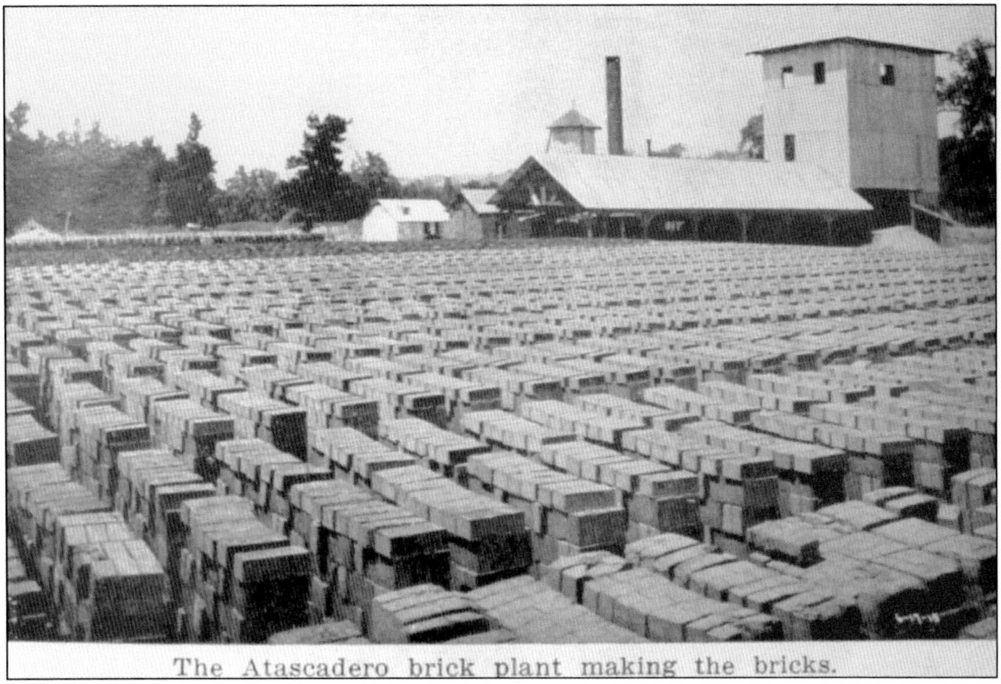

Bricks made of local materials still exist today in Atascadero's historical structures. (Courtesy of Kent Kenney Archives.)

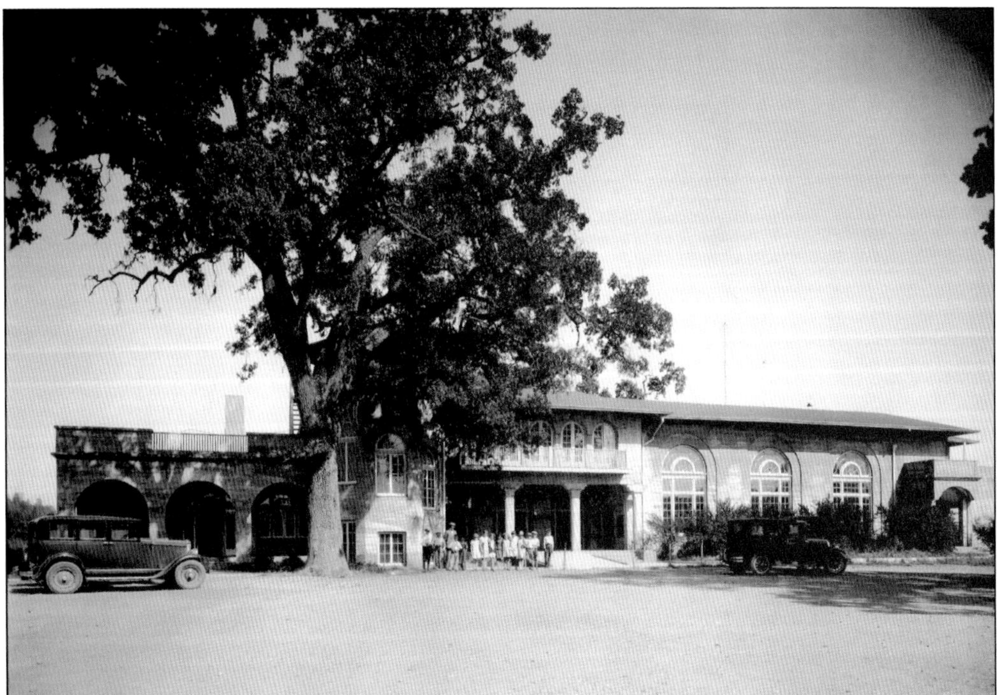

The original home of the Federated Church, this structure stands today as part of the complex developed by the Atascadero Bible Church (ABC). (Courtesy of Kent Kenney Archives.)

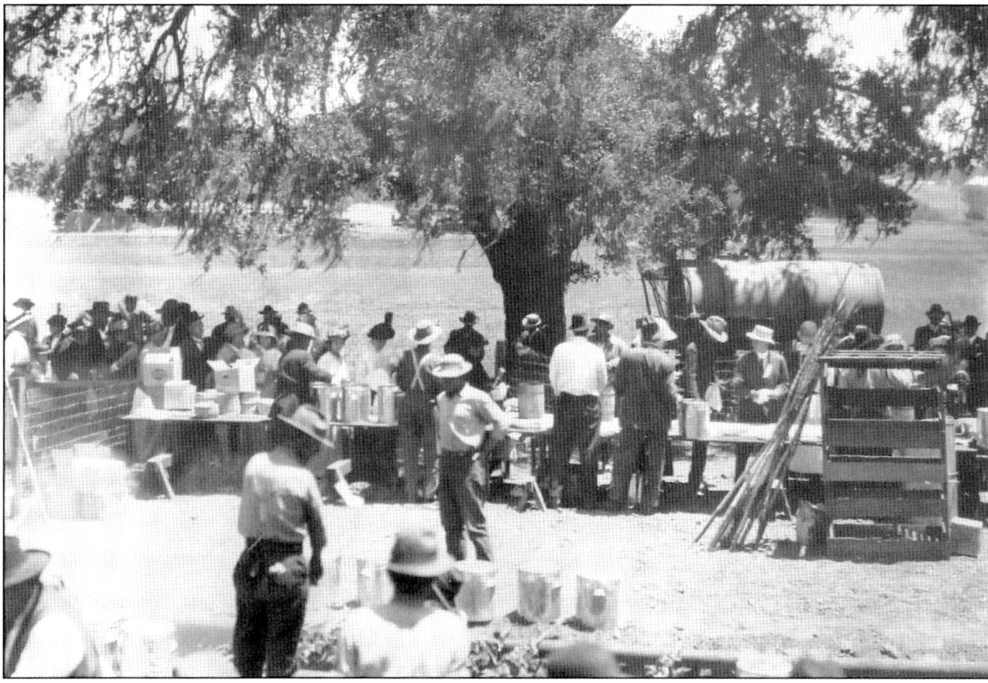

Community gatherings were obviously the order of the day in the young colony of Atascadero. This series of photographs depicts a huge picnic and barbecue. (Courtesy of Kent Kenney Archives.)

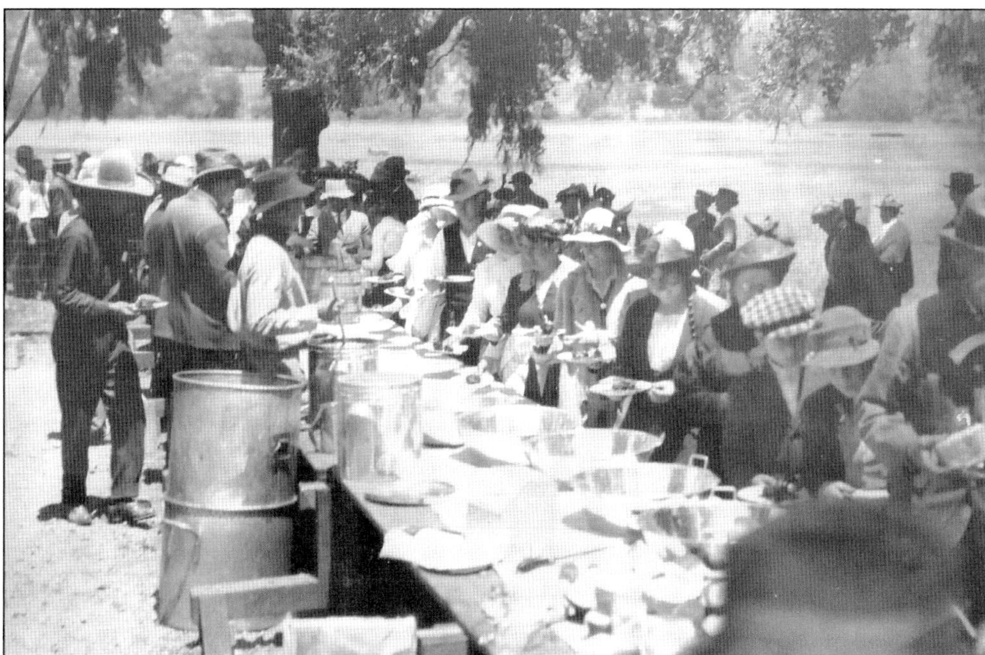

Residents and visitors can be seen queuing up for plates of food. Lewis used such occasions to promote Atascadero and impress visitors so they would spread the word when they went home. (Courtesy of Kent Kenney Archives.)

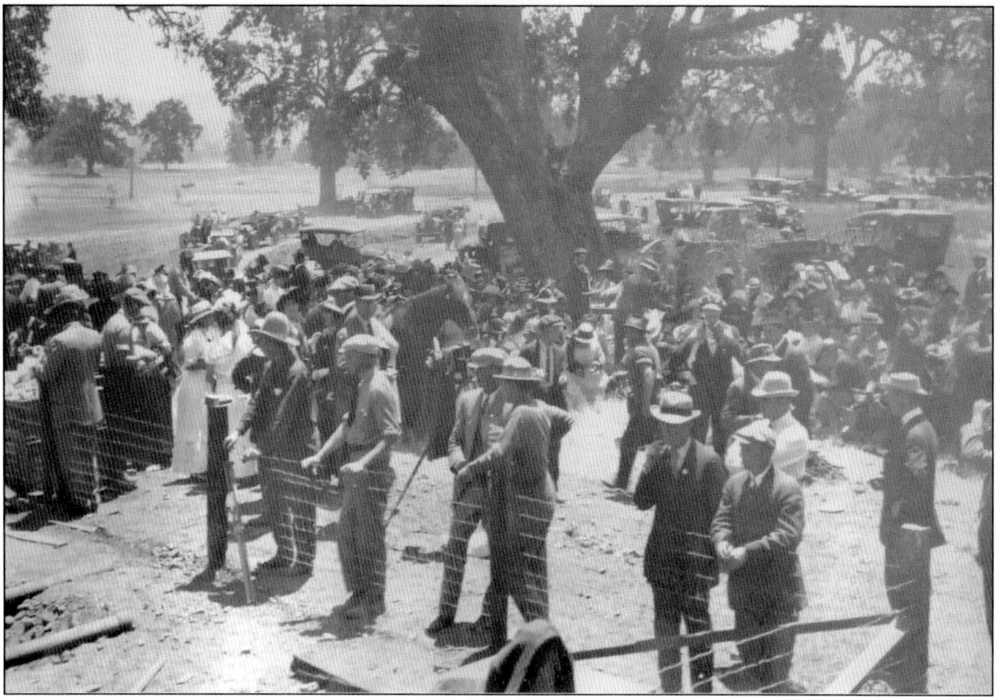

Guests and potential residents/investors arrive for one of Lewis's promotional gatherings. Notice the proliferation of automobiles. Lewis developed Atascadero to accommodate cars. (Courtesy of Kent Kenney Archives.)

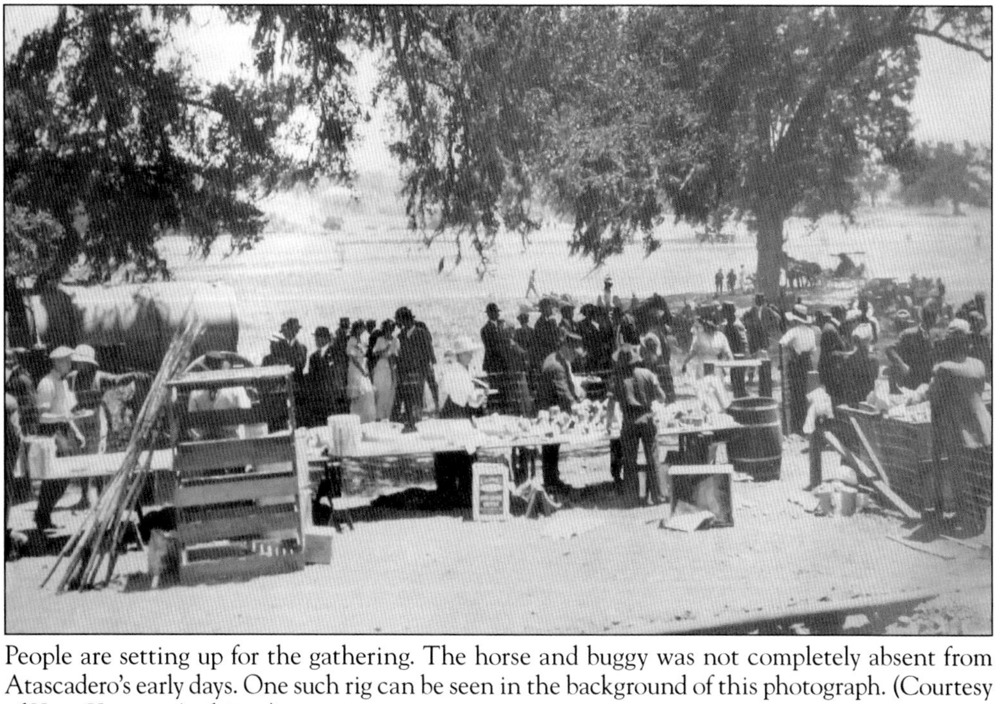

People are setting up for the gathering. The horse and buggy was not completely absent from Atascadero's early days. One such rig can be seen in the background of this photograph. (Courtesy of Kent Kenney Archives.)

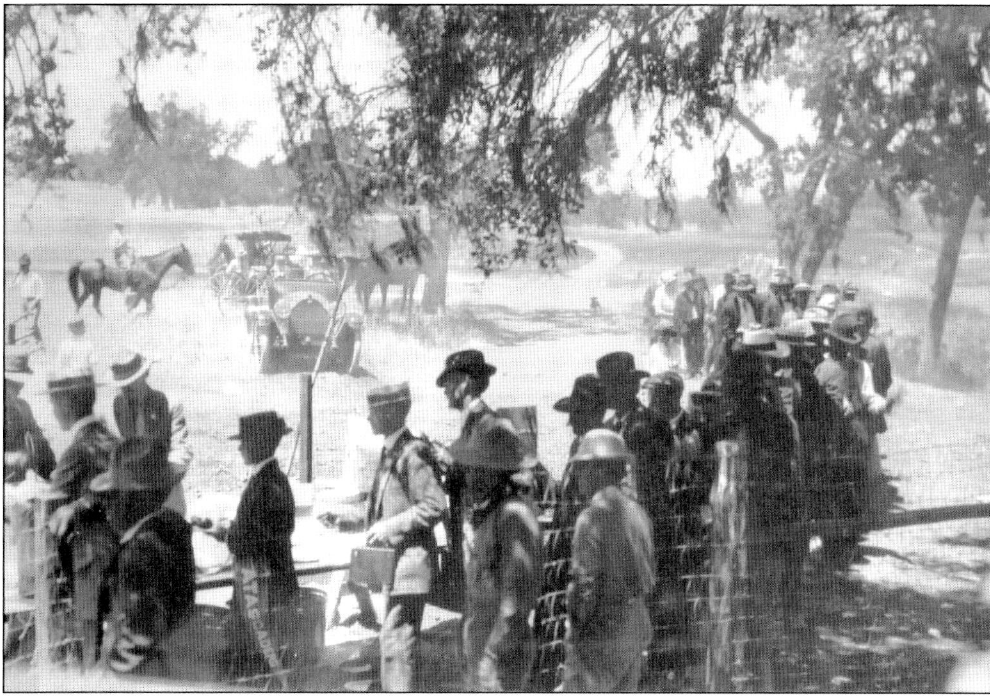

Guests queue up for a meal and materials promoting the new colony of Atascadero. (Courtesy of Kent Kenney Archives.)

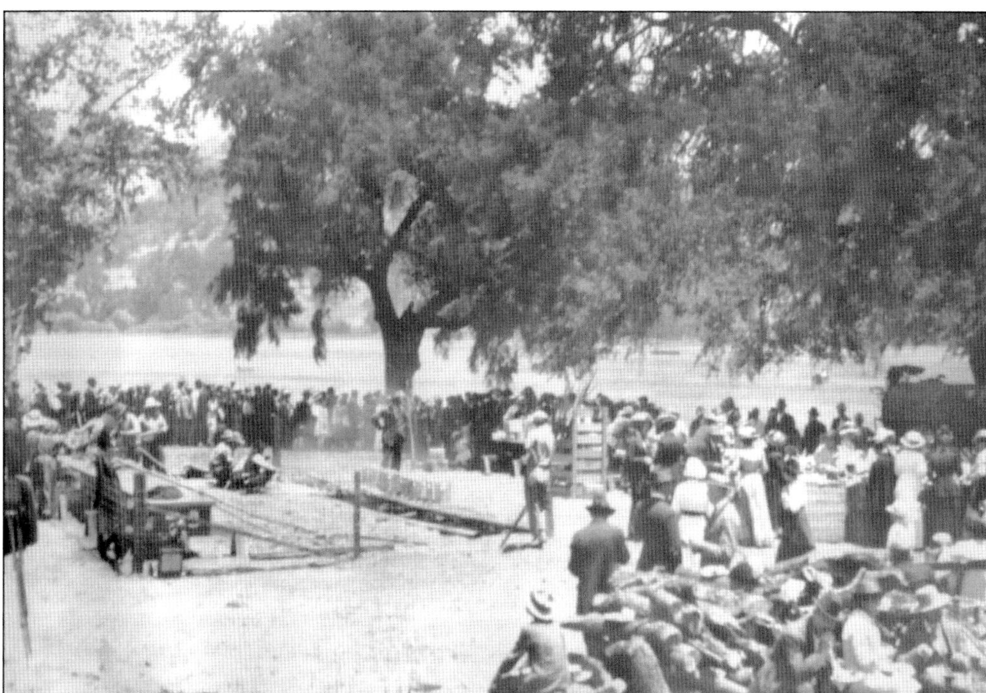

The crowd forms a circle around the open-pit barbecue. (Courtesy of Kent Kenney Archives.)

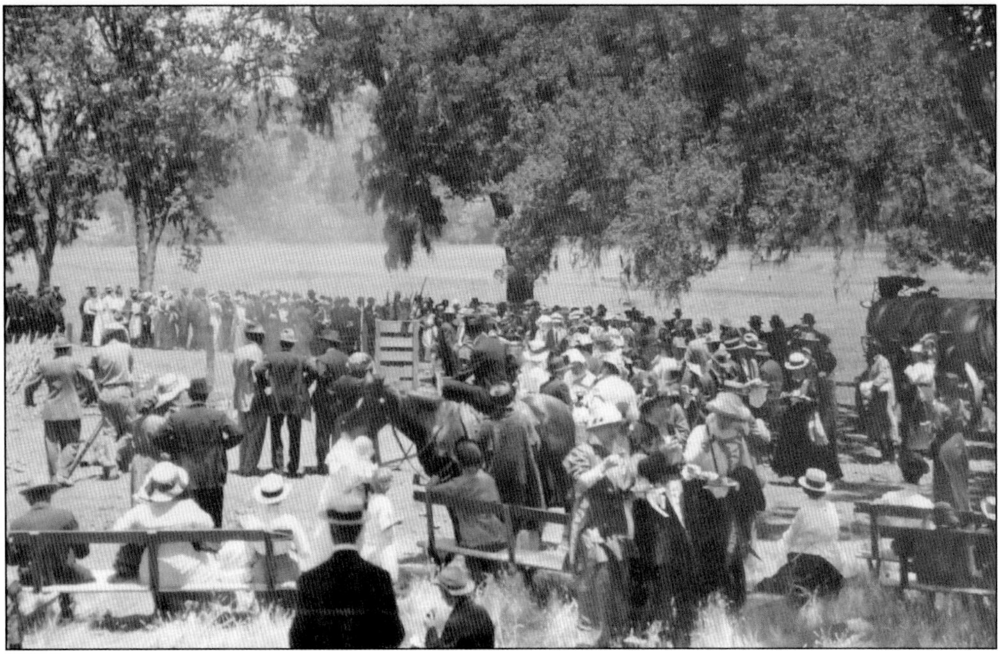

Men and women dressed up for the occasion, even though it was obviously held in an open, and probably dusty, area. Notice the formal attire: men and women in hats and suits and full dresses. (Courtesy of Kent Kenney Archives.)

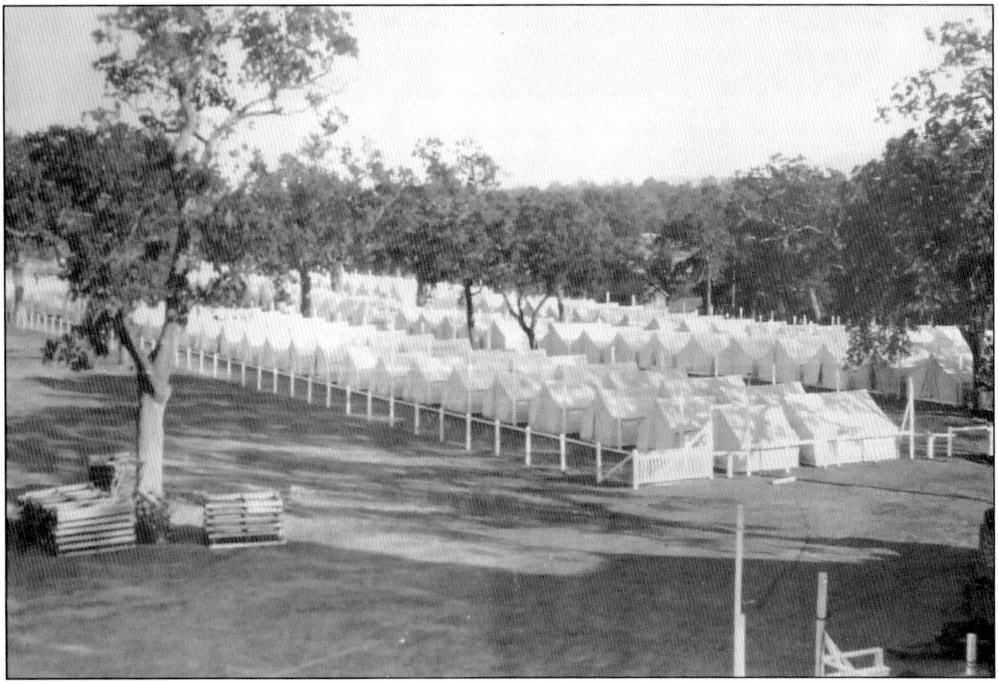

More than 1,000 tents were arranged in orderly fashion to house early residents and prospective investors before permanent lodgings were built. This Tent City contained everything needed for community life. There were residential tents, laundry tents, meeting tents, and even a grocery store. (Courtesy of Kent Kenney Archives.)

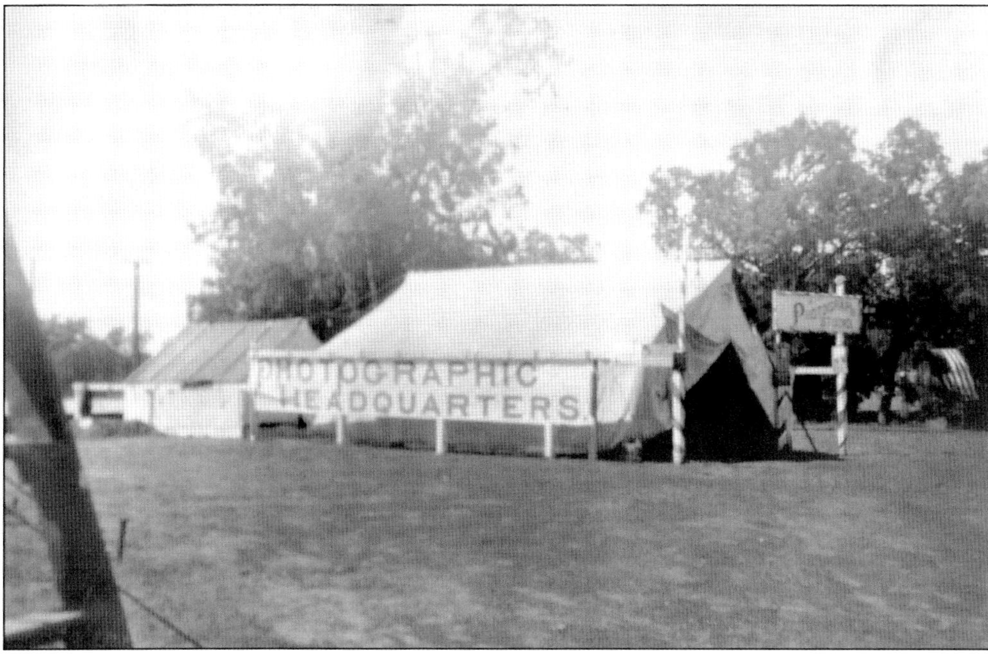

Ever the publicist, E.G. Lewis incorporated this photographic tent into the complex. (Courtesy of Kent Kenney Archives.)

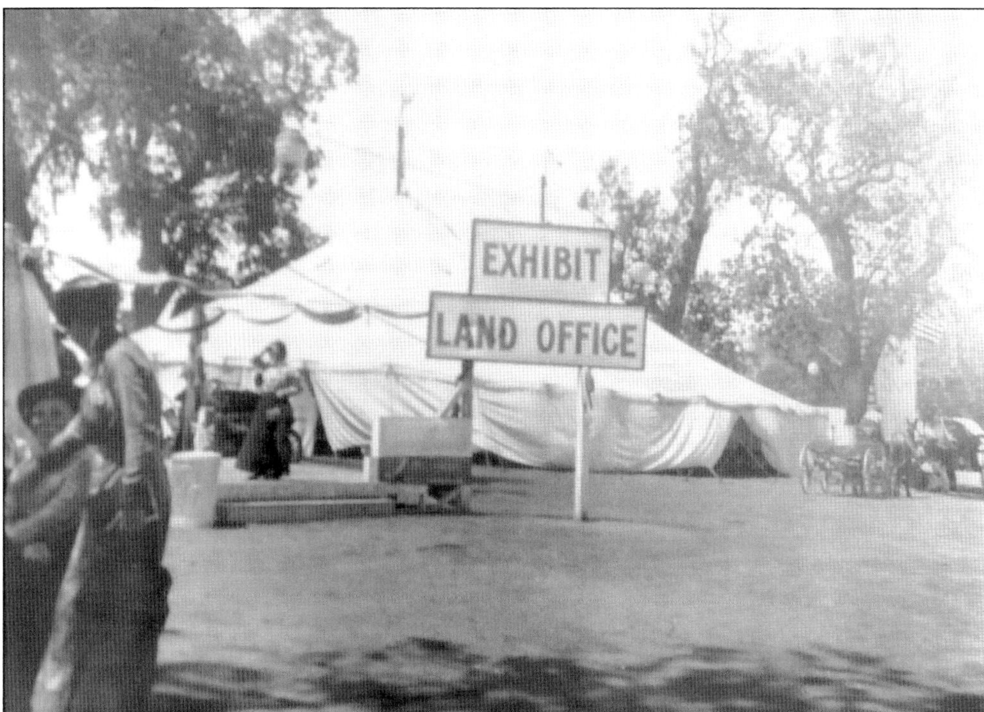

Lewis brought people in droves to inspect his property and select homesites. At the exhibit/homesite tent, he displayed a great map of the area. Visitors could select the lots they wished to view and were then whisked away to view their selections. (Courtesy of Kent Kenney Archives.)

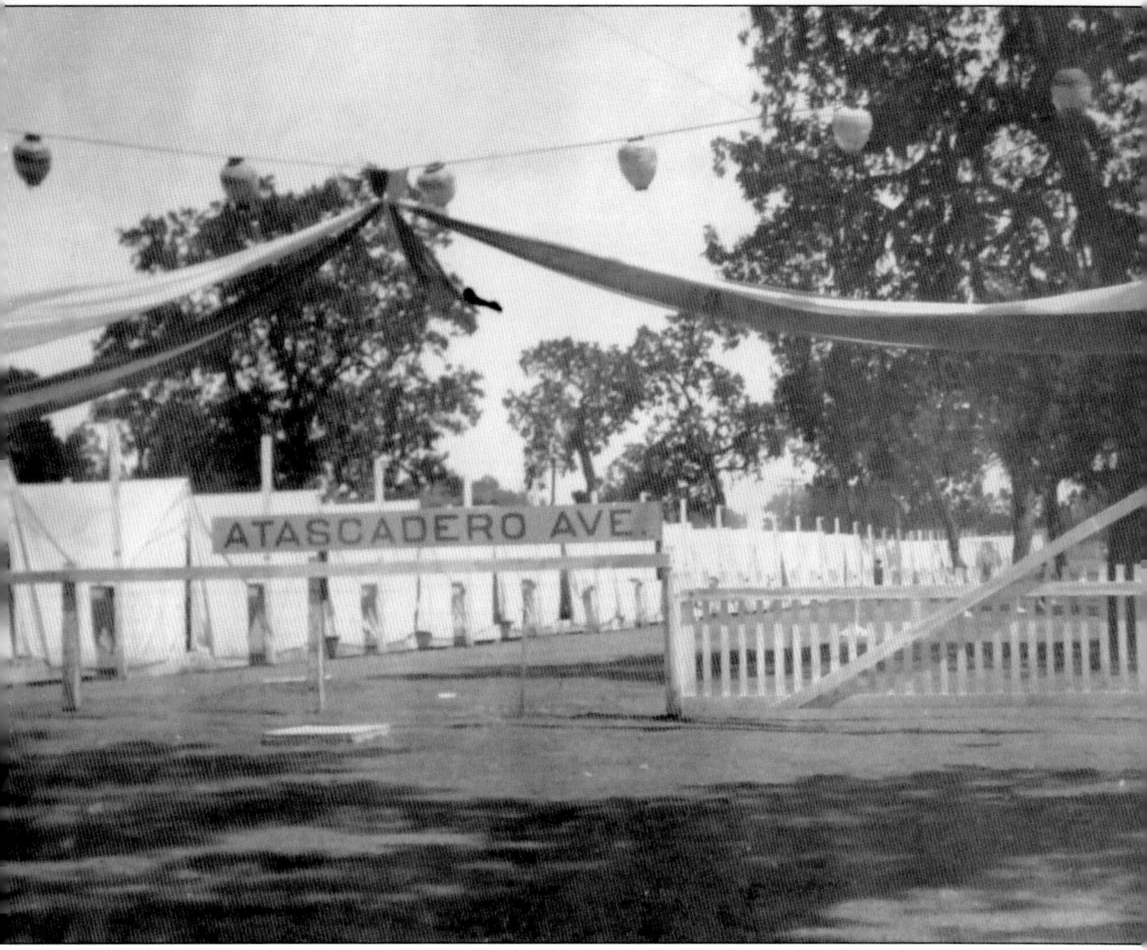

More than a campground, Tent City was laid out with city streets and lighted Japanese lanterns. (Courtesy of Kent Kenney Archives.)

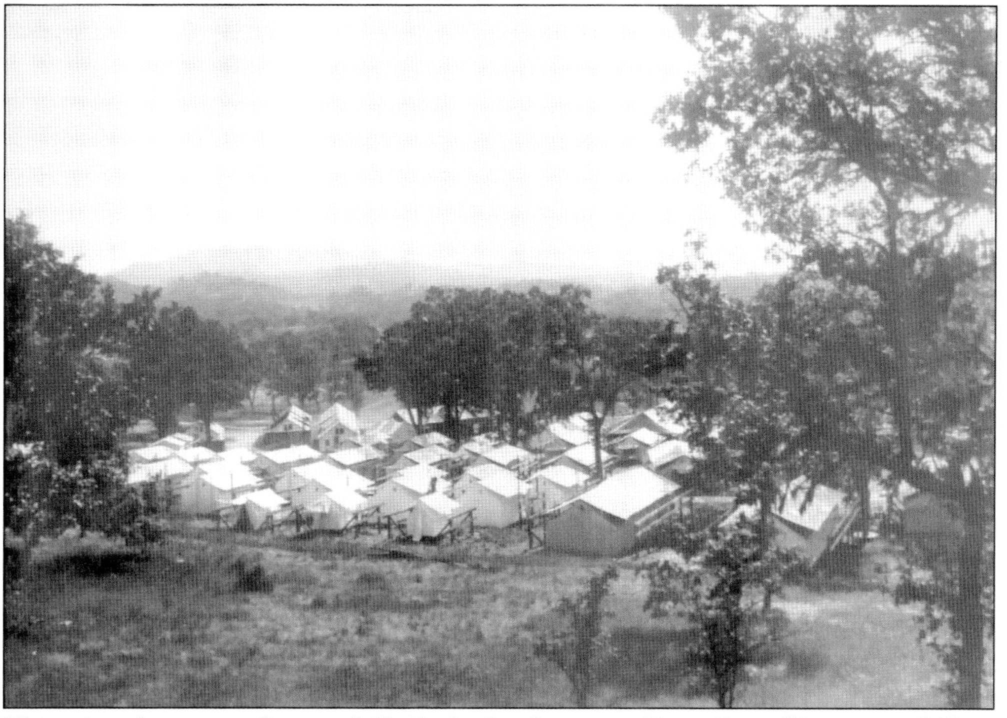

This view from an adjacent hillside looks down on Tent City. (Courtesy of Kent Kenney Archives.)

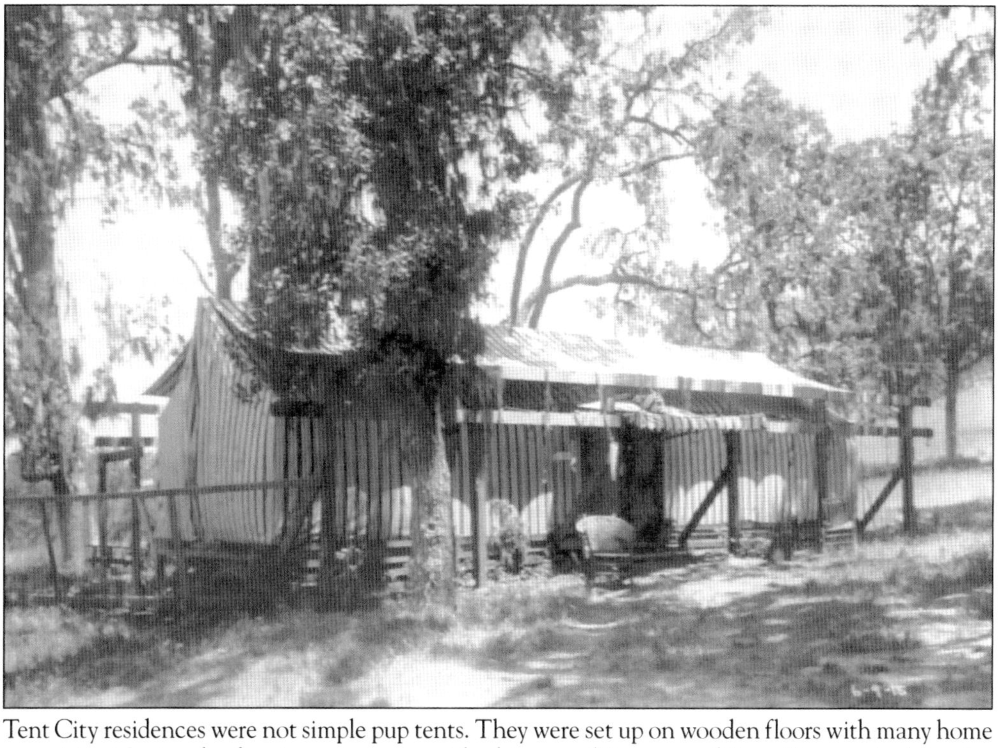

Tent City residences were not simple pup tents. They were set up on wooden floors with many home amenities. Notice the furniture sitting outside this tent. (Courtesy of Kent Kenney Archives.)

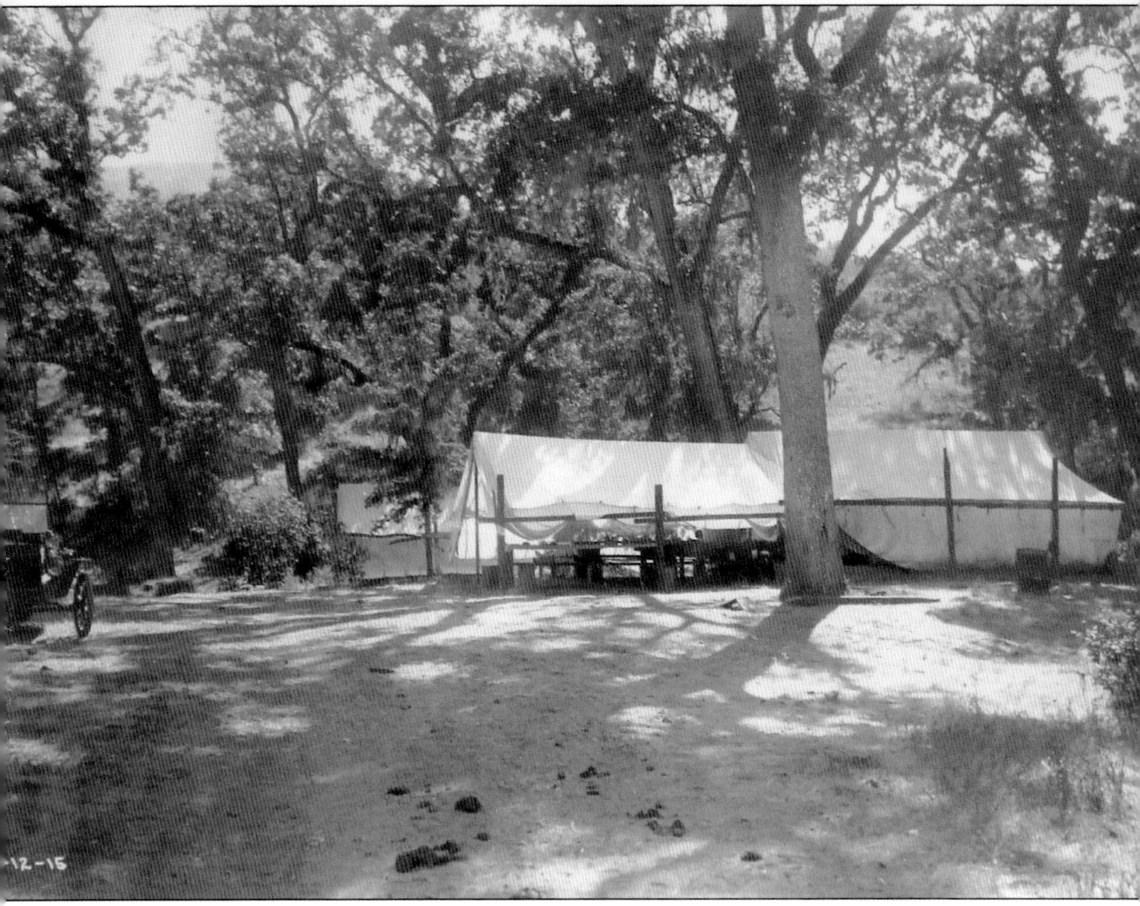

Pictured here is another view of Tent City residences. (Courtesy of Kent Kenney Archives.)

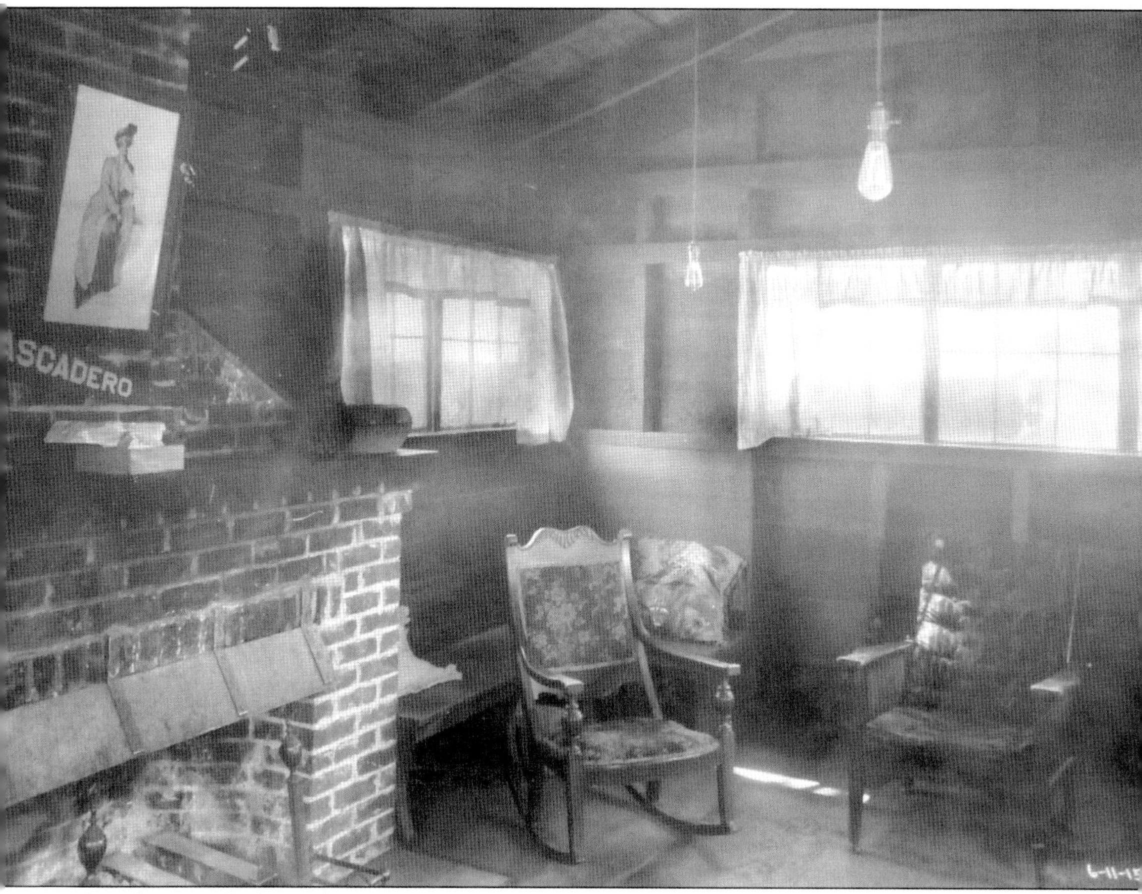

This photograph shows the interior of one of the dwelling structures at Tent City. Obviously more substantial than a tent, this residence even sports a brick fireplace. Tent City residents did enjoy a long list of amenities, including electric power. (Courtesy of Kent Kenney Archives.)

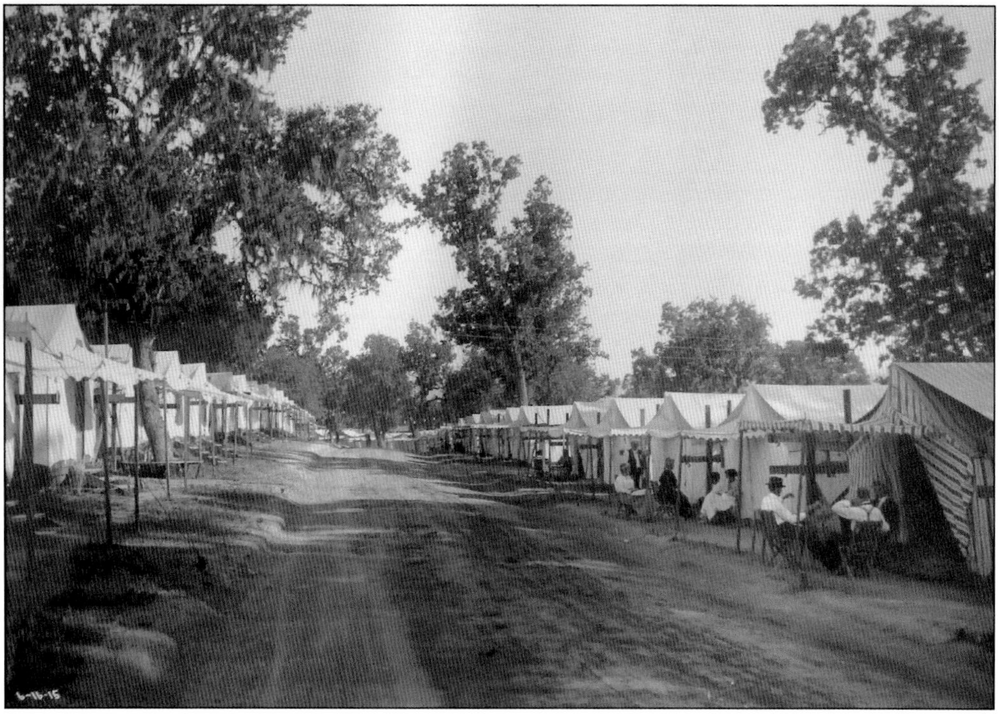

This is an additional view of the Tent City community. (Courtesy of Kent Kenney Archives.)

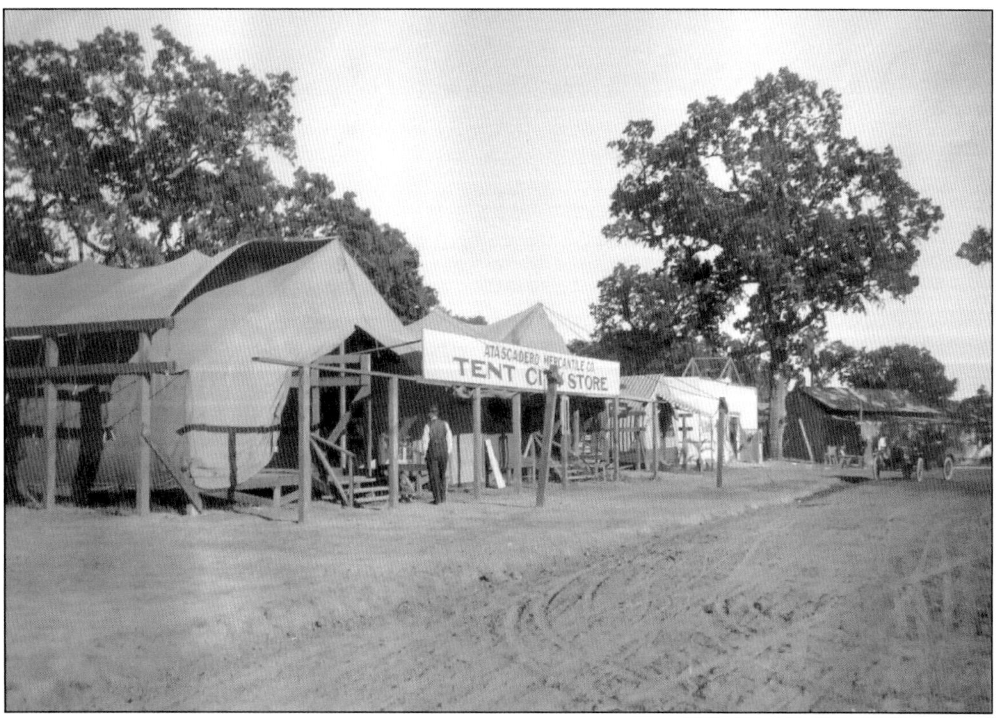

No decent Tent City can be without a general store. Under this tent, residents found the staples for everyday living. (Courtesy of Kent Kenney Archives.)

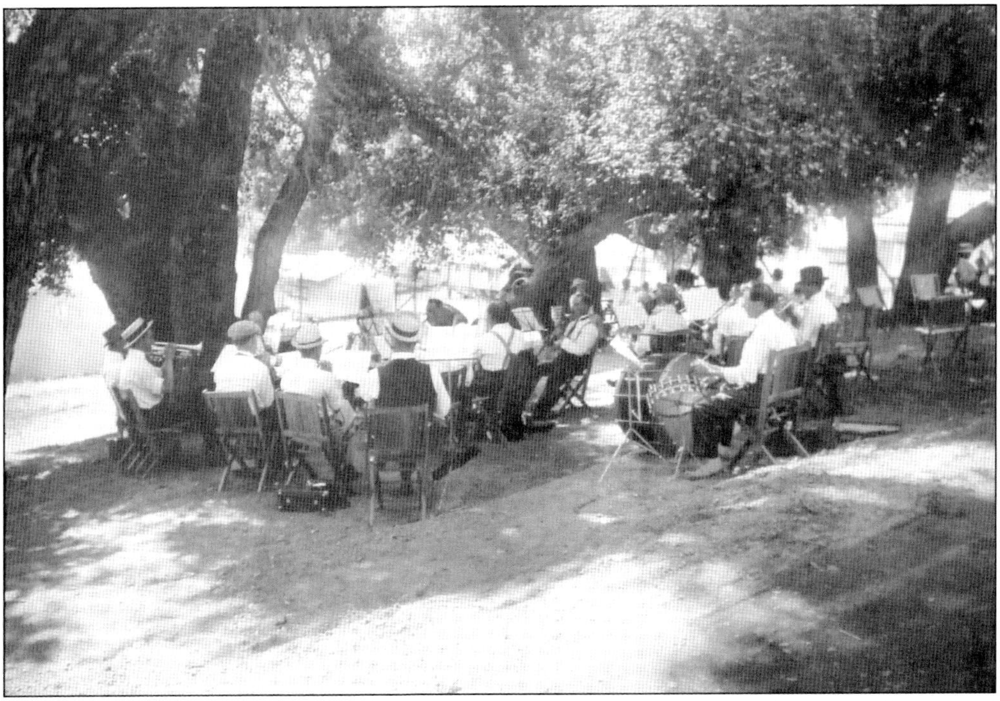

With Tent City in the background, local musicians take time to toss out a few tunes while seated comfortably in the shade. Music and the arts were important to early Atascadero residents. (Courtesy of Kent Kenney Archives.)

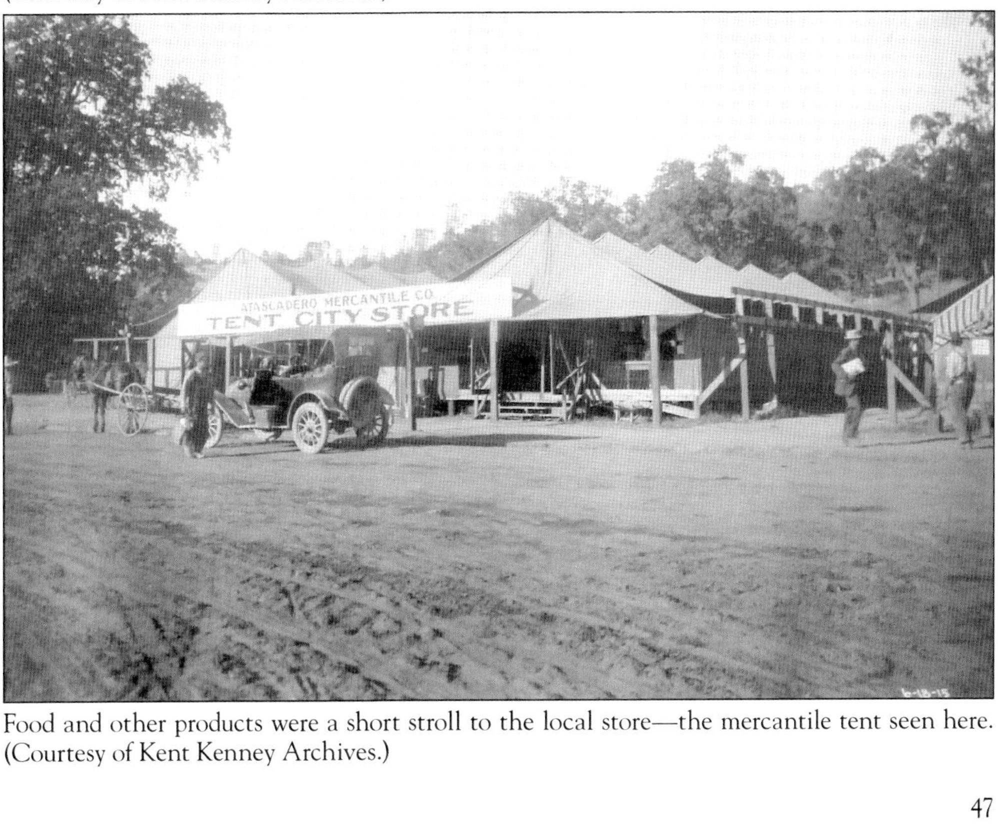

Food and other products were a short stroll to the local store—the mercantile tent seen here. (Courtesy of Kent Kenney Archives.)

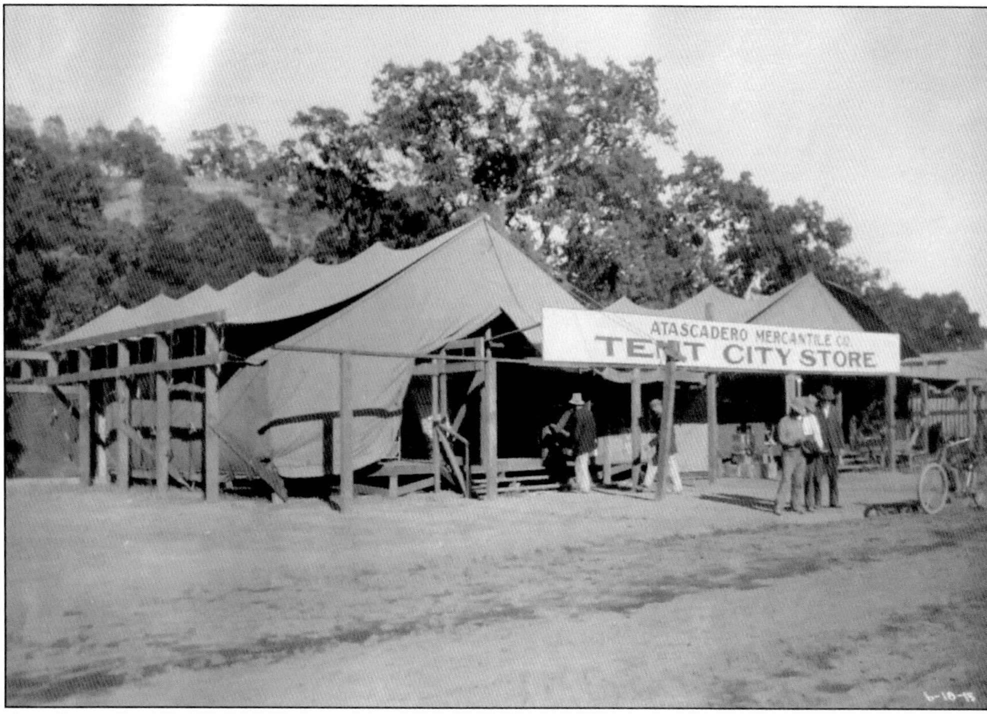

Another view of the Tent City store is pictured. (Courtesy of Kent Kenney Archives.)

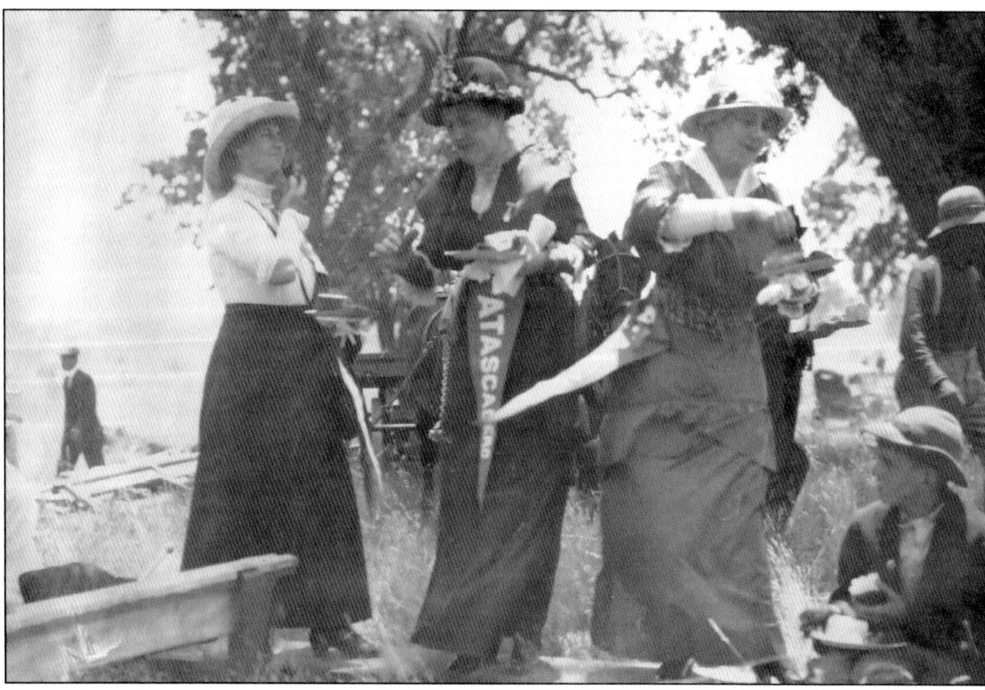

The ladies of Tent City join in the celebration and enjoy the offerings of the community barbecue. (Courtesy of Atascadero Historical Society.)

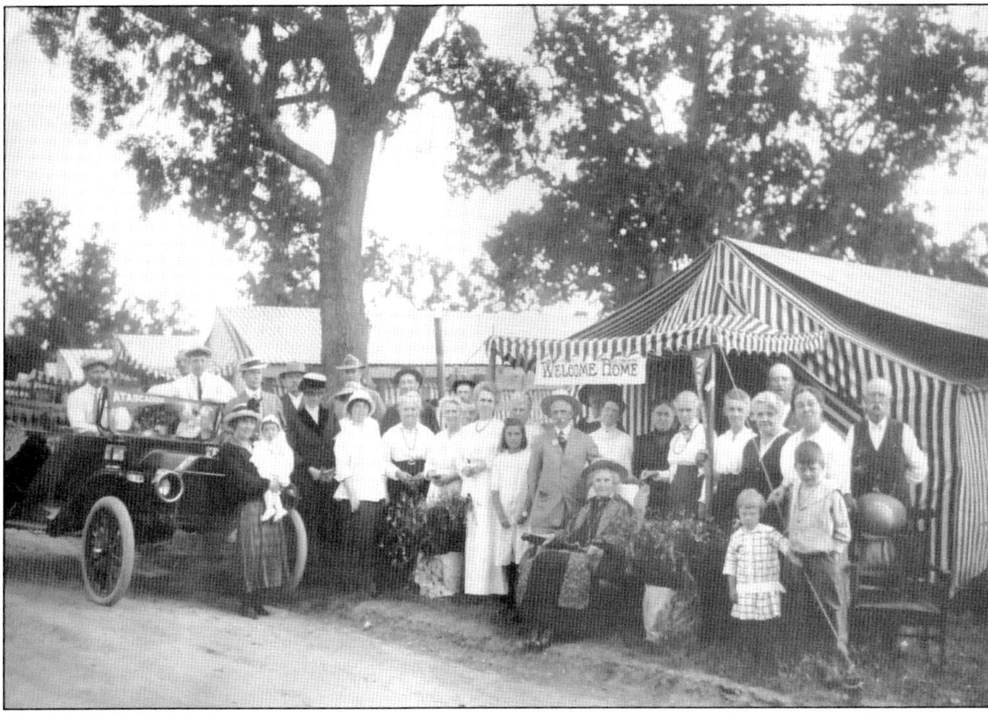

Welcome Home! Tent City residents greet newcomers to the colony of Atascadero. (Courtesy of Atascadero Historical Society.)

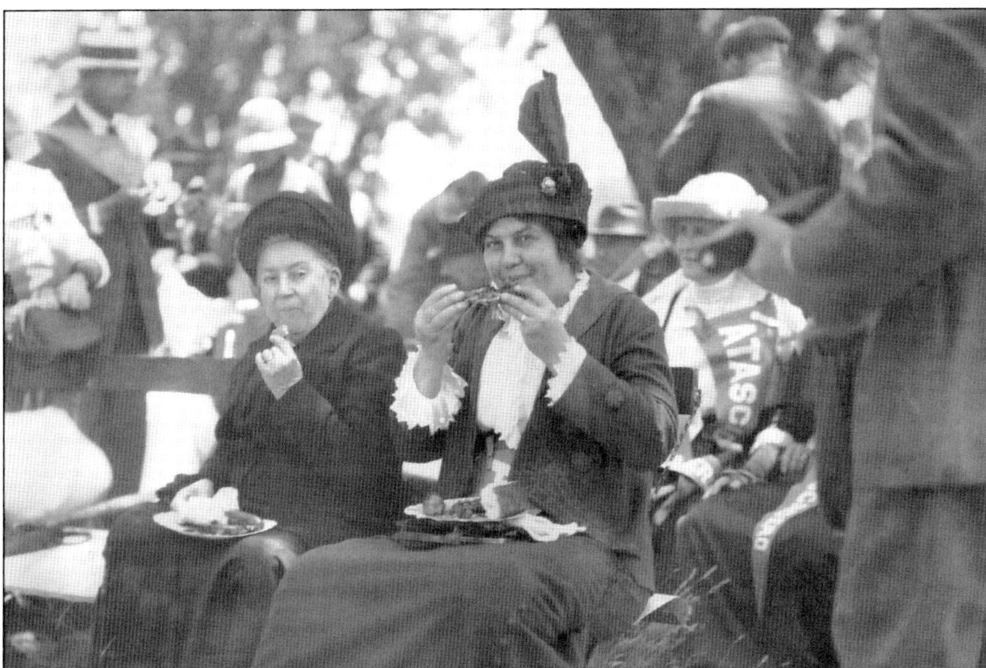

Mabel Lewis and friends participate in Tent City revelries. (Courtesy of Atascadero Historical Society.)

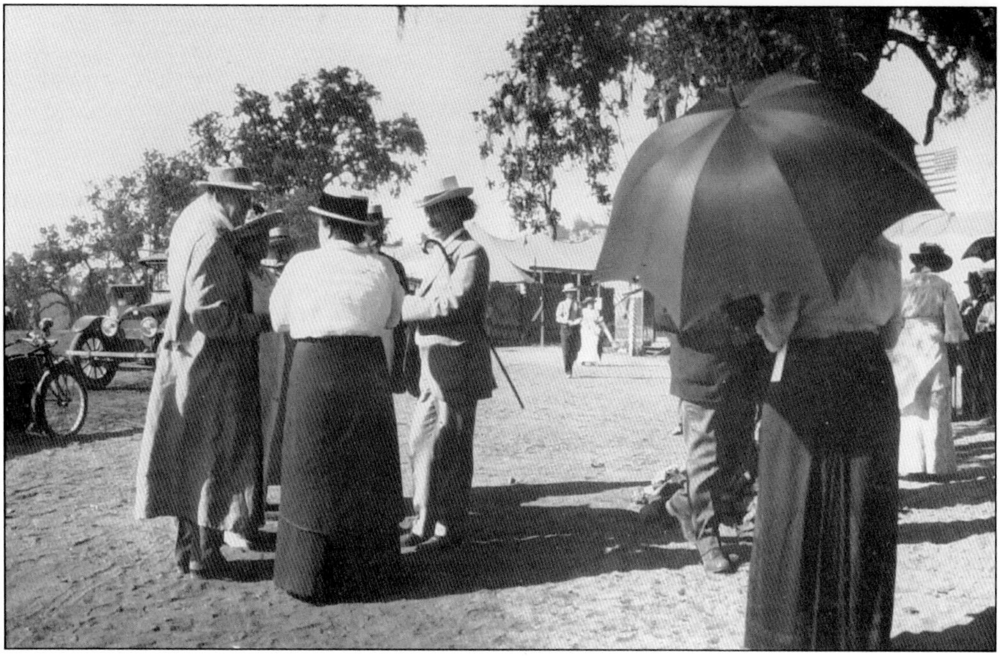

Atascadero was no stranger to the famous and influential of the day. Seen here, visiting with friends at Atascadero's Tent City, is world-famous pianist and, later, leader of Poland, Ignace Paderewski (the man in a white hat in the center of the picture). Paderewski owned vineyards in the Paso Robles area just 10 miles north of Atascadero. (Courtesy of Kent Kenney Archives.)

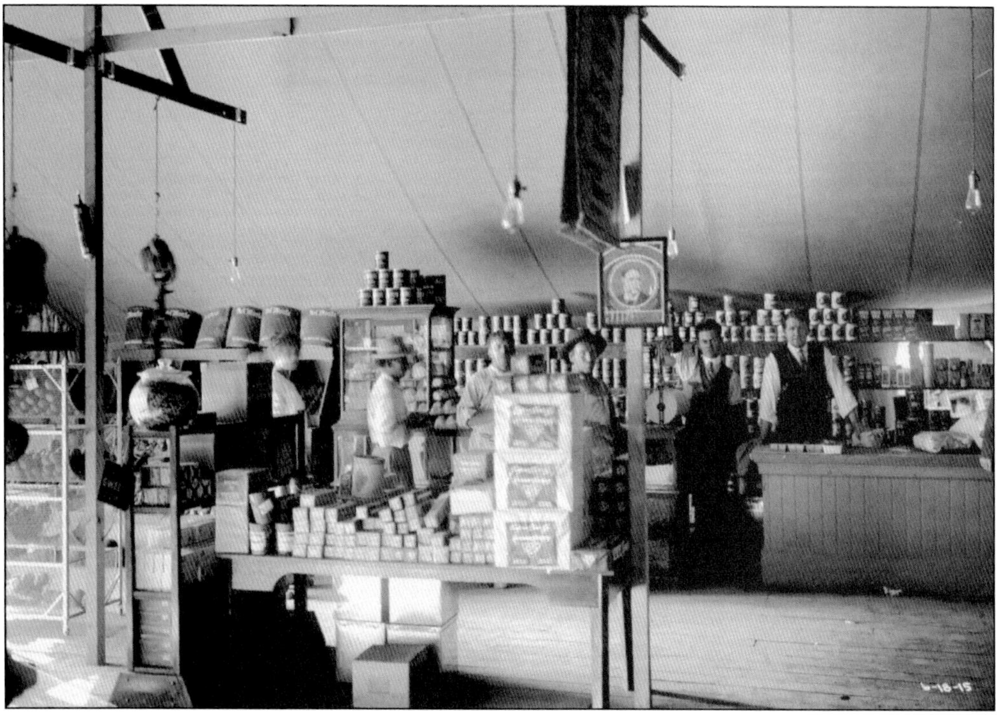

Tent City included most of the amenities found in a regular city, including a grocery store, as shown in this photograph. (Courtesy of Kent Kenney Archives.)

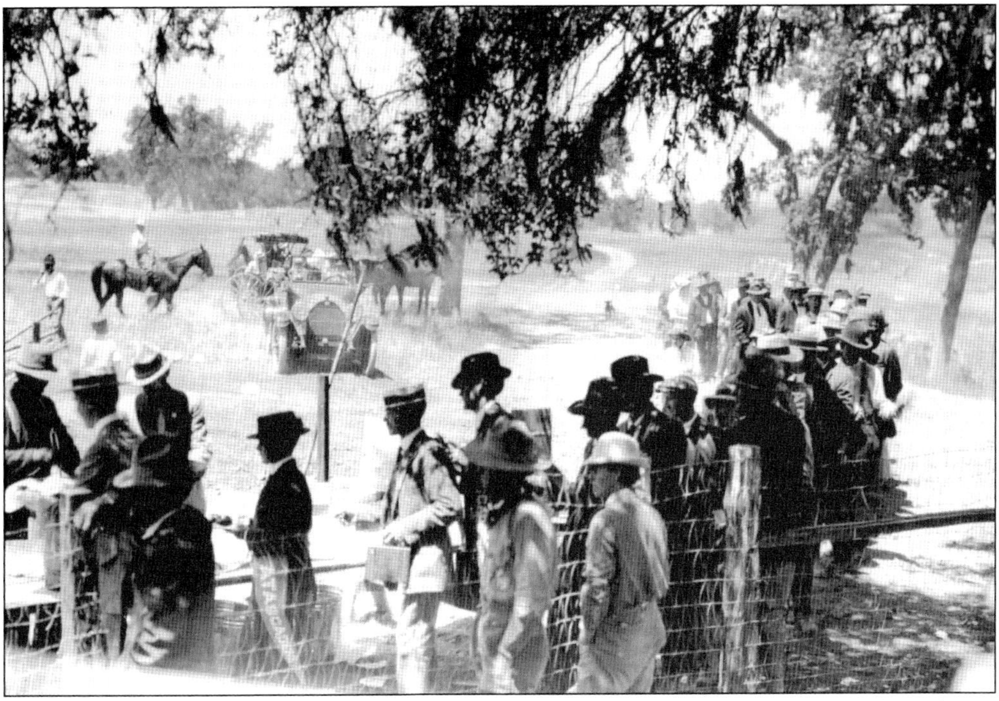

Crowds of Tent City residents, visitors, and potential investors enjoyed the hospitality of E.G. Lewis when he rolled out the red carpet to promote the features of his new utopia. (Courtesy of Kent Kenney Archives.)

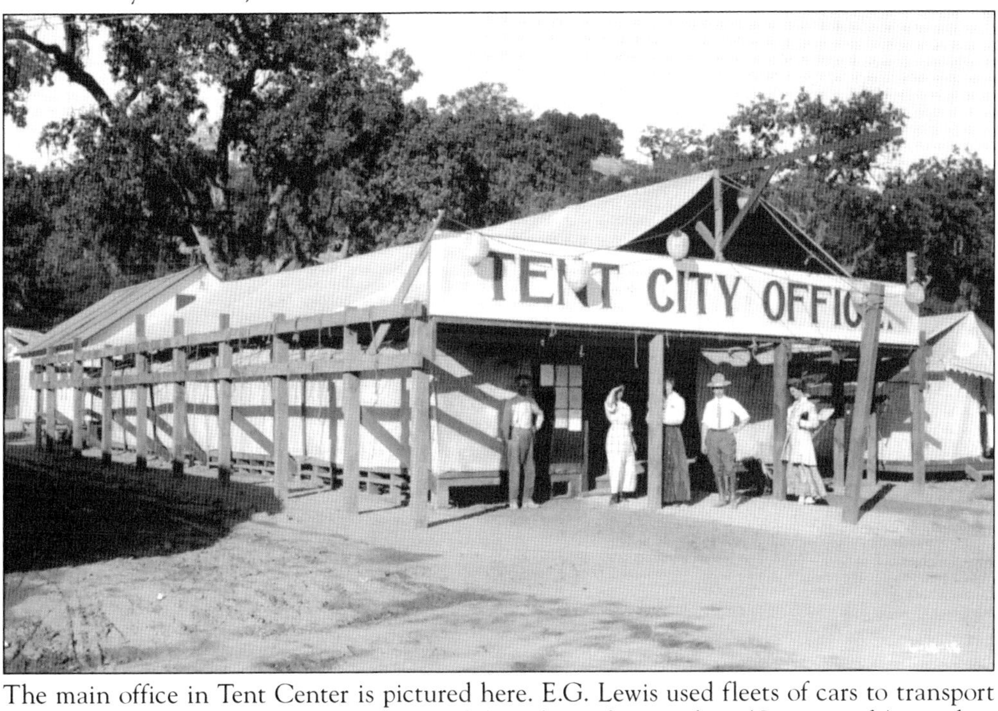

The main office in Tent Center is pictured here. E.G. Lewis used fleets of cars to transport potential investors to areas of interest around the colony of Atascadero. (Courtesy of Atascadero Historical Society.)

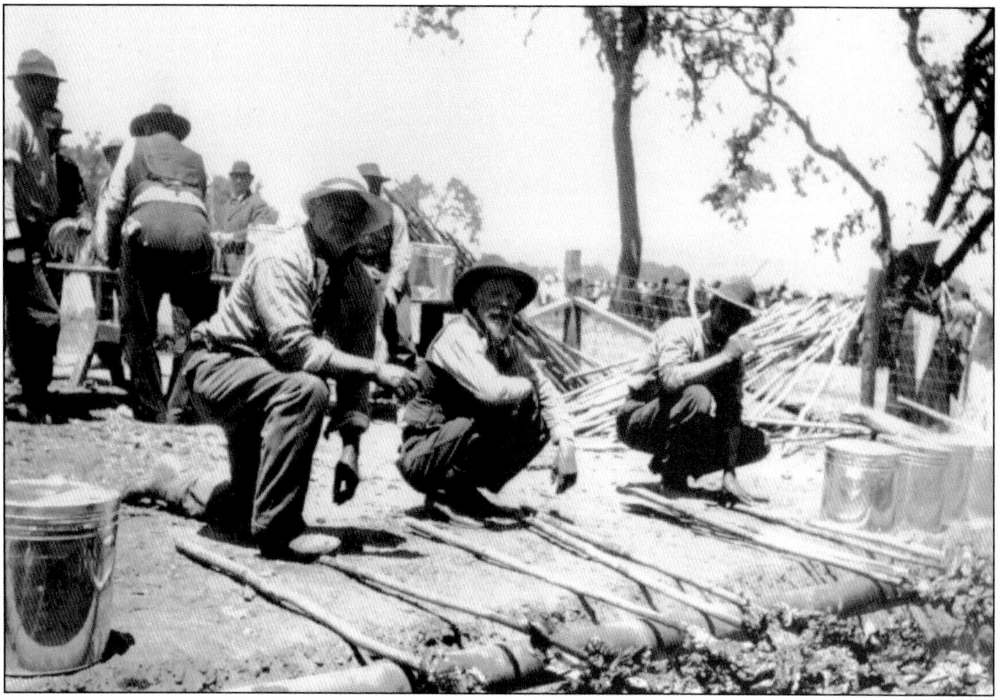

Food is being prepared for the masses. Atascadero cooks line the pit barbecues, preparing fare for residents and visitors. (Courtesy of Kent Kenney Archives.)

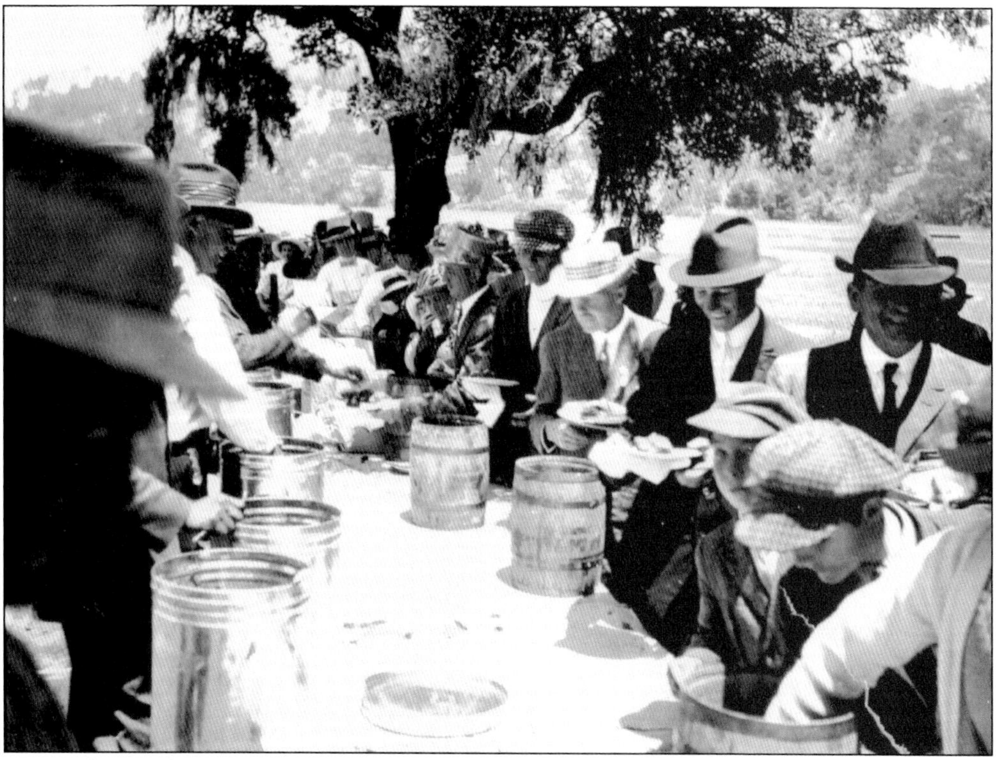

Visitors line up for food and refreshments. (Courtesy of Kent Kenney Archives.)

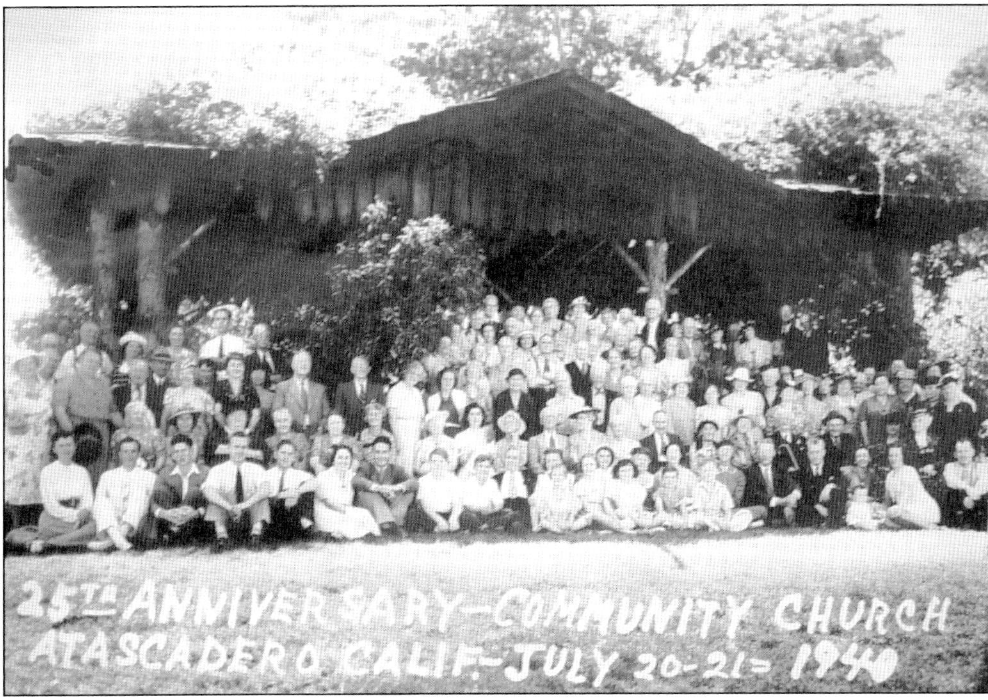

The Community Church was one of two congregations to be born from the original Federated Church. The Community Church still operates on Rosario Avenue. (Courtesy of Atascadero Community Church.)

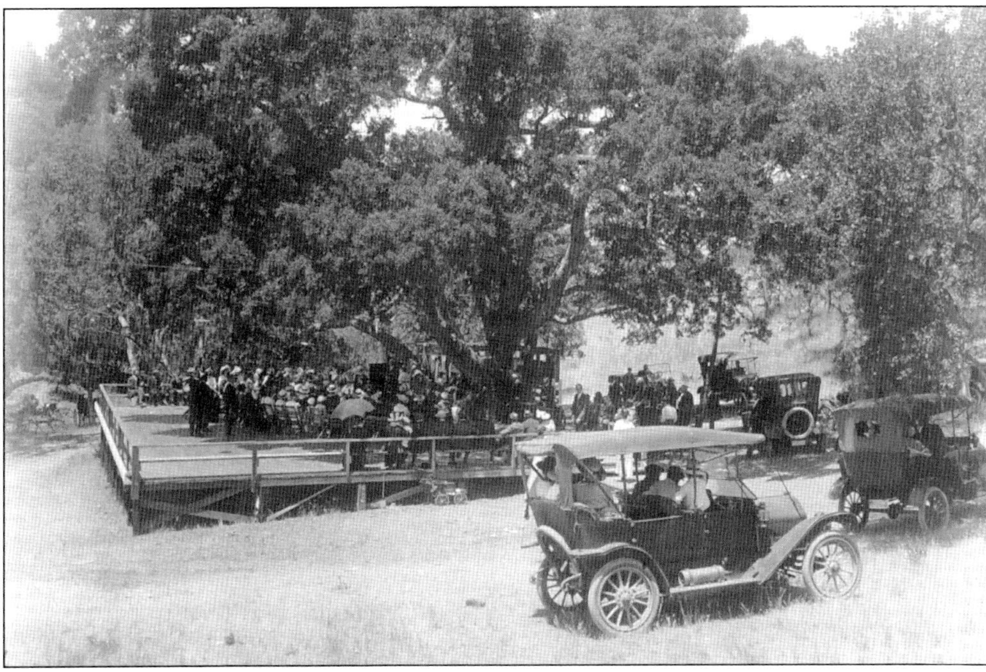

Stadium Park, a natural amphitheater near Tent City, was improved with a stage, seating, and electric power to accommodate social gatherings, weddings, and conventions. (Courtesy of Atascadero Historical Society.)

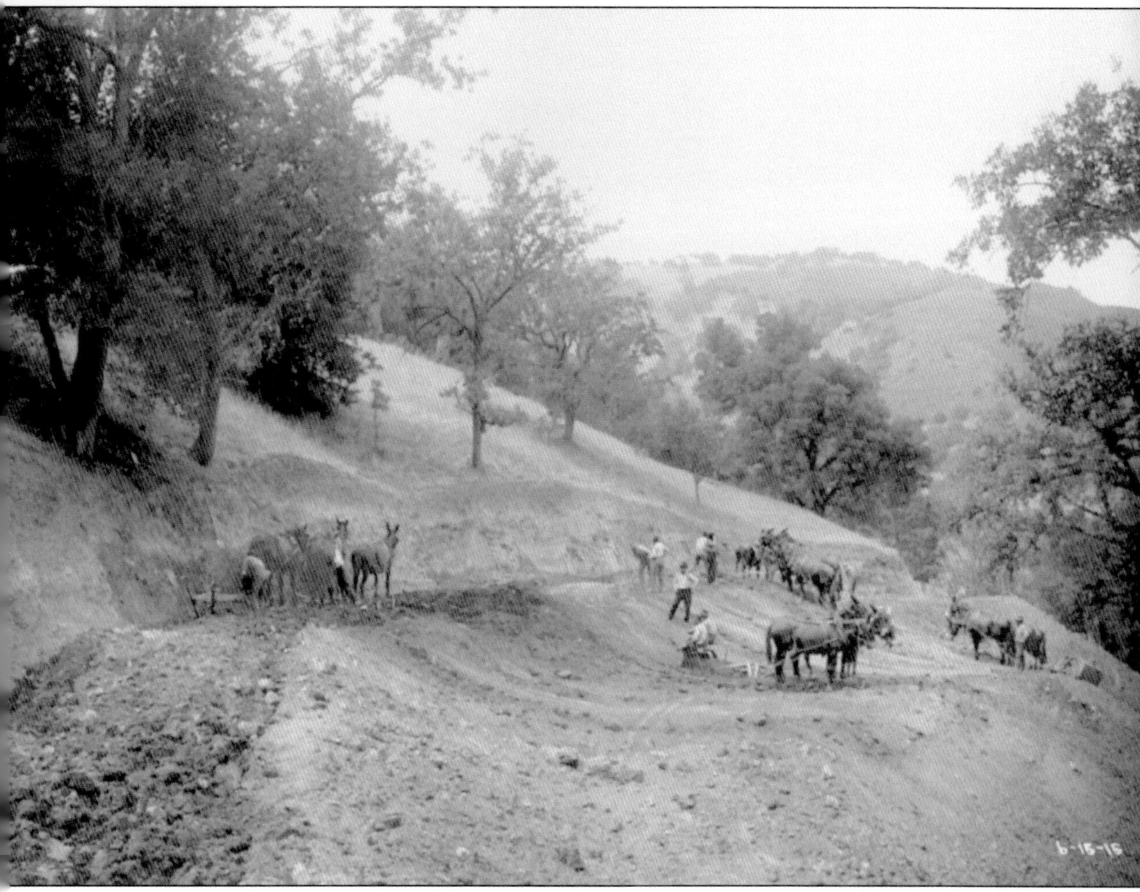

Explosives and equipment drawn by mules and horses were used to forge a 17-mile road through the Santa Lucia Mountains to the Pacific Coast. It linked the colony of Atascadero with the Cloisters resort and eventually came to be known as State Highway 41–E.G. Lewis Highway. (Courtesy of Atascadero Historical Society.)

Three

Commerce in Utopia

The first building constructed in Atascadero was an immense printery housing state-of-the-art rotogravure presses. Publications created at the printery included *Woman's National Magazine*, *Woman's National Weekly*, and the *Illustrated Review*. The *Illustrated Review* enjoyed incarnations as the *California Illustrated Review* and the *Atascadero Illustrated Review*. The building was adorned with an impressive arching entrance, a staircase, and murals of local scenes painted by Ralph Holmes, a noted artist from Chicago.

The Mercantile, or "La Plaza," was the first shopping center in California. It housed businesses on the first floor and the elegant Atascadero Inn on the second floor. The complex provided parking for up to 200 cars. Ironically, the Mercantile's fate was sealed when businesses began to emerge along El Camino Real, drawing motoring traffic away from the shopping center. In the 1920s, the building was remodeled. Notable guests included Hoot Gibson and Sally Rand. September 13, 1934, the structure was destroyed by fire

Agriculture played a large part in the story of Atascadero. Some 3,000 acres of fruit trees were planted. The Atascadero Seed Company was created, and the plan was for the company to provide small farms with seeds, supervision, and harvesting assistance. The result was to have been a kind of cooperative operation where residents would share in the bounty.

Lewis formed yet another business, the Caladero Products Company, to supply food for the military during World War I. Wars end, thankfully, but the end of the conflict also brought about cancellation of government food contracts. The dehydrating operation was a total loss.

The Dooley Doll and Toy Factory, founded by San Francisco resident Terrance Dooley, produced a unique line of dolls and other toys. The first Dooley products hit the market in 1919.

Abner and Warren Doble tried to produce the Doble Steam Car in Atascadero. They broke ground on a 100,000-square-foot assembly plant in 1922. Abner Doble told local residents he would hire 175 employees, construct 350 cars per year, and produce $1 million per year for local projects. The Dobles ran afoul of the State Commissioner of Corporations. Abner Doble wound up in San Quentin Prison, though he was later released on a technicality. The dream of a Doble steam-powered car produced in Atascadero came to an end, as did the Doble Steam Car Company.

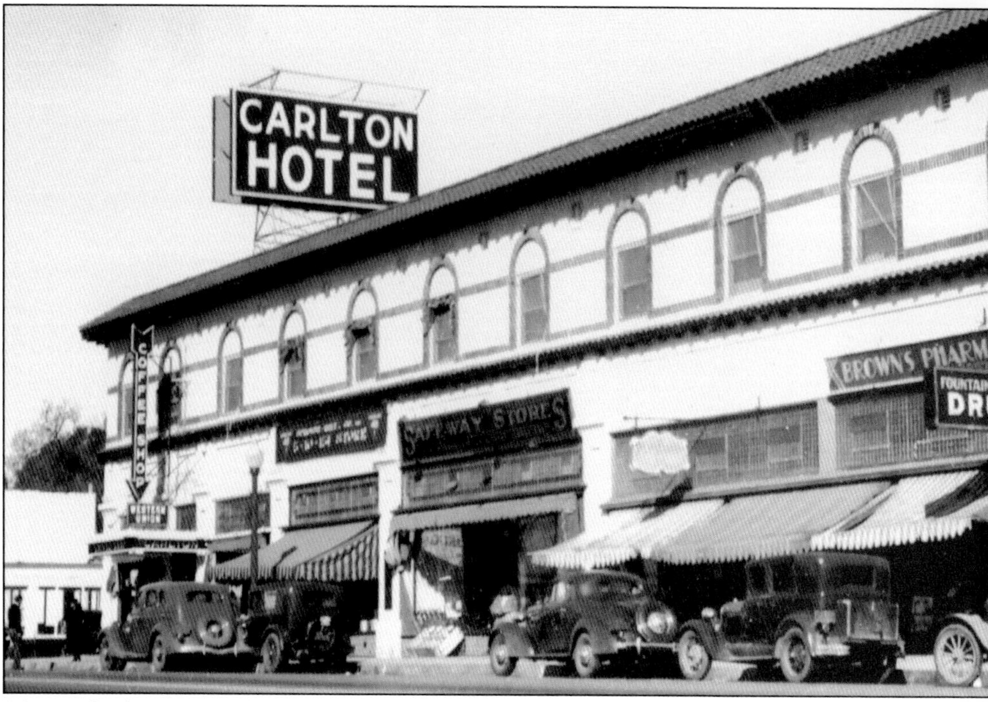

This is the historic Carlton Hotel in the center of downtown Atascadero. The hotel has since been torn down and replaced with a new Carlton Hotel created to resemble the original. (Courtesy of Kent Kenney Archives.)

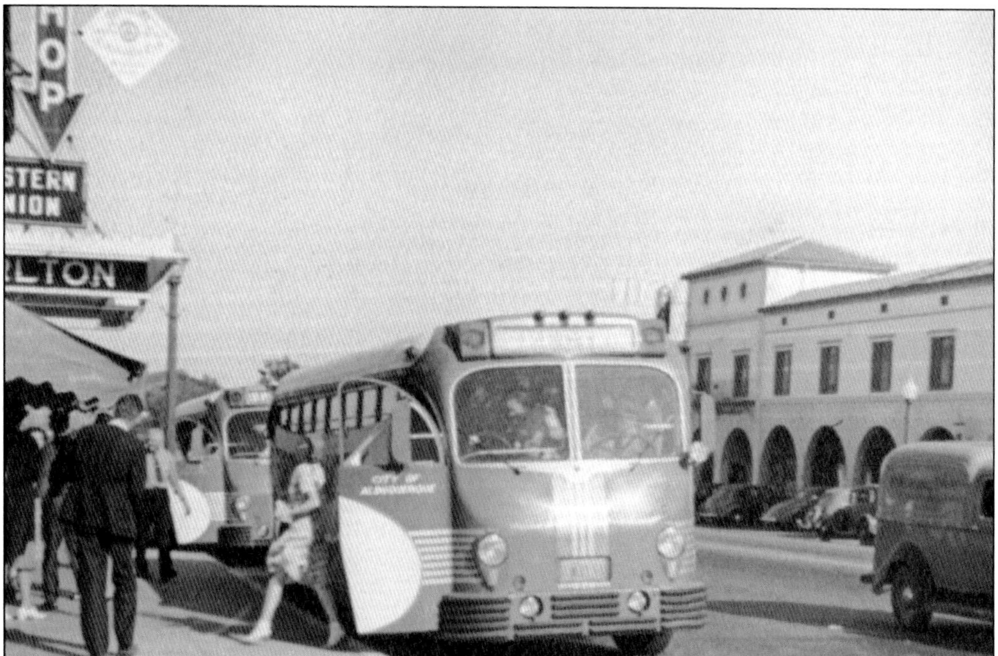

Here, a bus traveling El Camino Real stops to allow passengers to exit in front of the Carlton Hotel at the intersection with Traffic Way in this photograph of Atascadero's bustling downtown. (Courtesy of Atascadero Historical Society.)

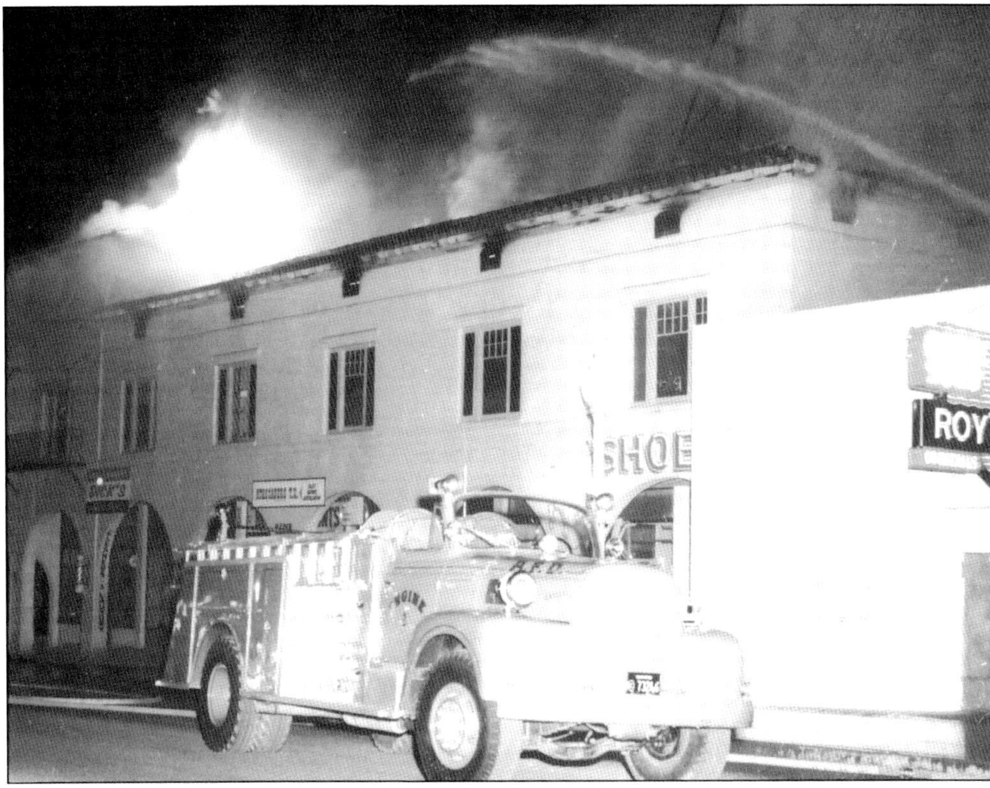

The Atascadero Hotel (not to be confused with the earlier Atascadero Inn) joined the ranks of historic buildings that have fallen to fire. The building burned in 1965. (Courtesy of Atascadero Historical Society.)

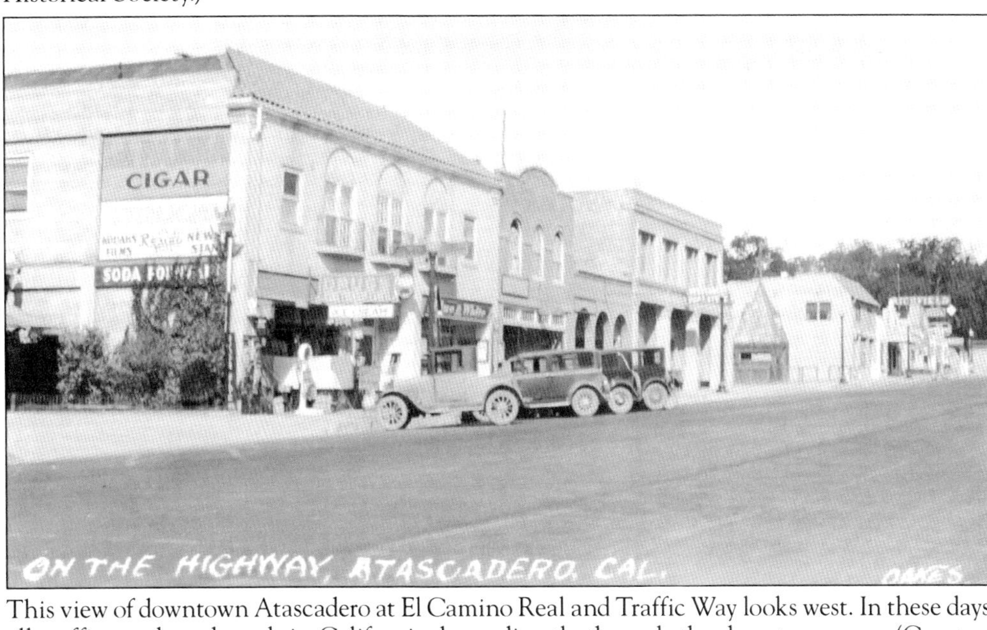

This view of downtown Atascadero at El Camino Real and Traffic Way looks west. In these days, all traffic north and south in California drove directly through the downtown area. (Courtesy of Kent Kenney Archives.)

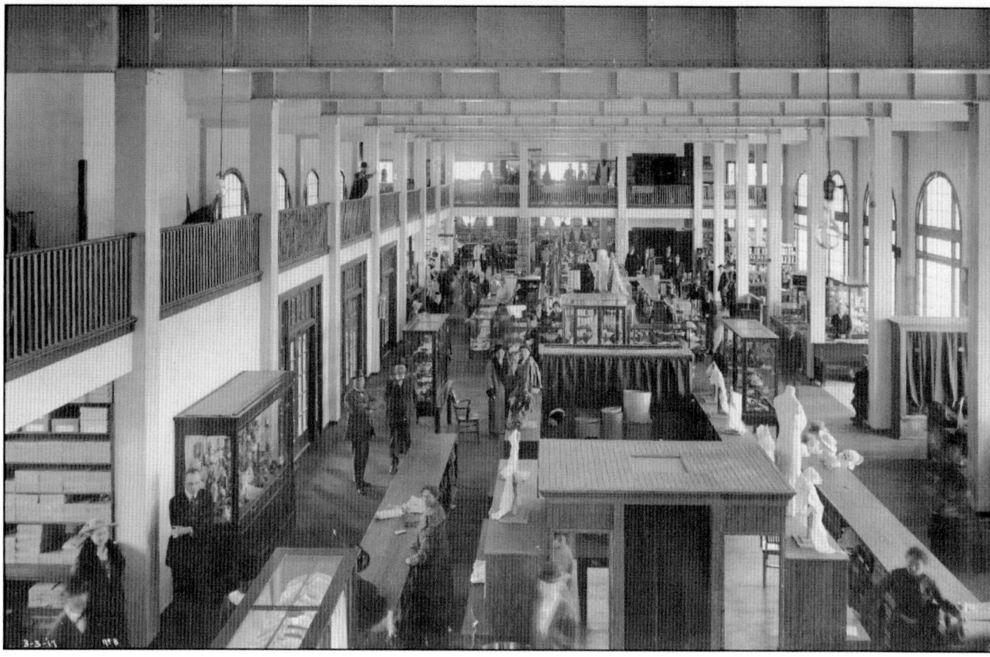

This is an interior view of the shopping area in the Mercantile/La Plaza building. This shopping center was unique in the 1920s. (Courtesy of Atascadero Historical Society.)

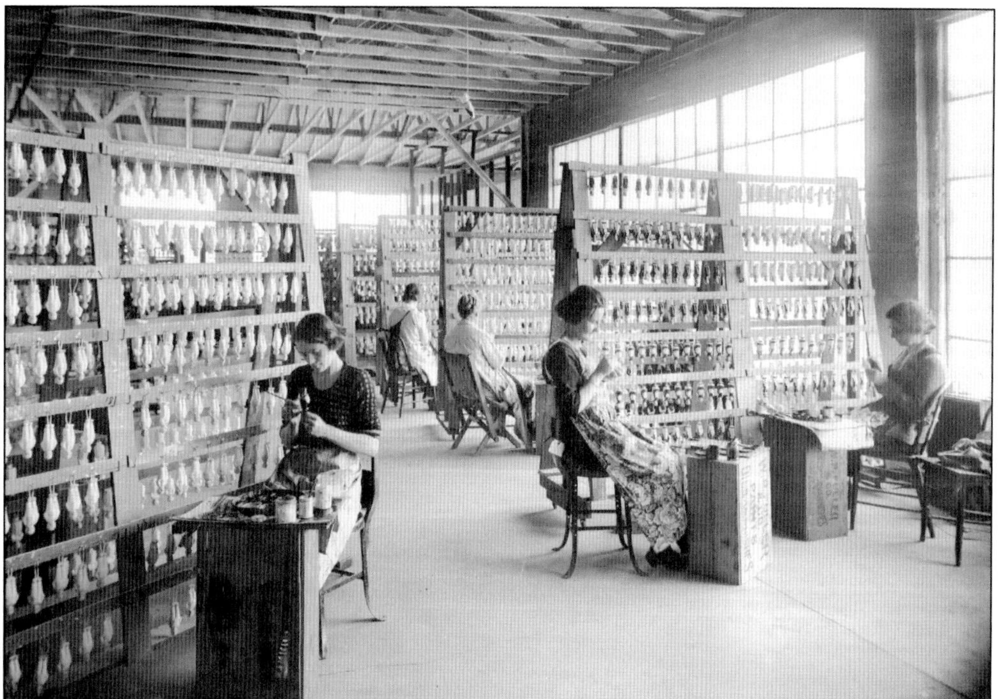

Local Atascadero ladies were hired by the Dooley Doll and Toy Factory in the 1920s. Those pictured are putting the final paint on the dolls before they are ready to be sold. Surviving dolls are quite collectible and may sometimes be found for sale with other Atascadero memorabilia on various websites. (Courtesy of Kent Kenney Archives.)

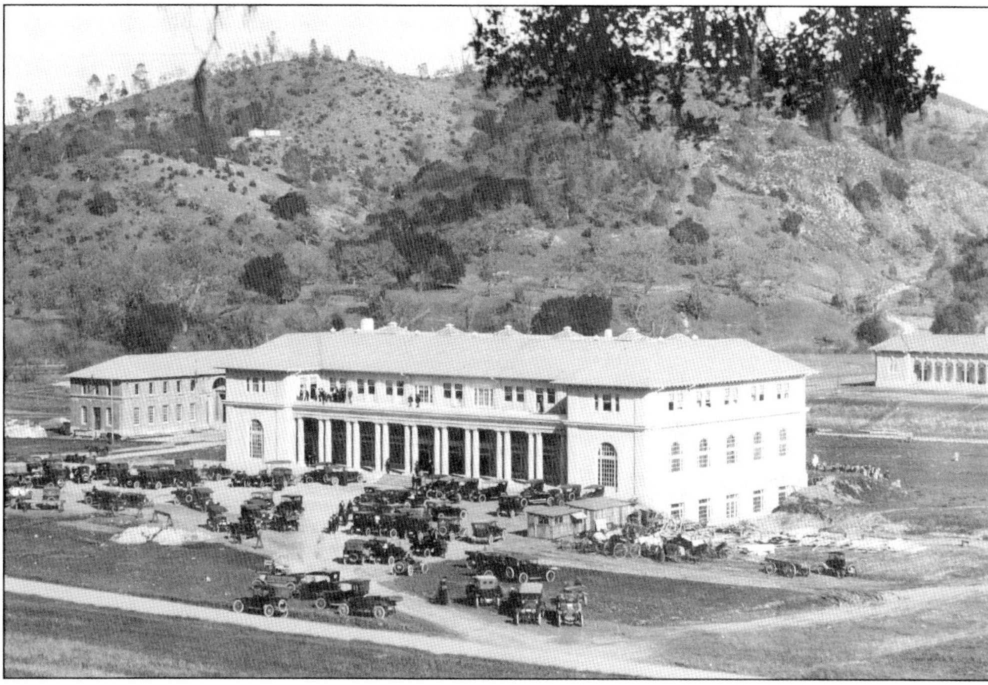

This is a wide shot of the Mercantile/La Plaza building on Traffic Way. Note the ample space for automobile parking. (Courtesy of Atascadero Historical Society.)

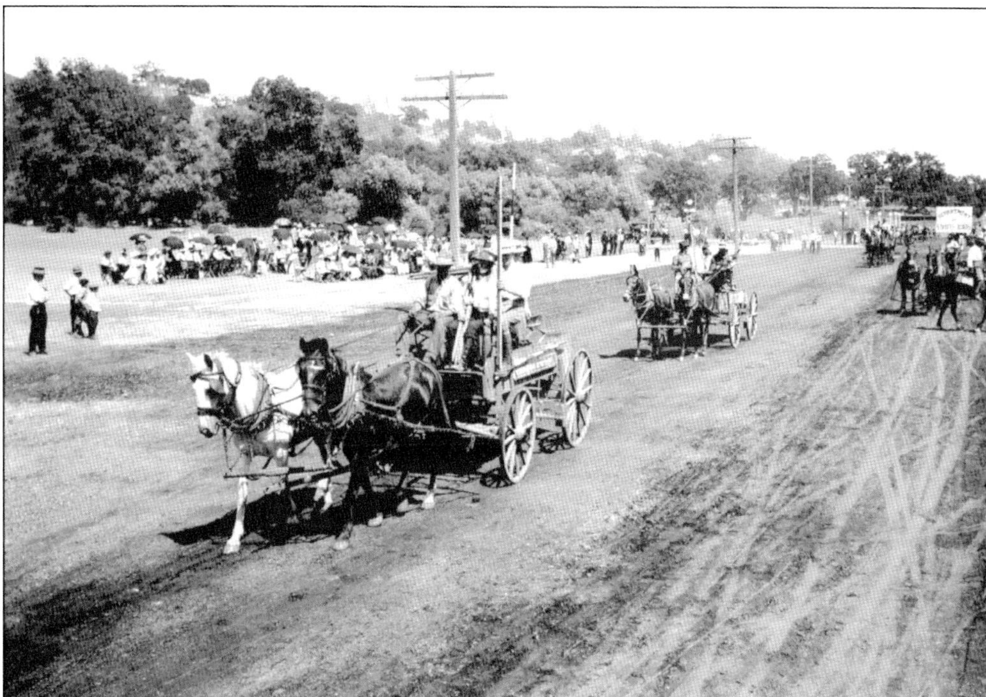

To impress potential customers, an Industry Parade was staged very early in the history of the colony. Wagons from every construction profession were represented as wave after wave of workers joined in. (Courtesy of Atascadero Historical Society.)

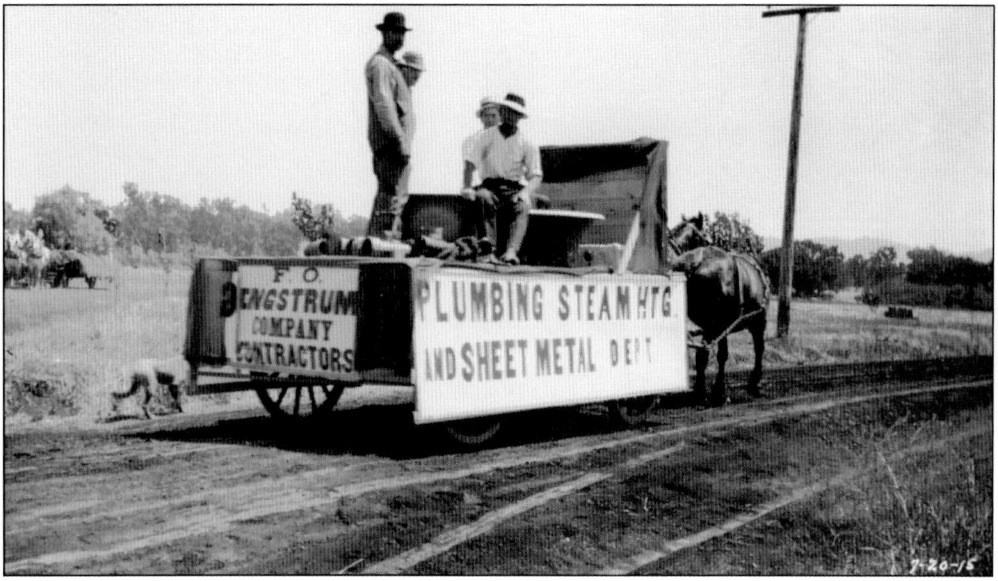

F.O. Engstrum Company was the contractor for Atascadero's great civic center and administration building. This 1917 photograph shows one entry in the parade of progress that accompanied the construction of that building. (Courtesy of Atascadero Historical Society.)

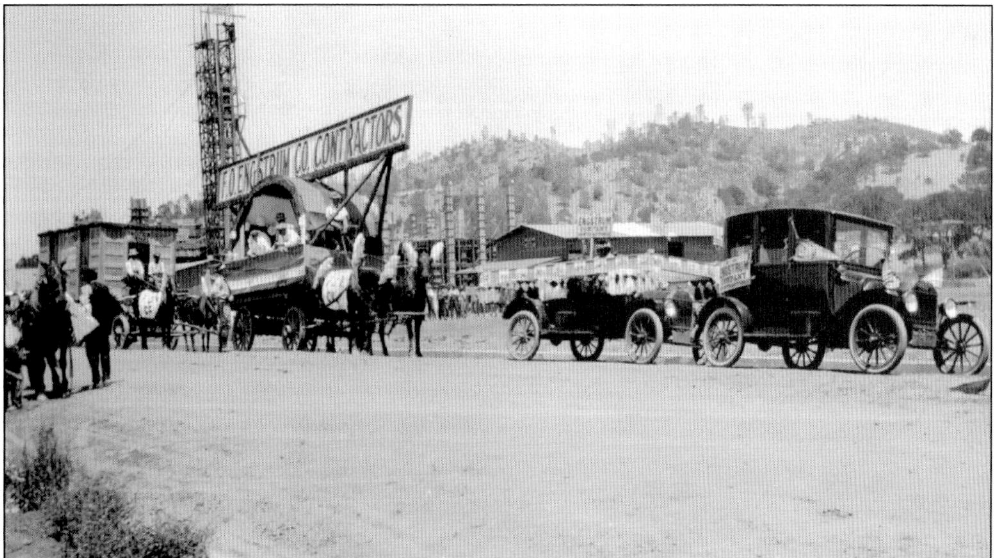

The beginnings of the civic center, the second building constructed in Atascadero, emerge in the background; F.O. Engstrum vehicles, among others, pass in front. (Courtesy of Atascadero Historical Society.)

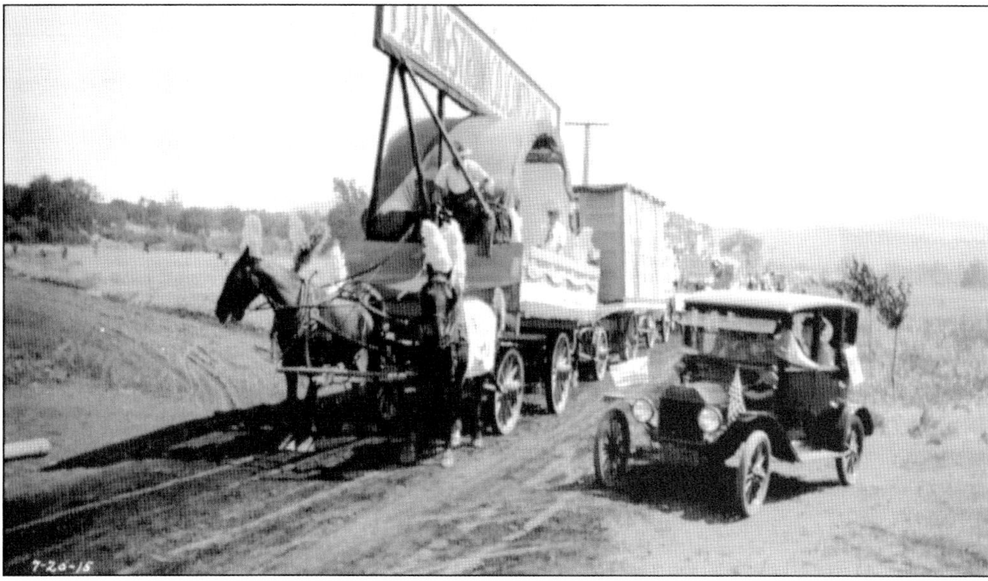

Pomp and circumstance were standard fare for E.G. Lewis's promotions. Here, an F.O. Engstrum vehicle is towed by adorned horses. (Courtesy of Atascadero Historical Society.)

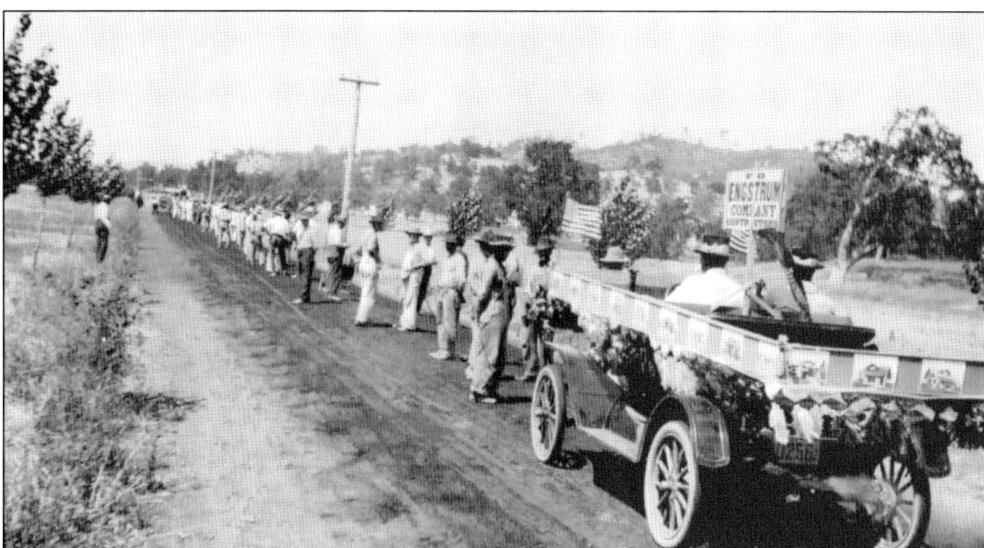

This 1920 image shows a procession of construction vehicles. Note the photographs of colony homes attached to the trailing vehicle. (Courtesy Atascadero Historical Society.)

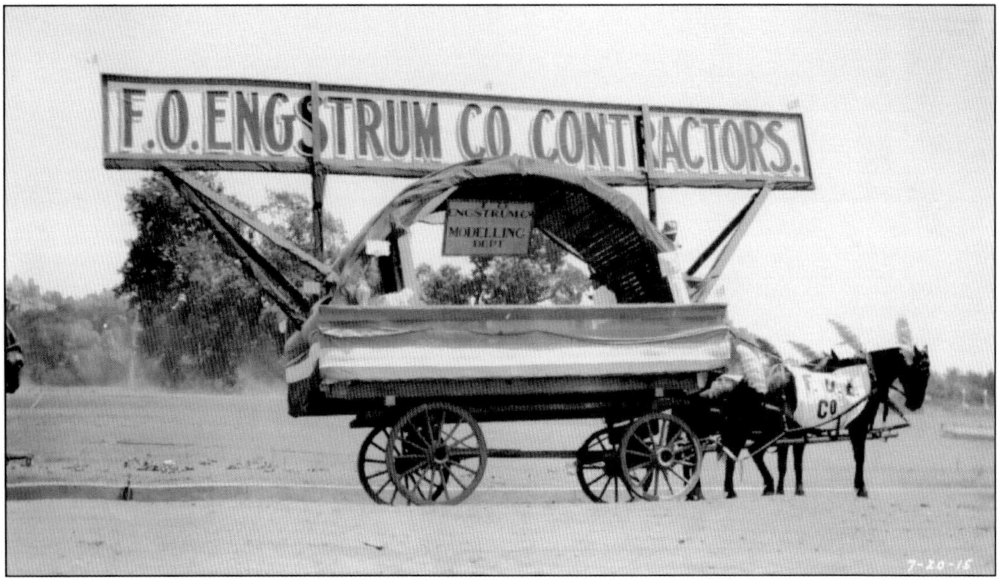

A vehicle containing offerings from F.O. Engstrum's modeling department sits parked curbside near the site of the civic center building. (Courtesy of Atascadero Historical Society.)

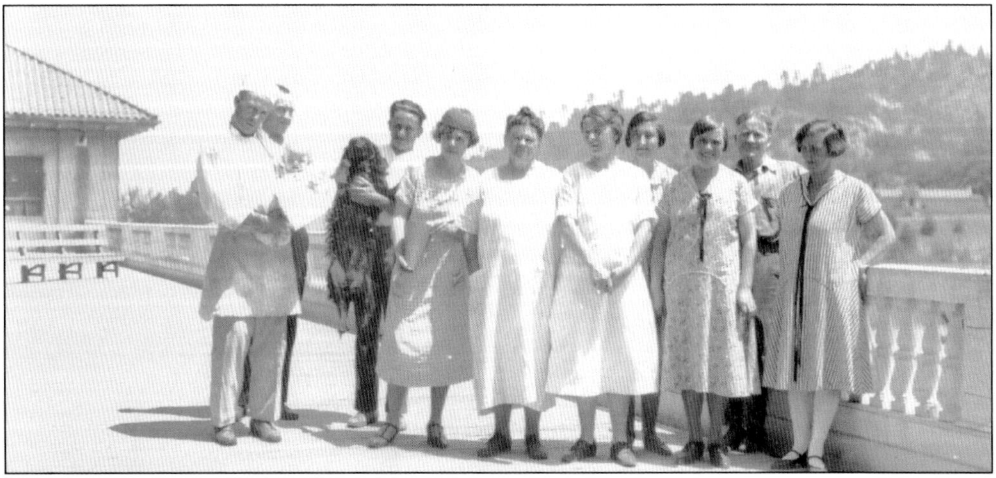

The staff of the Atascadero Inn on the second floor above the Mercantile pauses for a photograph. (Courtesy of Kent Kenney Archives.)

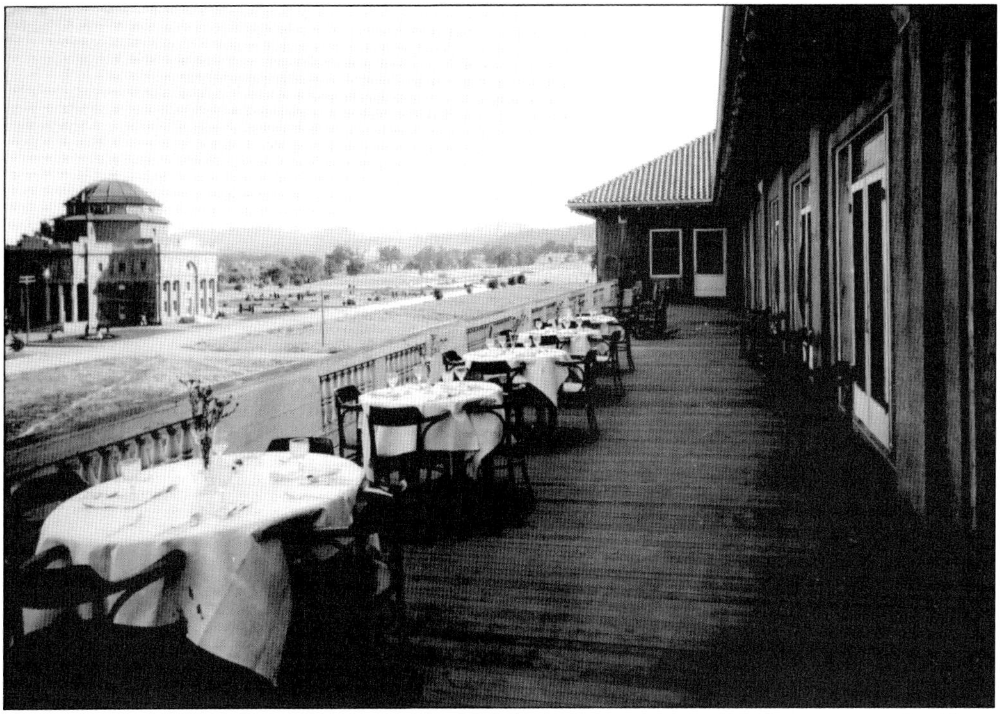

The view from the balcony at the Atascadero Inn looks west towards the administration building. (Courtesy of Atascadero Historical Society.)

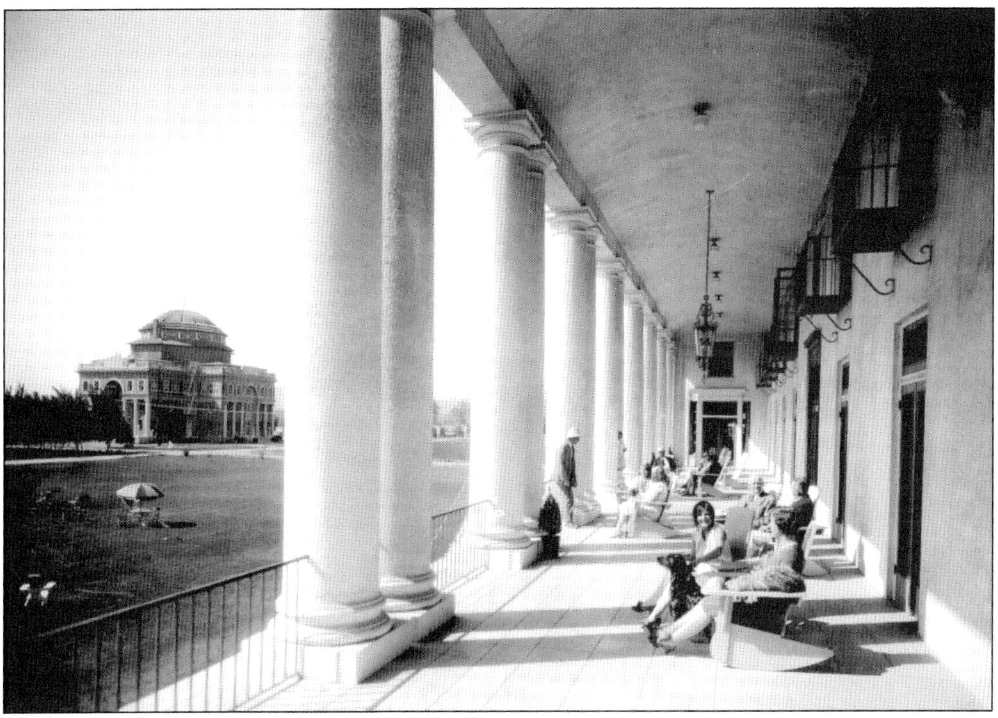

The view from the first floor at the Atascadero Inn looks west towards the administration building. (Courtesy of Atascadero Historical Society.)

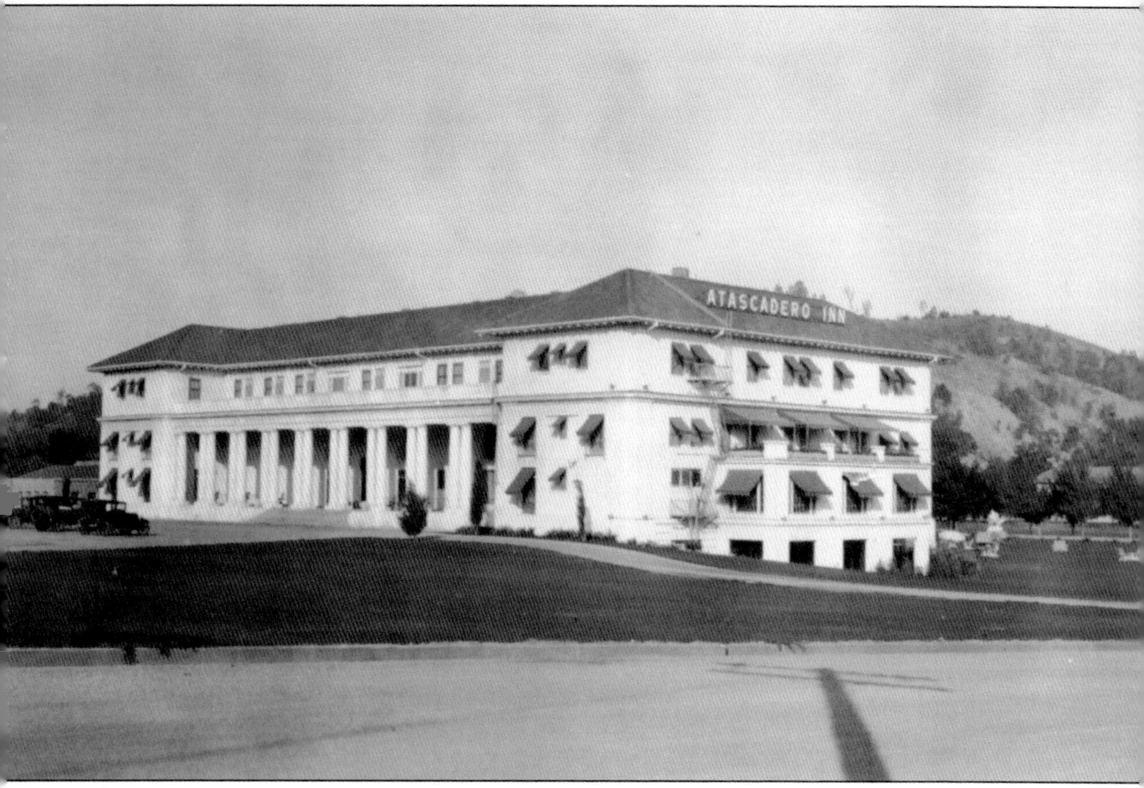

The historic Atascadero Inn featured a plaza containing multiple shops on the first floor and a luxury hotel accommodating 70 guests on the second floor. In keeping with E.G. Lewis's regard for the automobile, this facility featured parking for 200 cars. (Courtesy of Atascadero Historical Society.)

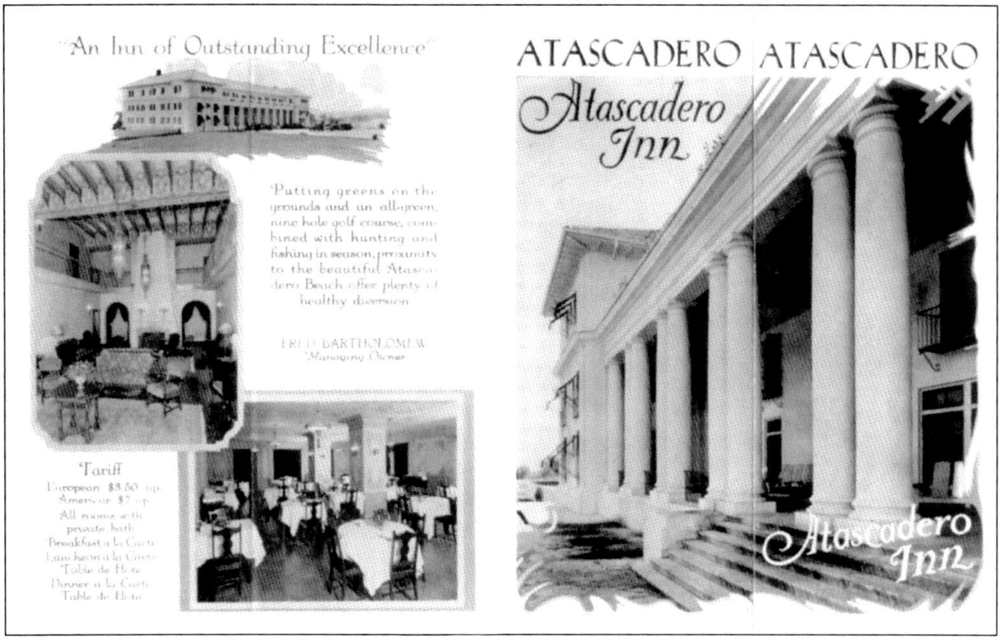

An advertising flyer promotes the Atascadero Inn. Through his publishing business, founder E.G. Lewis was able to turn out a great deal of promotional material and distribute it nationwide. (Both, courtesy of Kent Kenney Archives.)

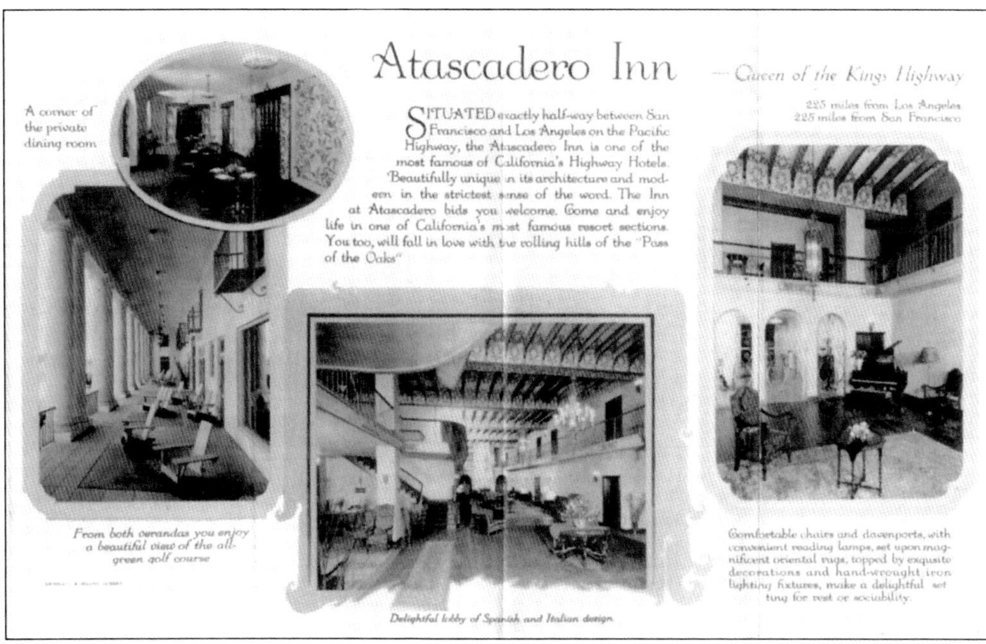

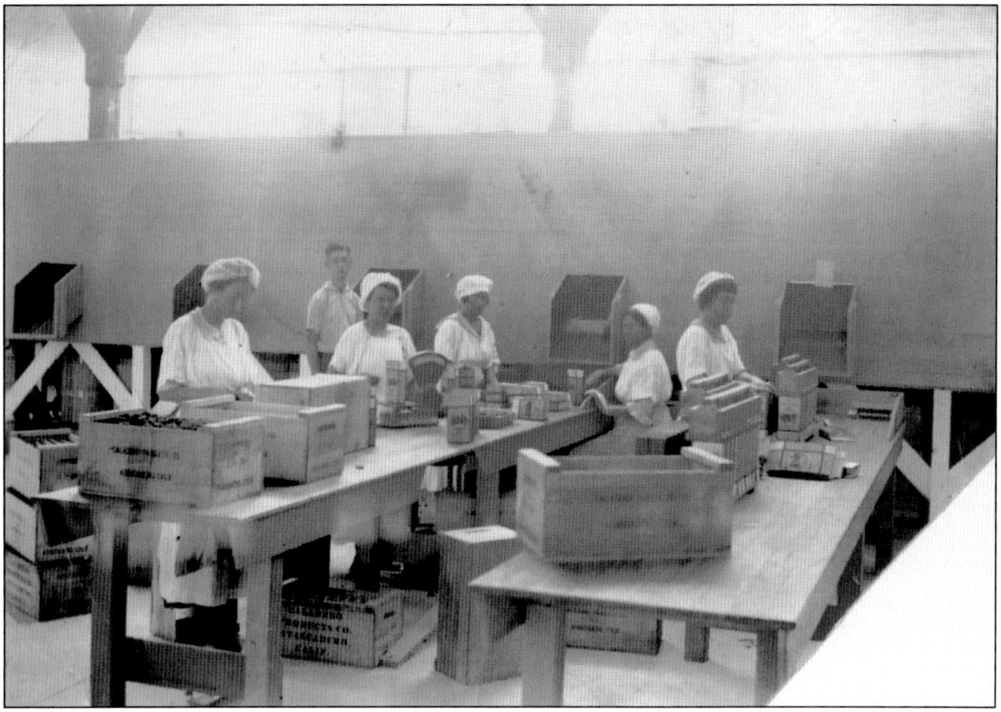

Workers were employed by Lewis to package dehydrated fruits and vegetables for soldiers in Europe. Produce was grown locally in Atascadero. (Both, courtesy of Kent Kenney Archives.)

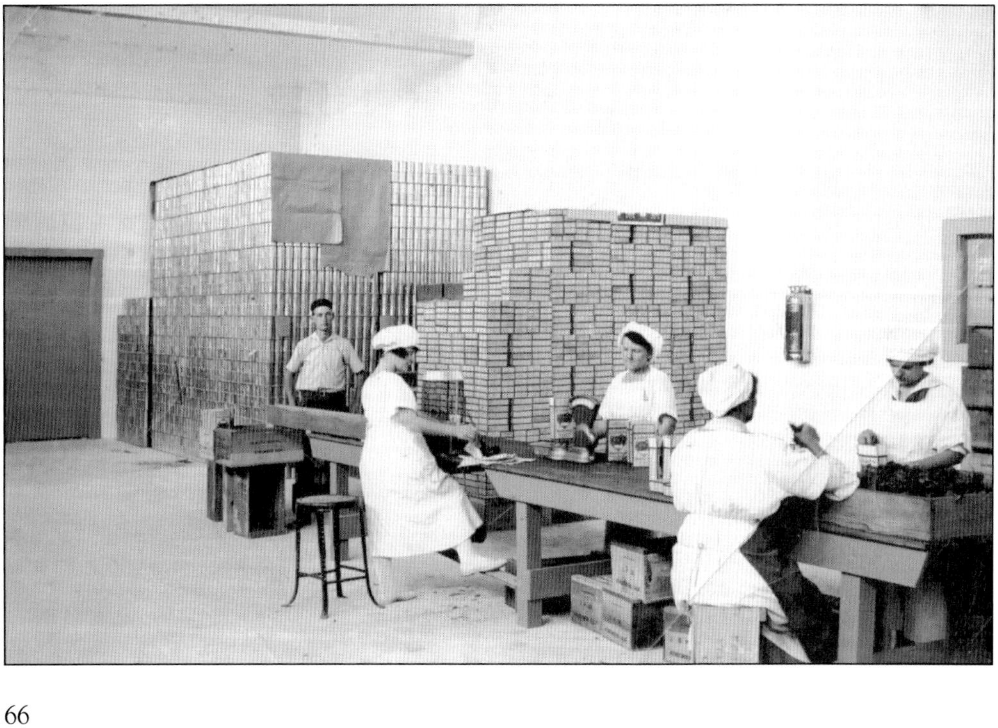

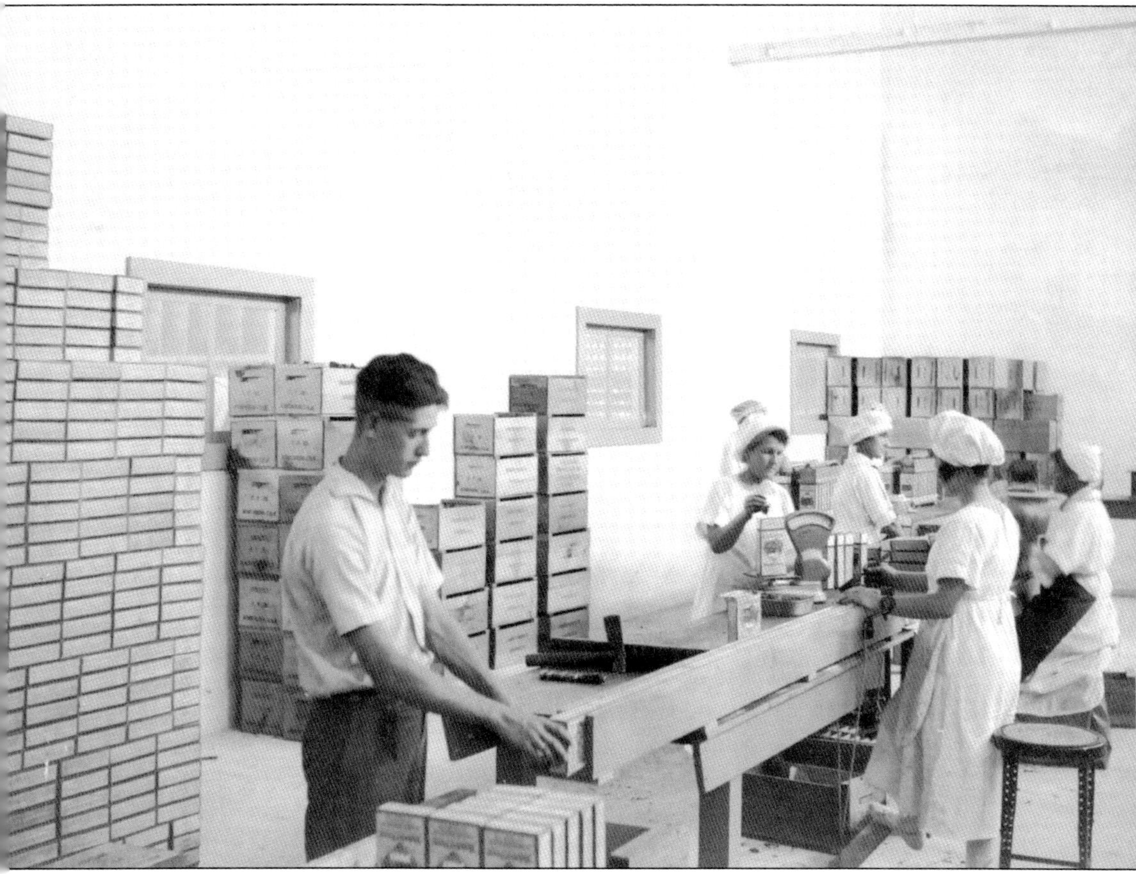

Thousands of boxes containing local produce were prepared for shipment. In the early days of Atascadero, a railroad spur provided shipping access to and from the outside world. (Courtesy of Kent Kenney Archives.)

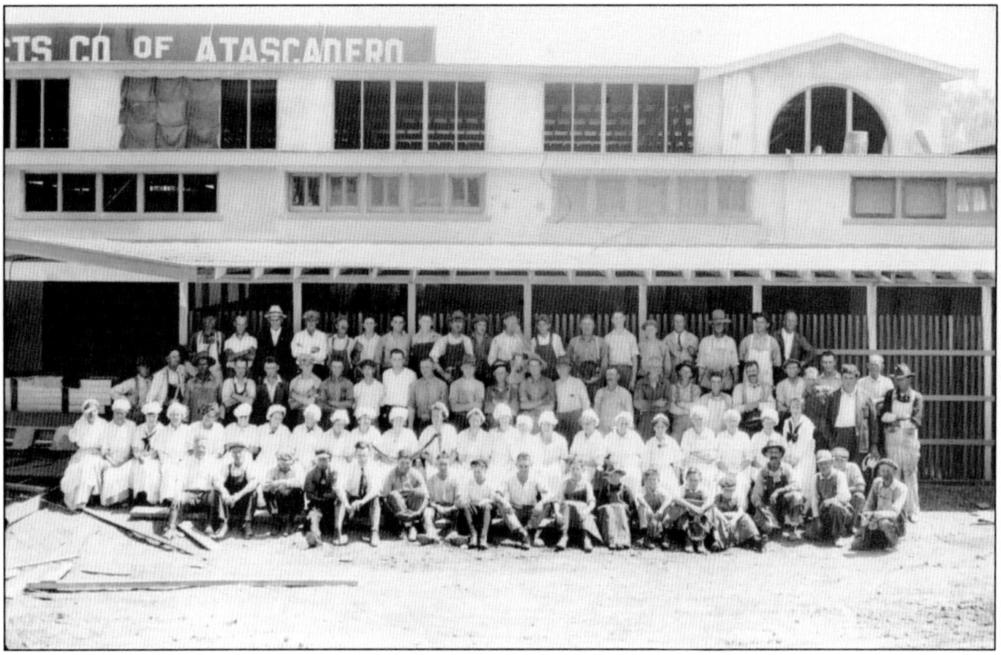

Seen here are employees at the fruit and vegetable dehydrating plant built to prepare food for World War I troops. When the war ended, so did the plant. (Both, courtesy of Kent Kenney Archives.)

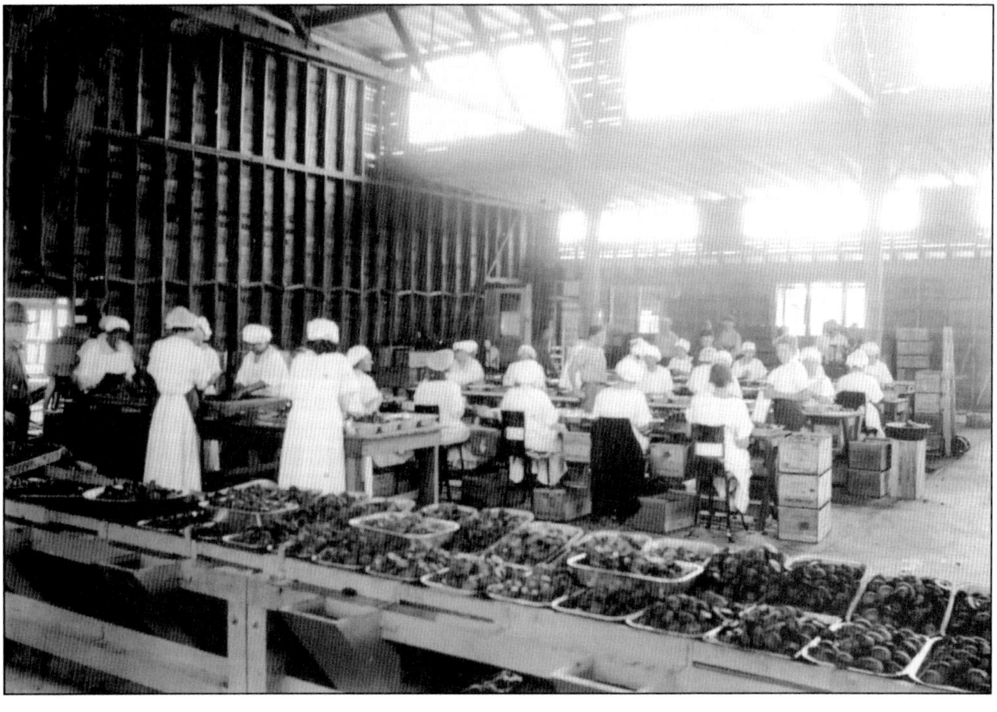

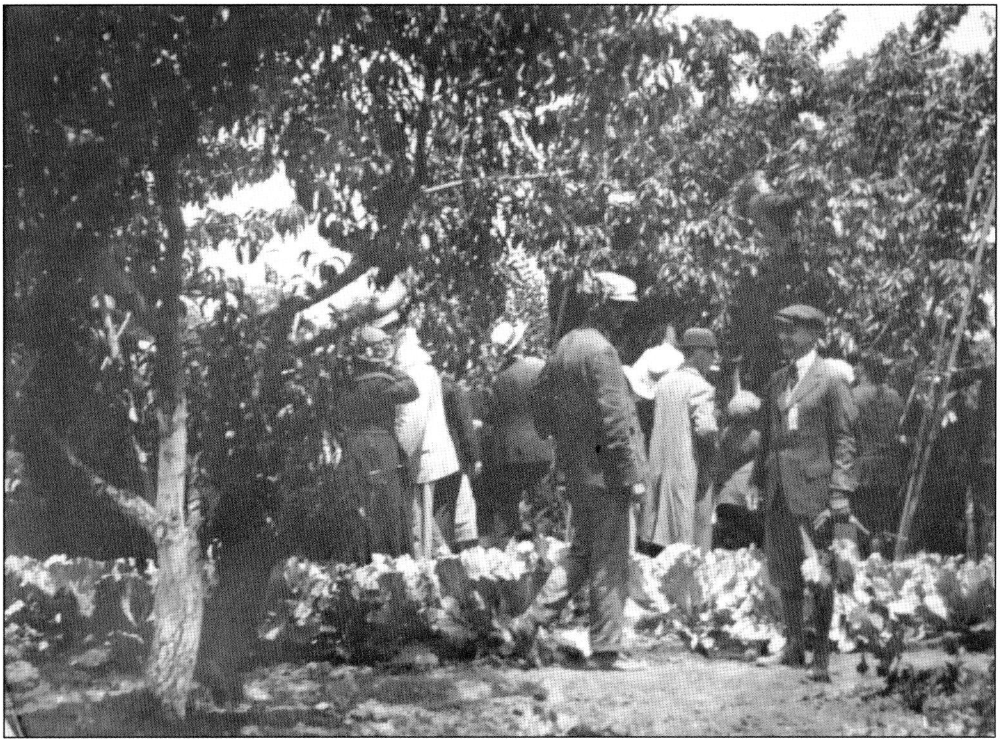

E.G. Lewis planted acres of fruit trees as part of his utopian plan to create a community where residents could enjoy the serenity of rural life with the amenities of urban life. (Courtesy of Kent Kenney Archives.)

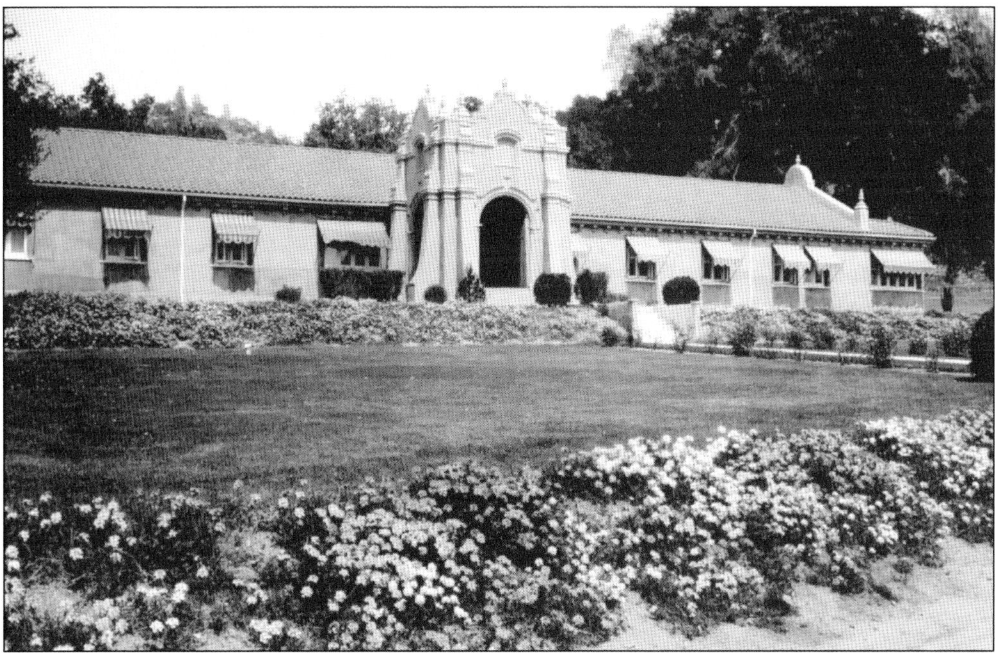

This is the W.H. Lewis Community Hospital. Today, this building is home to San Luis Obispo County Public Health offices. (Courtesy of Atascadero Historical Society.)

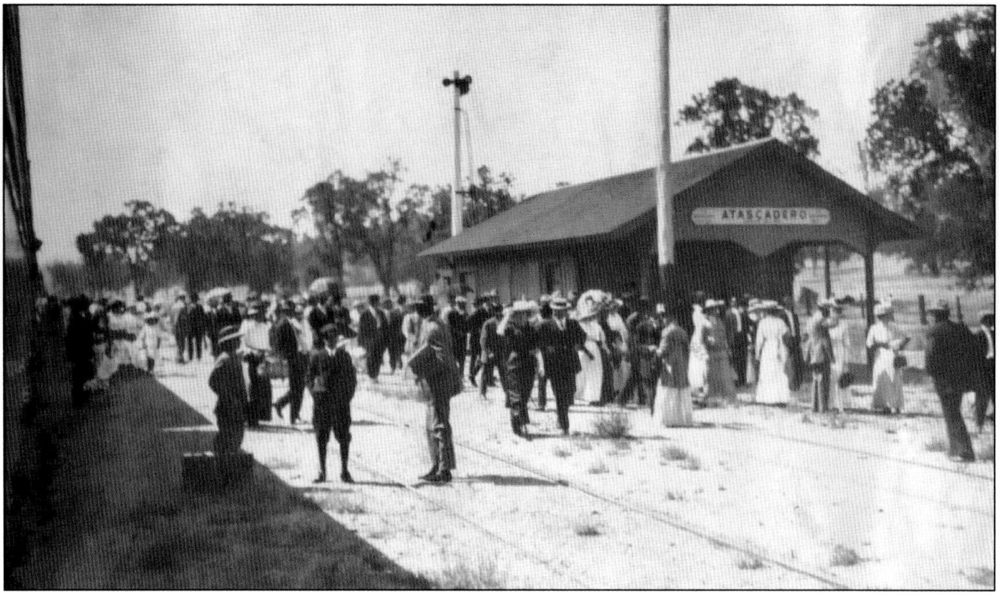

Passengers get off the train and prepare to make their way into town. (Courtesy of Kent Kenney Archives.)

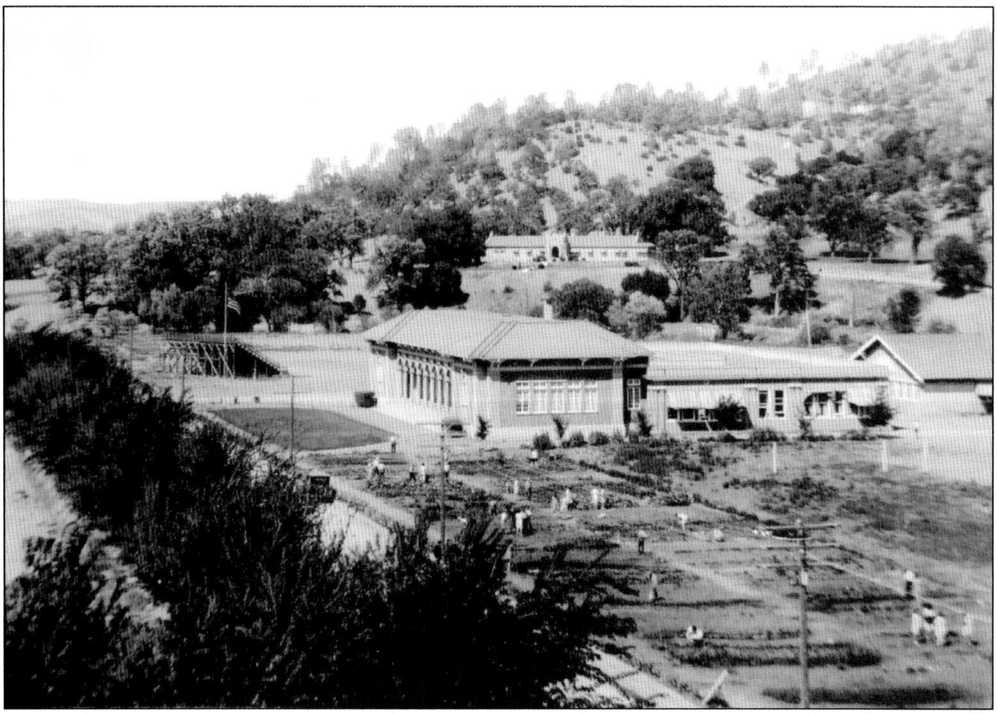

This picture shows construction of the original grammar school, one of the first municipal buildings, near the Atascadero Civic Center. In the background on the hillside, the W. H. Lewis Community Hospital can be seen. (Courtesy of Atascadero Historical Society.)

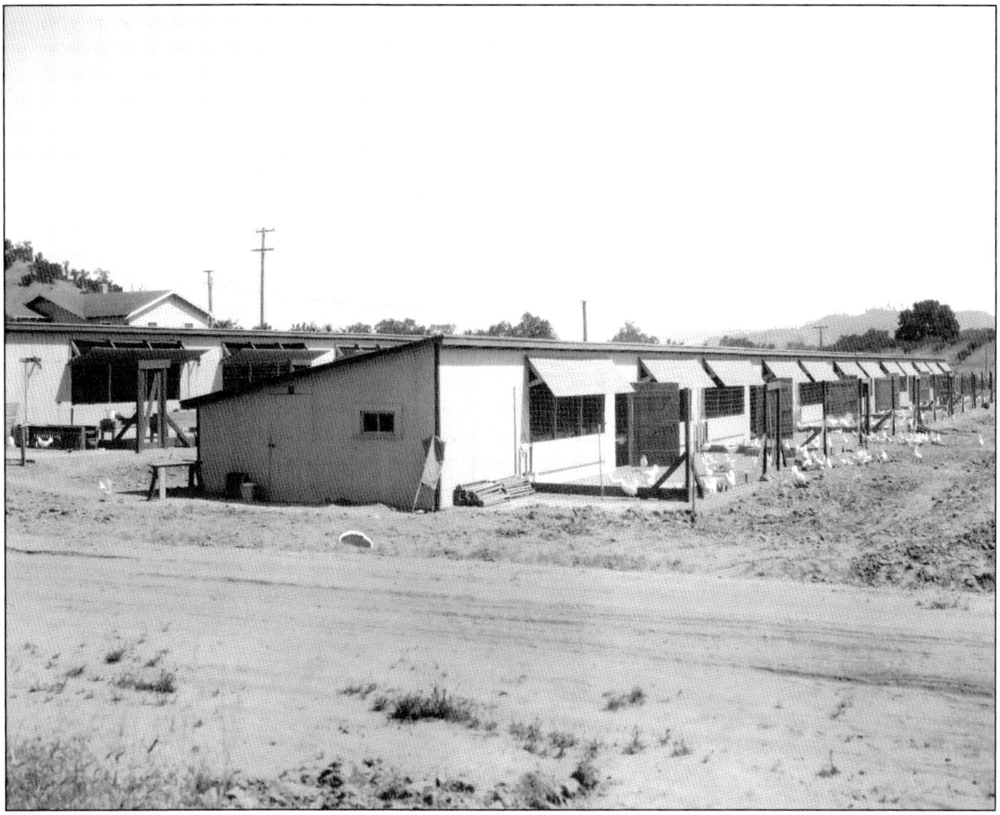

Poultry farming was quite extensive for a while in Atascadero. Some of the hundreds of chicken coops are shown here. (Courtesy of Kent Kenney Archives.)

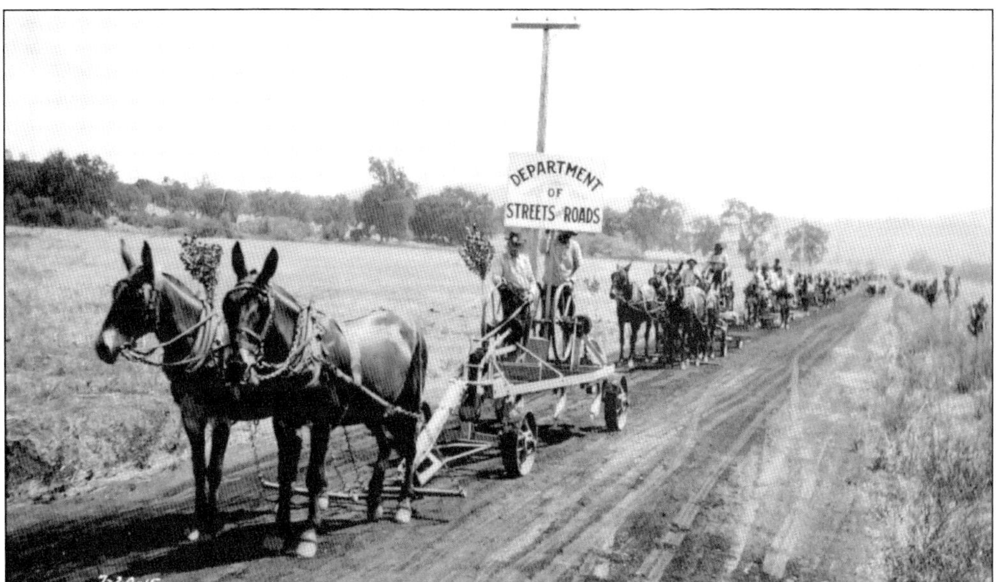

This Industry Parade featured the Department of Streets and Roads. (Courtesy of Atascadero Historical Society.)

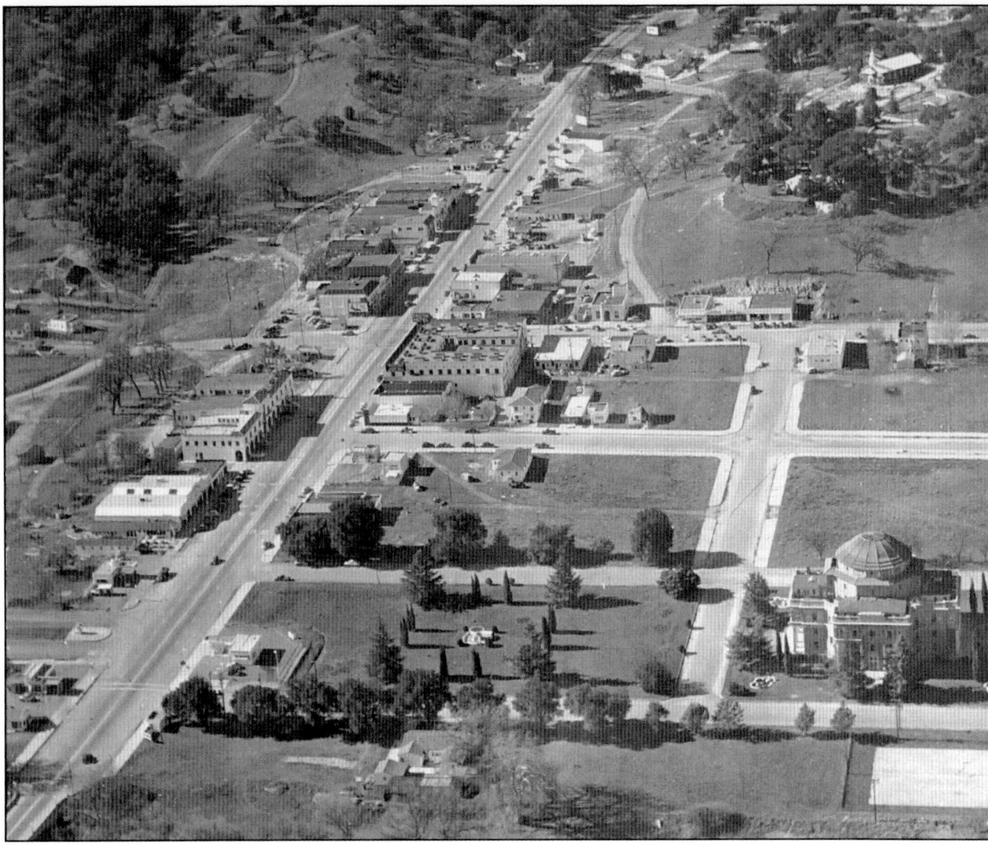

An aerial view, probably from the 1930s, shows the Atascadero Civic Center in the lower right-hand corner and the beginnings of downtown development along El Camino Real. (Courtesy of Atascadero Historical Society.)

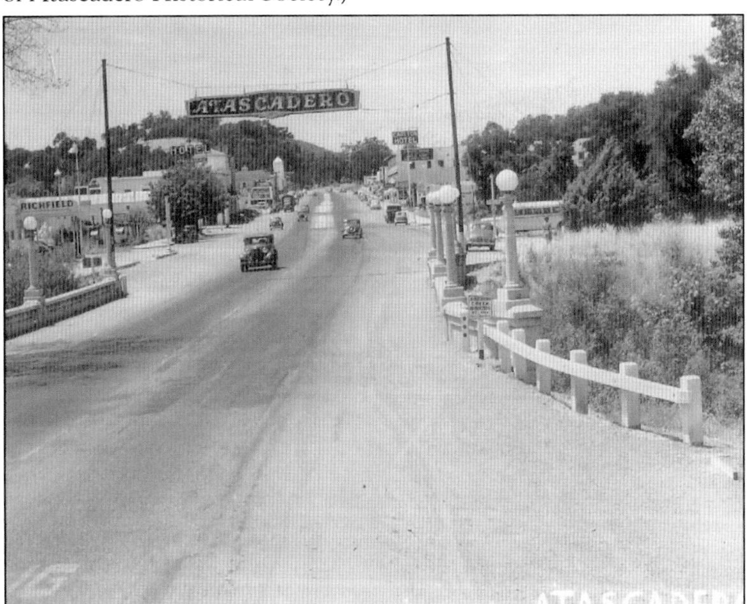

This view looks north along El Camino Real at the Atascadero Creek Bridge. (Courtesy of Atascadero Historical Society.)

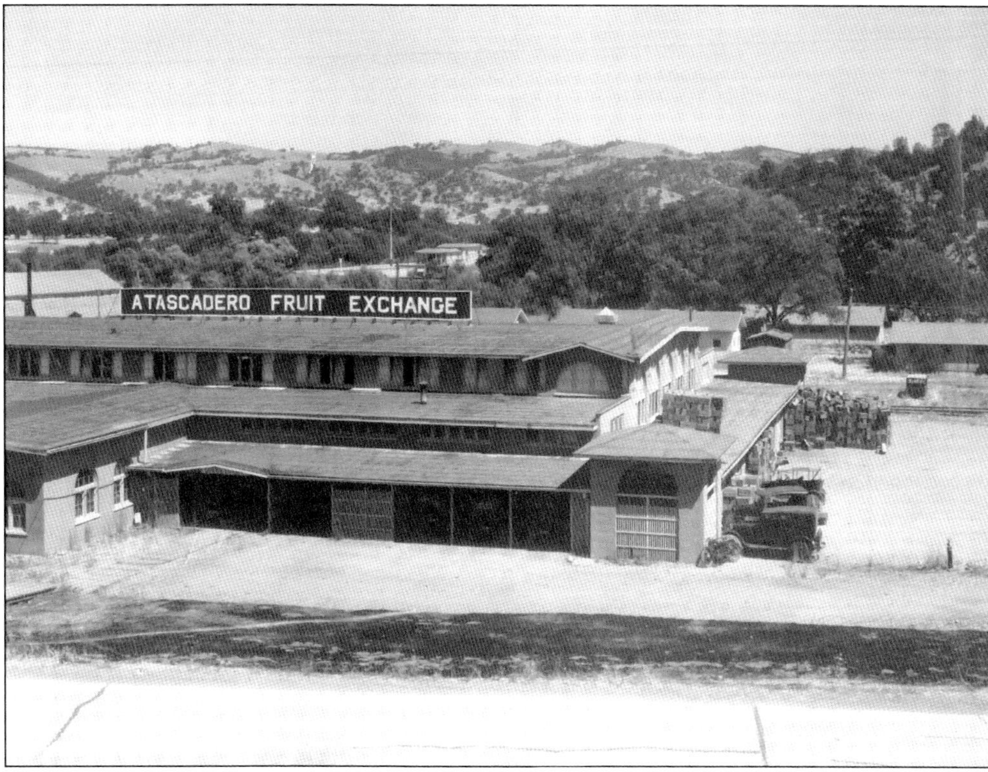

This is an exterior view of Lewis's huge agricultural processing plant. Vestiges of these structures still exist on Traffic Way. (Courtesy of Kent Kenney Archives.)

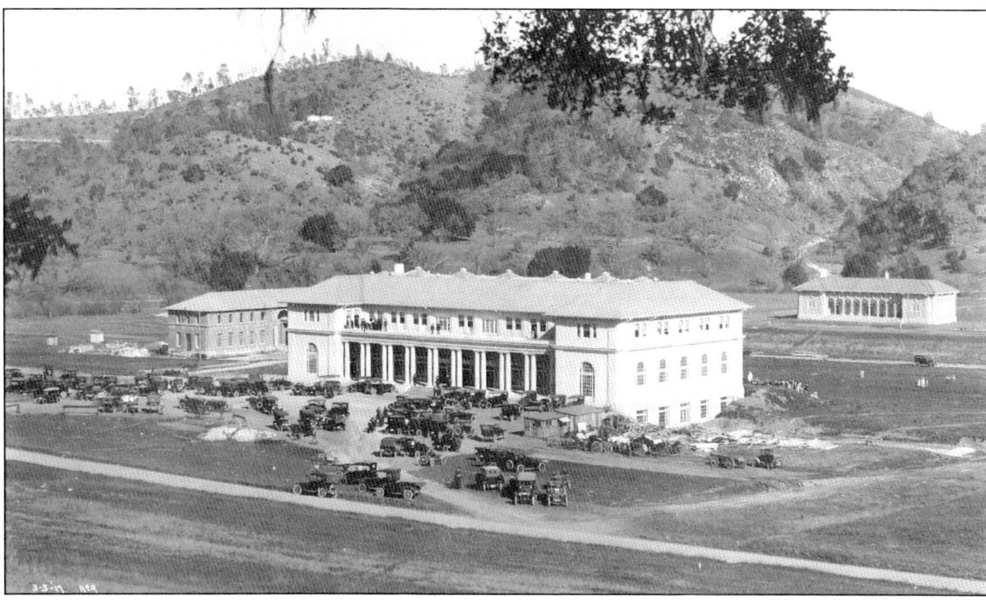

Note the extensive area for automobile parking in this exterior view of the Atascadero Inn/La Plaza. Also note that nowhere in the colony are there any overhead power lines. Part of Lewis's planning for a beautiful city was the mandate for underground electrical utilities, a practice not adopted elsewhere for many years. (Courtesy of Atascadero Historical Society.)

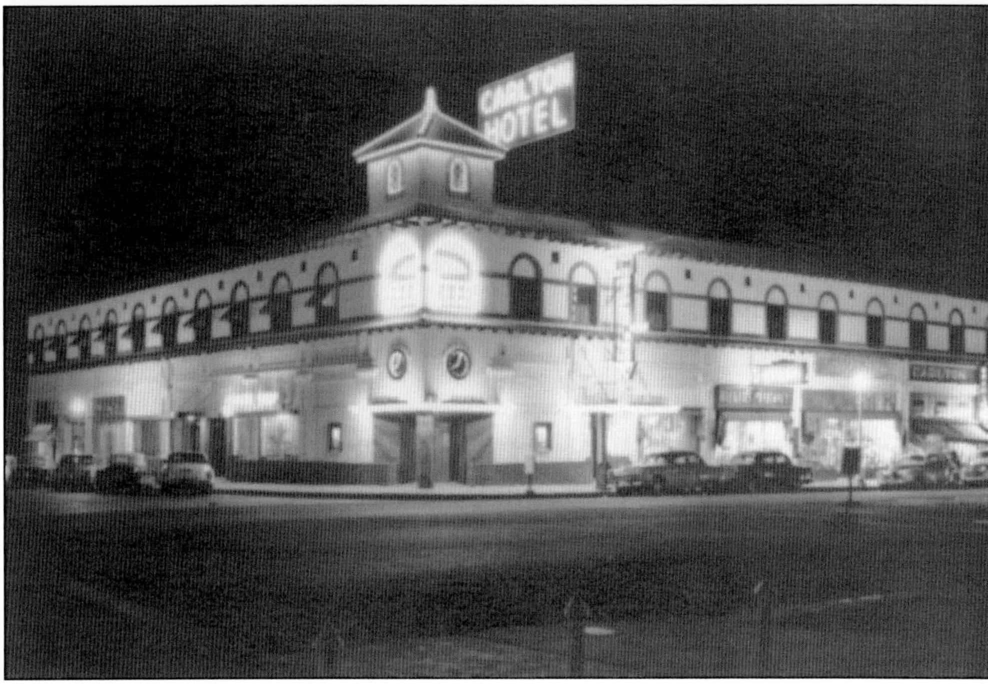

The Carlton Hotel is pictured here at night in the 1940s. (Courtesy of Atascadero Historical Society.)

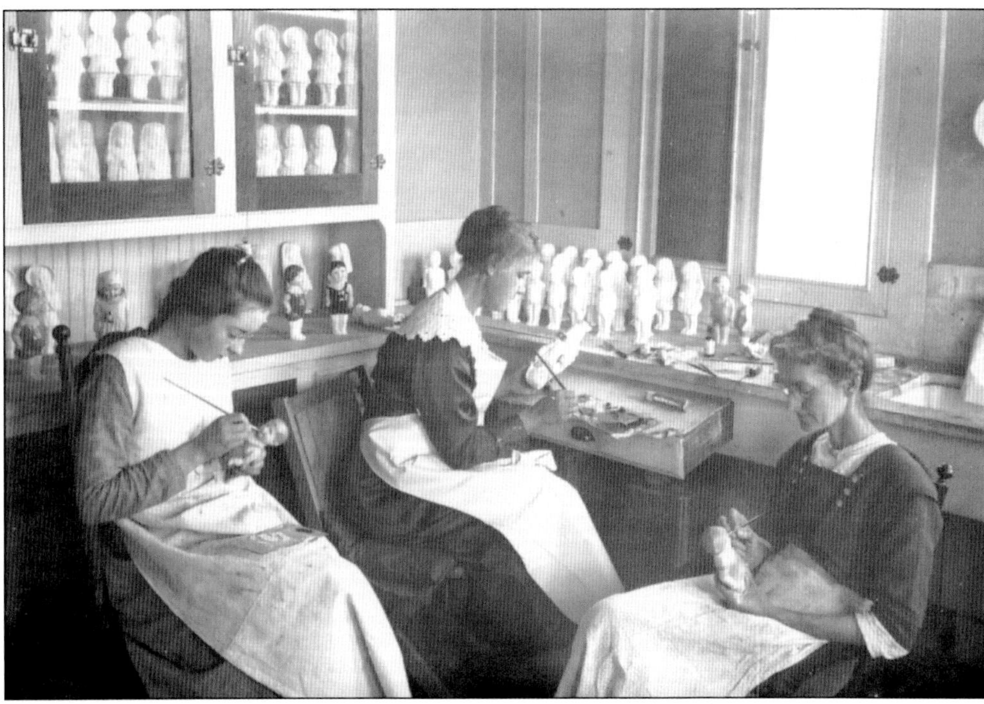

Local women were hired to paint products in the Dooley Doll and Toy Factory. (Courtesy of Atascadero Historical Society.)

Shown here is a doll constructed in the factory in Atascadero. The company was the Dooley Doll and Toy Factory. The label on this product, however, reads "Atascadero Doll and Toy Factory." (Courtesy of Atascadero Historical Society.)

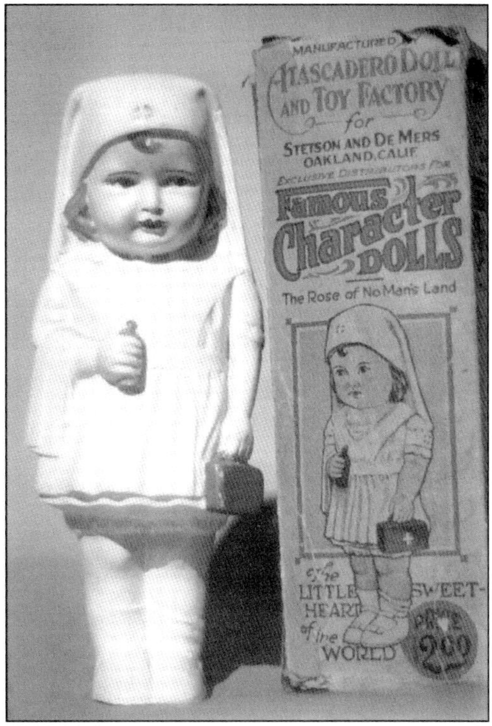

The Dooley Doll and Toy Factory employed Atascadero residents to manufacture products and prepare them for sale. (Courtesy of Kent Kenney Archives.)

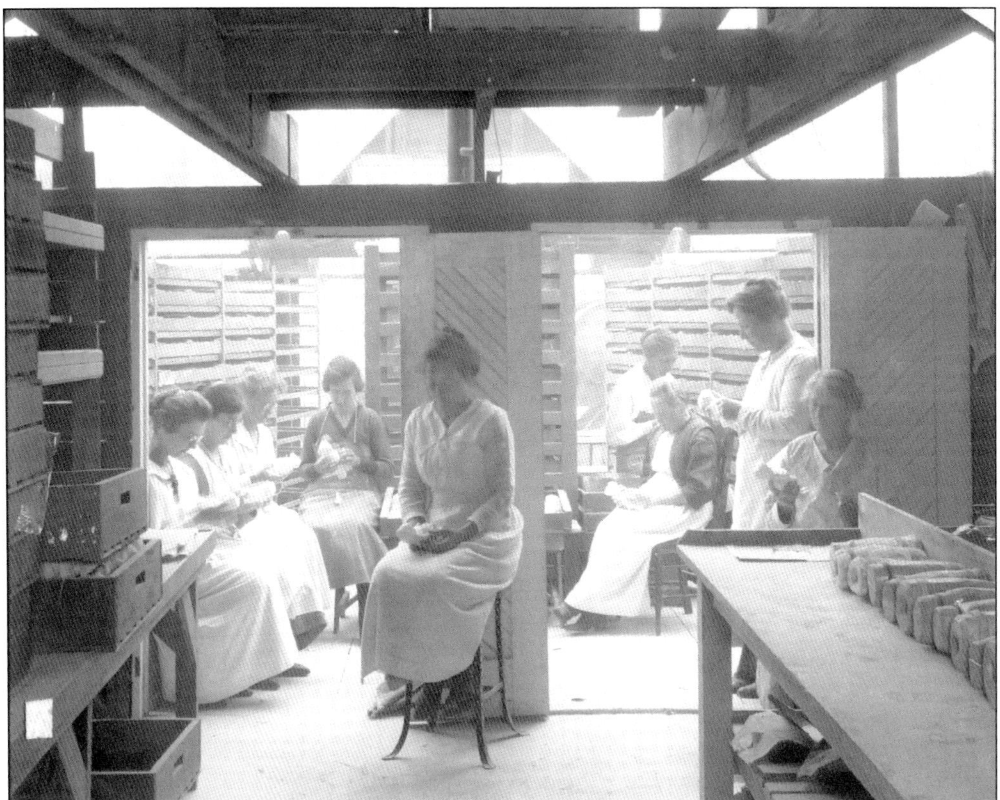

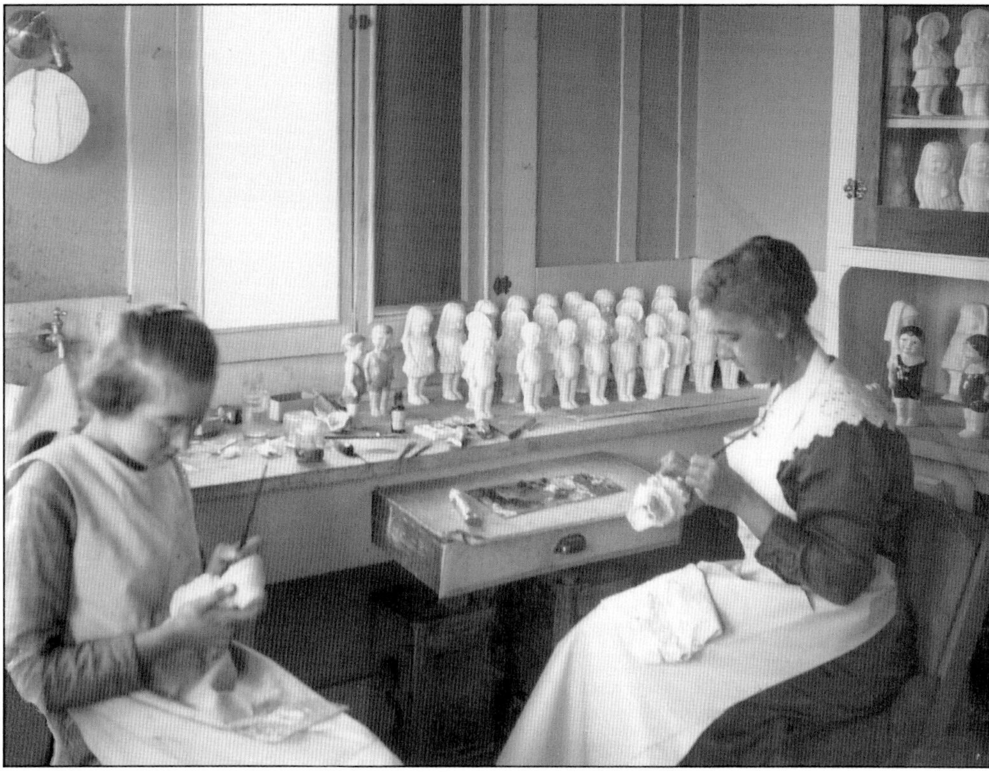

Women paint the faces and bodies of dolls made at the Dooley Doll and Toy Factory in this close-up shot. (Courtesy of Kent Kenney Archives.)

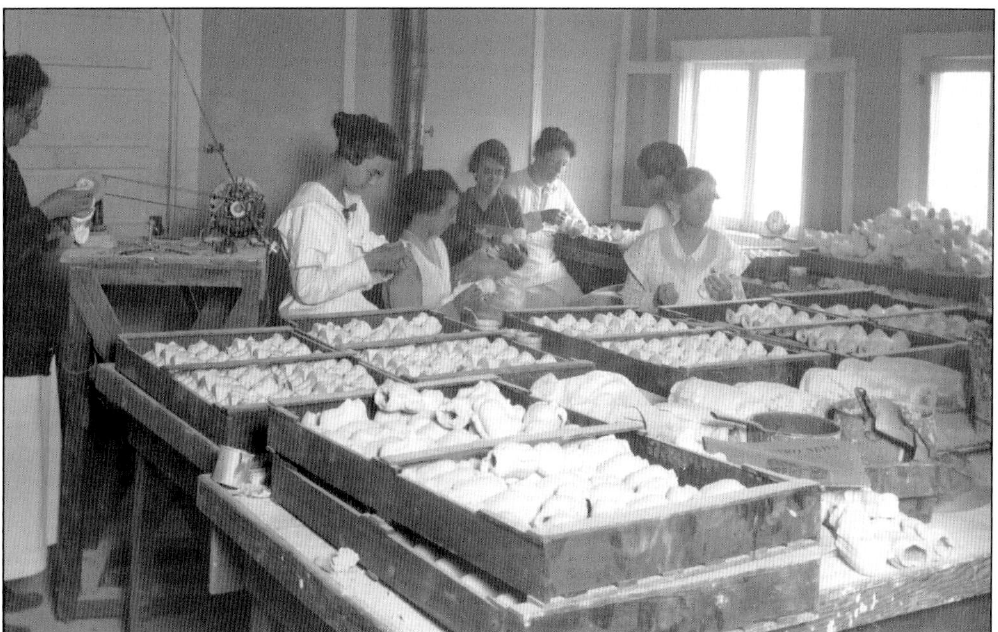

Local ladies assemble Dooley dolls. Notice a copy of the *Atascadero News* lying on top of a crate. (Courtesy of Kent Kenney Archives.)

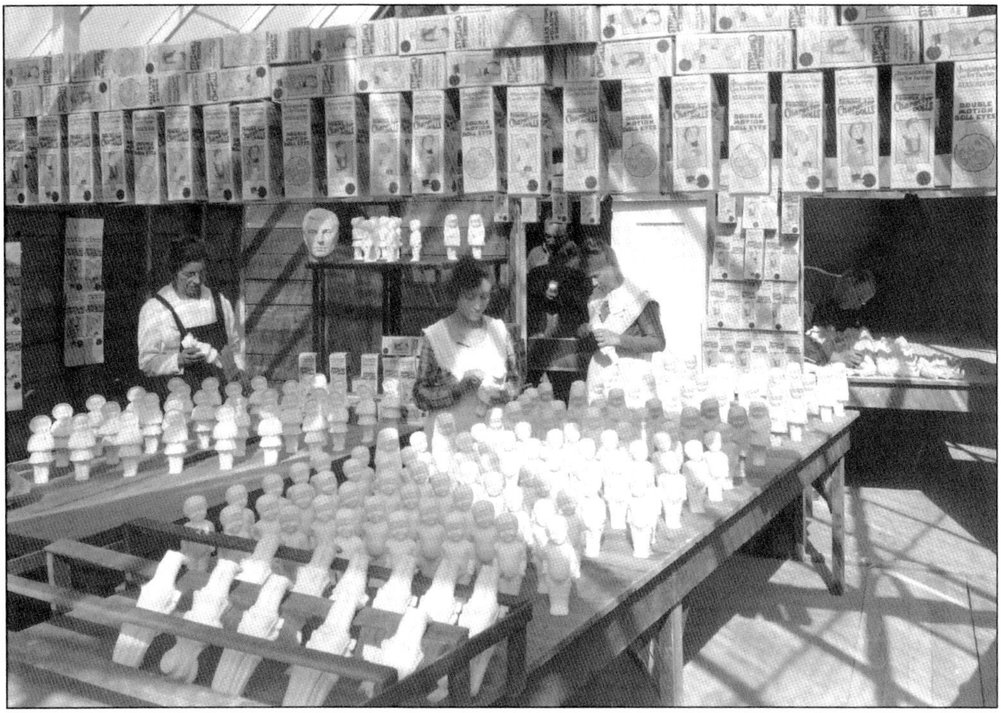

Processing and packing at the Dooley Doll and Toy Factory is pictured here. Notice the various labels on the packing boxes along the wall at the rear of the work area. (Courtesy of Kent Kenney Archives.)

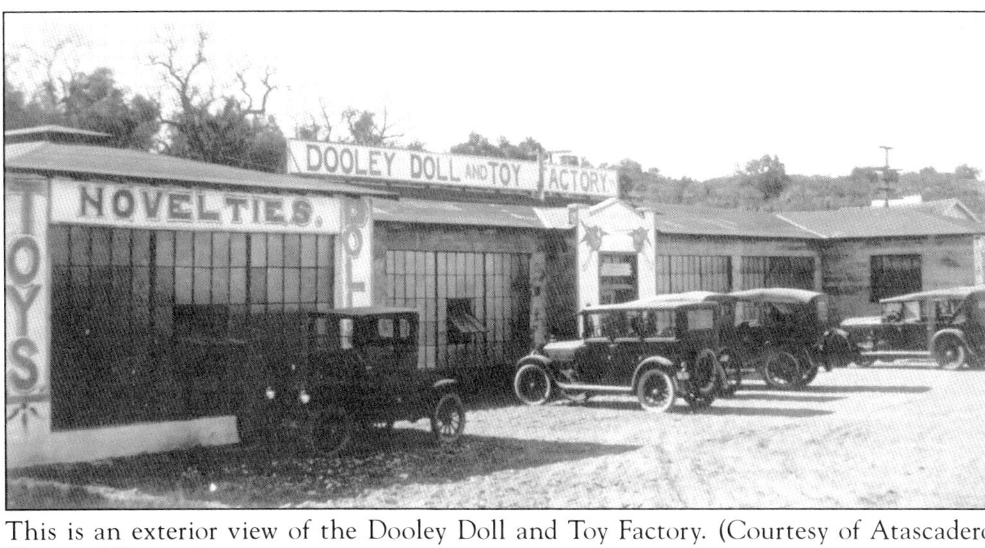

This is an exterior view of the Dooley Doll and Toy Factory. (Courtesy of Atascadero Historical Society.)

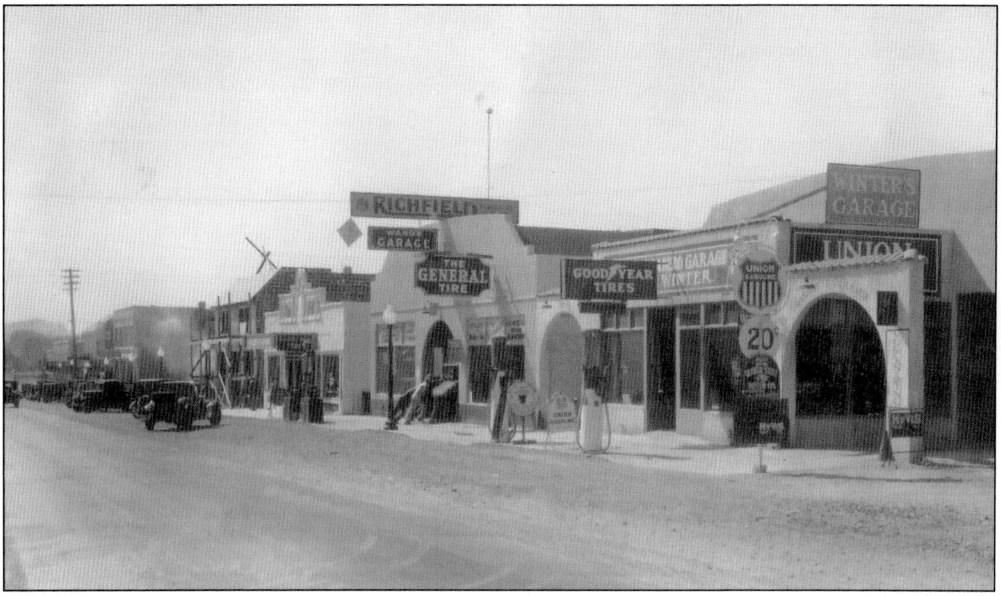

Located across El Camino Real from the domed civic center, the Golden Way Auto Camp was prominent for many years in downtown Atascadero. This cluster of businesses was in operation before the Carlton Hotel was built. Later, automotive services were abandoned, and the 10,000-square-foot building was converted into a thrift store. On March 6, 2009, it burned down. (Courtesy of Atascadero Historical Society.)

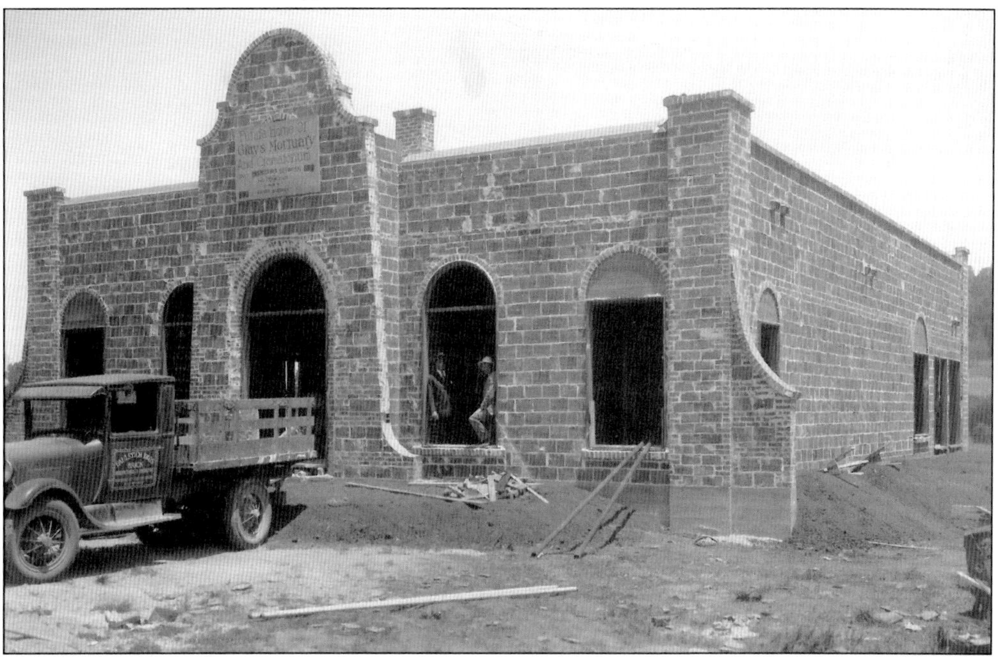

Gray's Mortuary, built in 1929 by Faulstich Brothers Brick Company of San Luis Obispo, was owned and operated by Harry Gray until 1947. It was purchased by Victor Desrosier and became the Chapel of the Roses. It is claimed to have the only crematory service between Santa Barbara and San Francisco. When the business was moved to a new location, this building was leveled to make way for Century Federal Savings. (Courtesy of Atascadero Historical Society.)

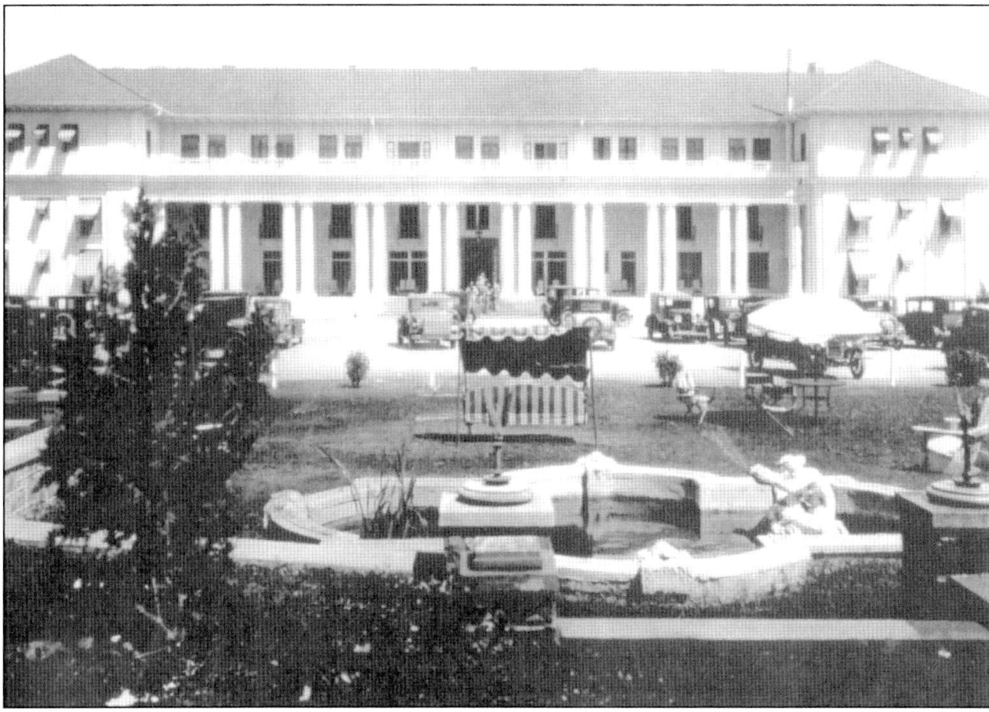

This photograph of the exterior of La Plaza shows a lady and swan fountain. (Courtesy of Atascadero Historical Society.)

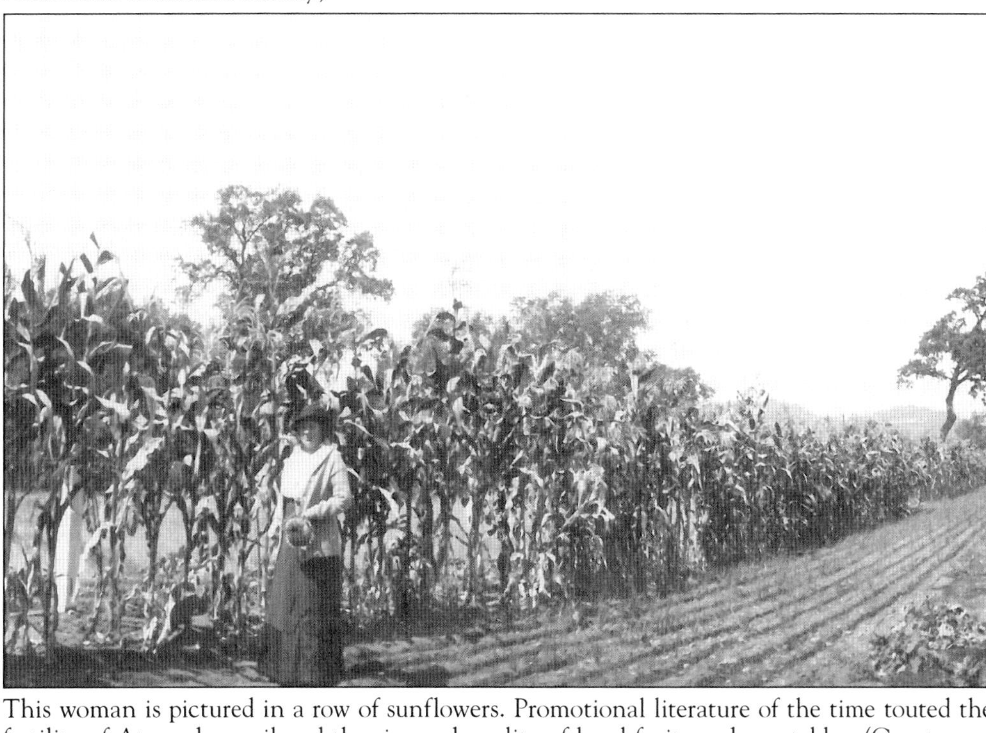

This woman is pictured in a row of sunflowers. Promotional literature of the time touted the fertility of Atascadero soil and the size and quality of local fruits and vegetables. (Courtesy of Kent Kenney Archives.)

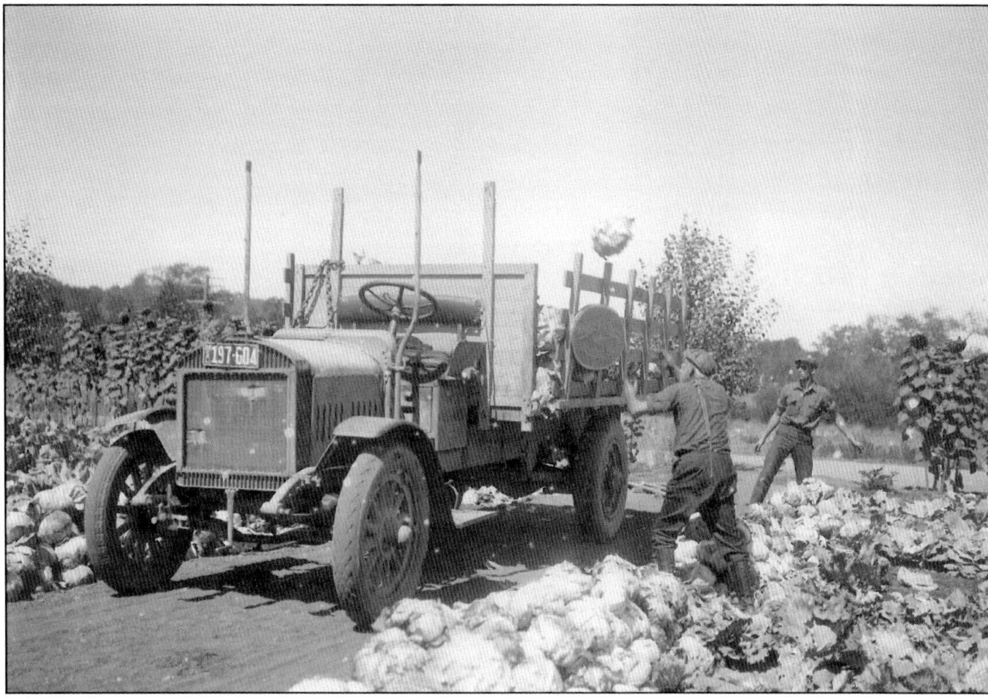

Atascadero workers harvest vegetables. (Courtesy of Atascadero Historical Society.)

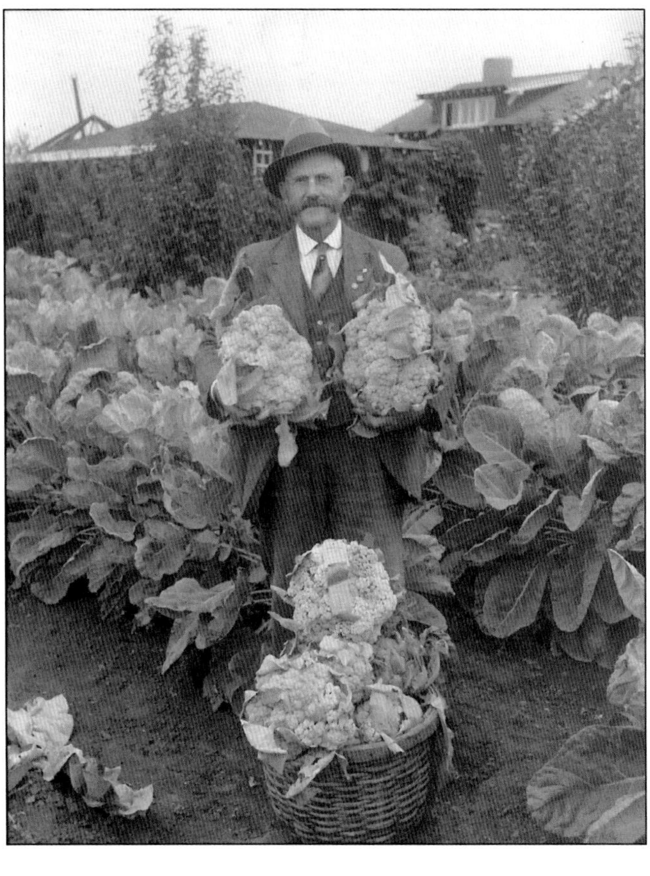

An Atascadero man shows off a bumper crop of vegetables. (Courtesy of Atascadero Historical Society.)

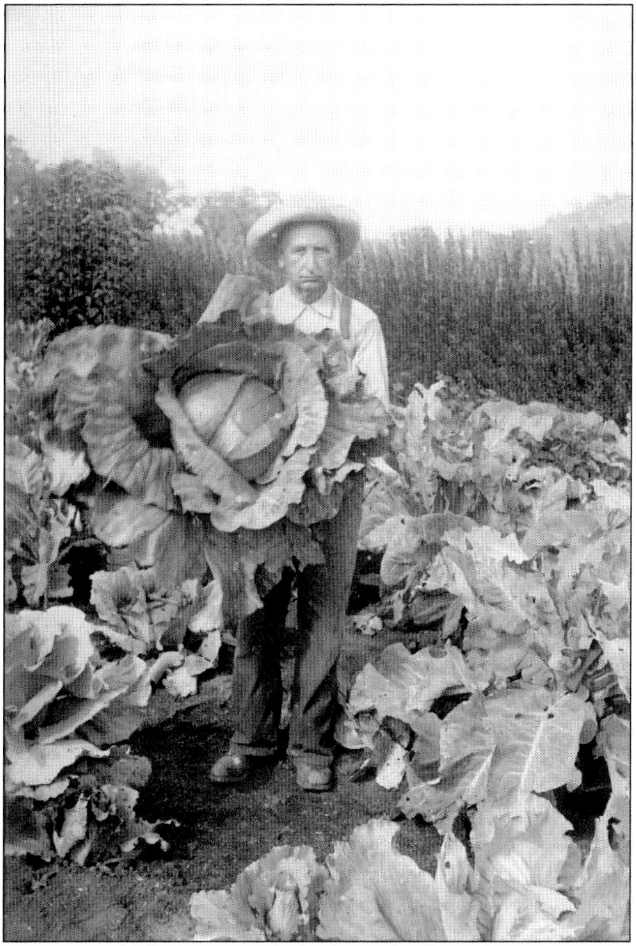

Another proud Atascadero farmer is pictured. Many local residents planted flower and food gardens. The agricultural component of Lewis's utopia was intended to provide financial incomes for participants. Many residents who had moved from cities found it difficult to raise crops and abandoned the gardens. (Courtesy of Atascadero Historical Society.)

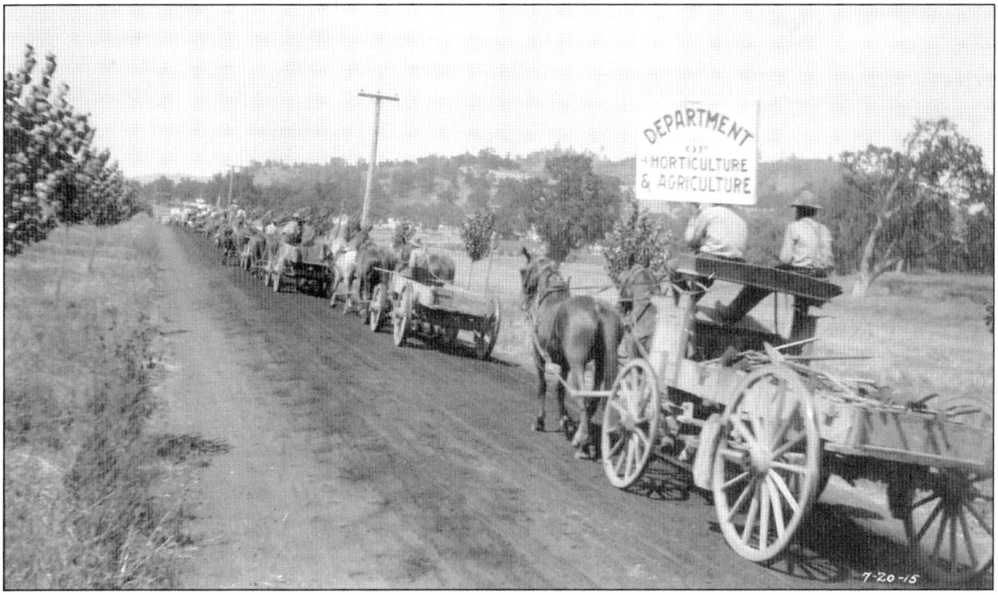

The Department of Horticulture and Agriculture takes part in the Industry Parade. (Courtesy of Atascadero Historical Society.)

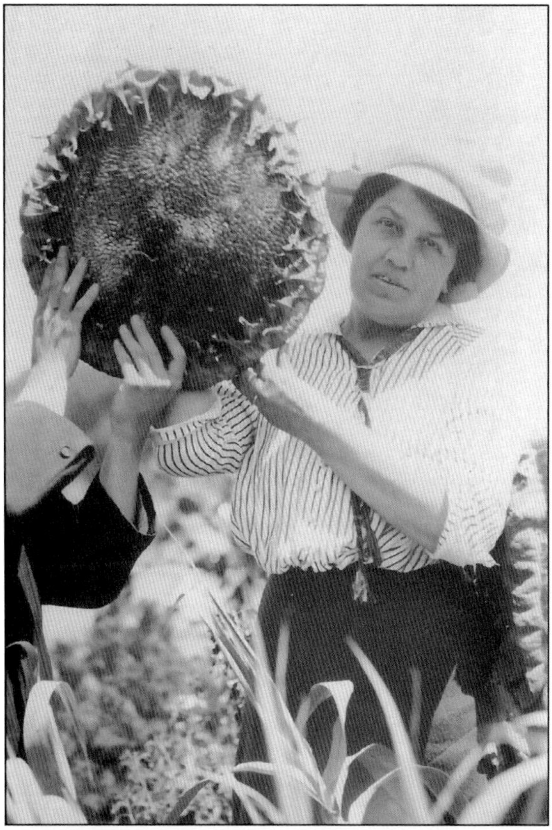

Mabel Lewis is pictured with a huge sunflower. (Courtesy of Atascadero Historical Society.)

This boxed fruit was grown and packaged in the colony. (Courtesy of Atascadero Historical Society.)

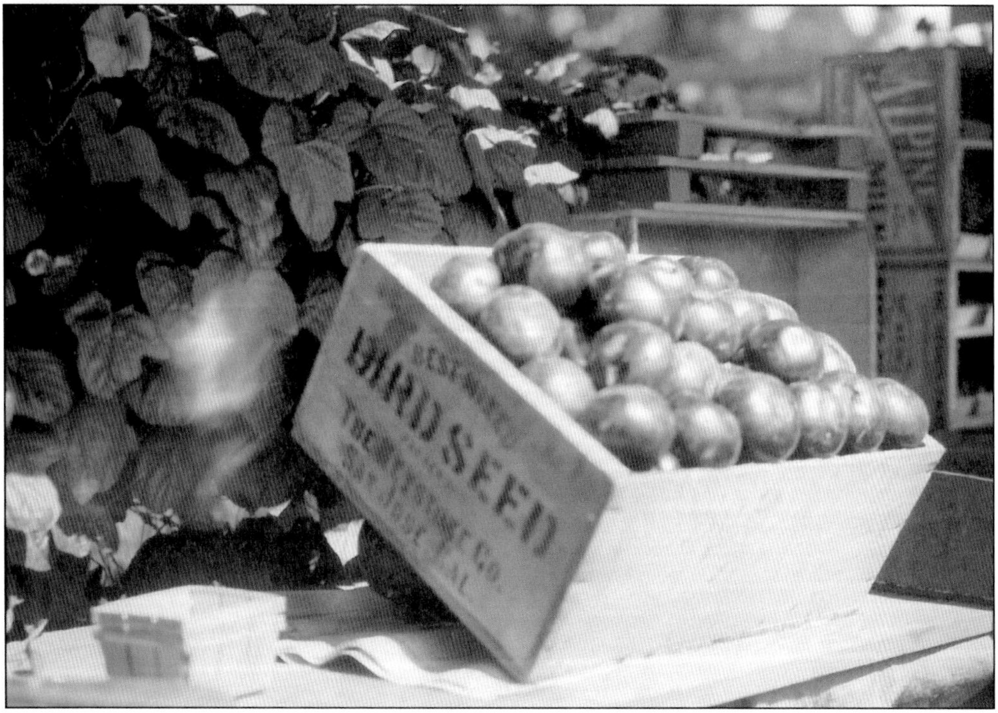

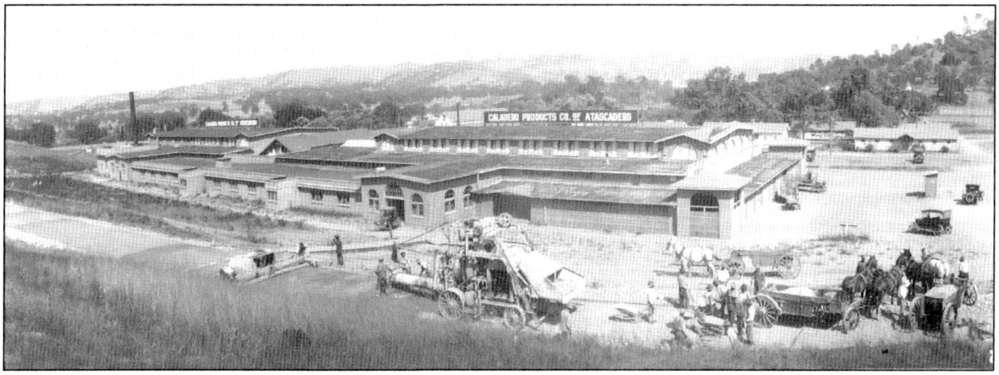

The Caladero Packaging Plant was E.G. Lewis's huge food-processing facility. Lewis claimed a few tablespoons of dried pumpkin would suffice to make a whole pie. (Courtesy of Atascadero Historical Society.)

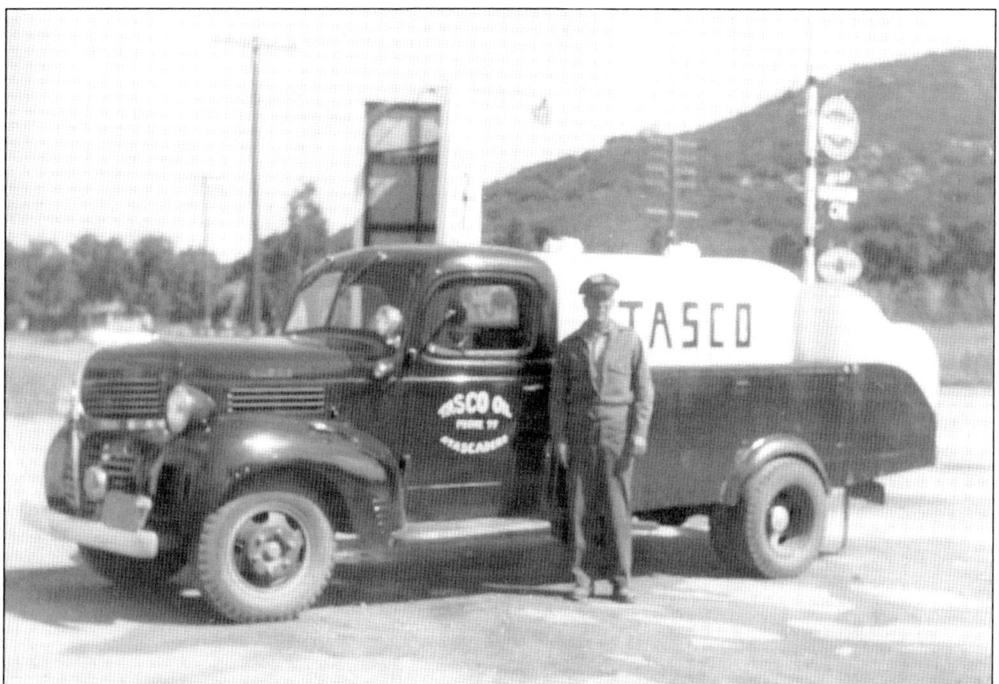

When planning a community around the automobile, all the support services are a necessity. Tasco Oil was one of several purveyors of petroleum products in the 1940s. (Courtesy of Atascadero Historical Society.)

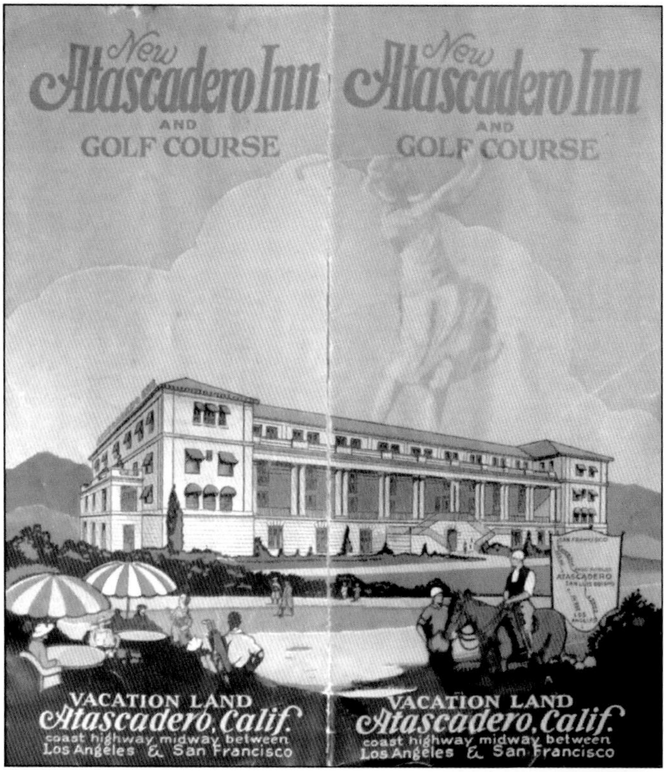

This is an advertising flyer for the Atascadero Inn. Lewis's publishing company made it easy for him to create endless promotional pieces and distribute them nationwide. (Courtesy of Kent Kenney Archives.)

Pictured is dedication day for a bank that did business out of the historic Atascadero Administration Building. (Courtesy of Atascadero Historical Society.)

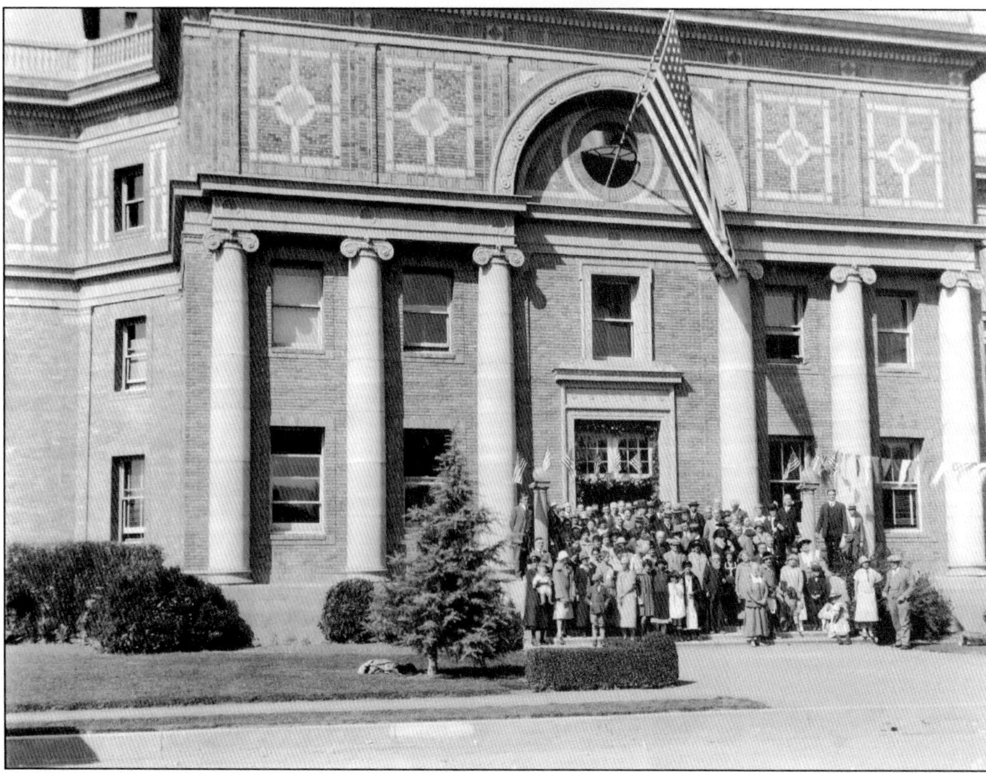

This is an early picture of the historic administration building. The decorative fountains still exist, although they have been damaged over time. Water no longer flows through these statues. (Courtesy of Atascadero Historical Society.)

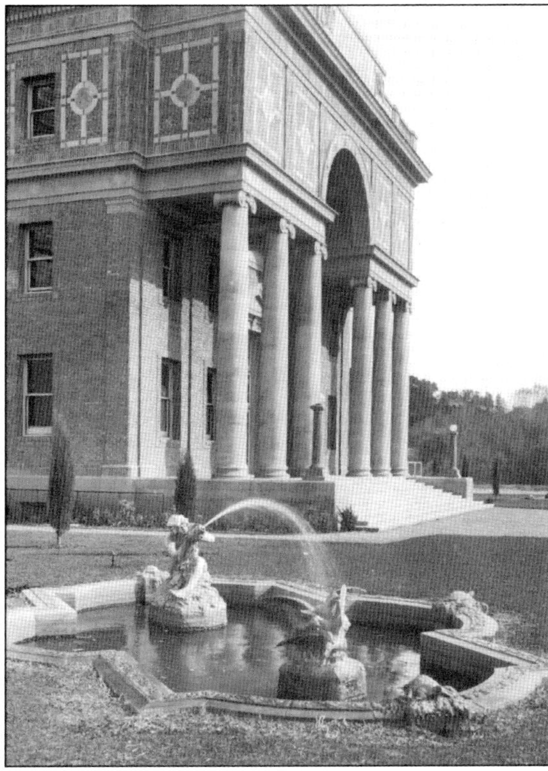

This view of La Plaza was taken from Palma and West Mall. (Courtesy of Atascadero Historical Society.)

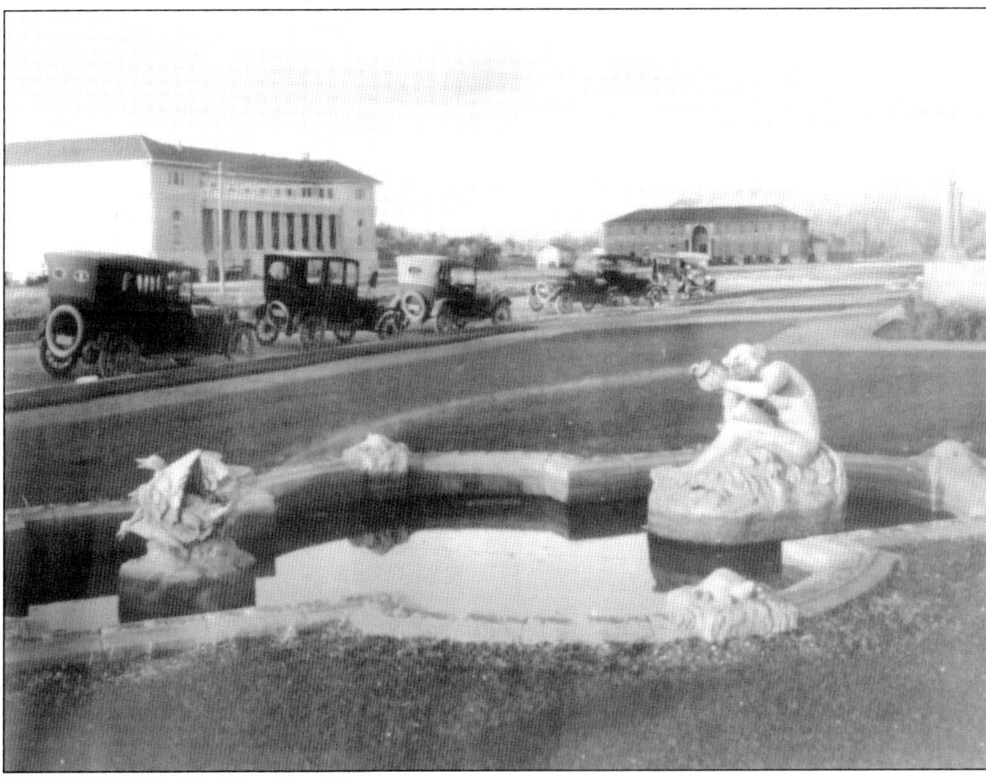

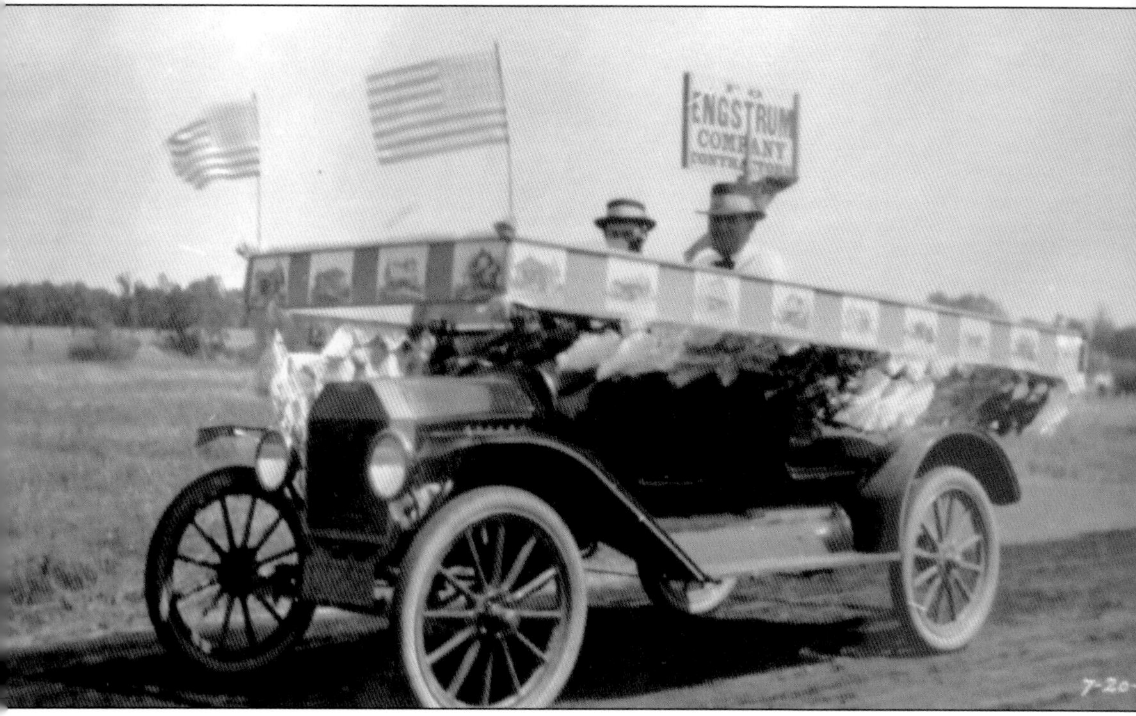

The F.O. Engstrum Company was contractor for the construction of the Atascadero Administration Building in the center of town. This entry in the Industry Parade on July 20, 1915, was photographed by representatives of the Colony Holding Corporation as part of a series of promotional pictures to show the progress in the town. (Courtesy of Atascadero Historical Society.)

Four

Atascadero Administration Building

Known as the Atascadero Civic Center, Atascadero Administration Building, Atascadero Veterans Memorial Building, and the historic City Hall, this structure is designated as State Historical Landmark No. 958. Its cornerstone was laid on June 12, 1914, and it was designed by Walter D. Bliss of the San Francisco architectural firm Bliss & Faville. The building contains nearly 50,000 square feet of space. F.O. Engstrum was the general contractor for the $458,000 construction project. It took four years to build. In 1990, the building was used in the filming of *My Blue Heaven*, starring Steve Martin and Rick Moranis.

The design includes two domes stacked one above the other. Interior stairways lead to the upper floors that are also accessible via a small elevator. The building may be entered by climbing cement staircases on all four sides of the structure. Upon entering the building and after crossing an interior corridor, visitors enter a large domed chamber. This is the lower rotunda. A huge, ornate chandelier (which survived the 2003 earthquake) hangs from the rotunda ceiling, and the room is embraced by ornate pillars and artistic reliefs. Large doorways lead into and out of the rotunda on three sides. Until the building was seriously damaged in the 2003 San Simeon Earthquake, the lower rotunda housed the extensive collection of the Atascadero Historical Society. There is a second domed chamber in the upper rotunda. Outside, over each of the entryways, there are different inscriptions, one from Abraham Lincoln, two from poet George Sterling, and the final one from E.G. Lewis, which reads, "Let us keep our faces to the sunshine and we will not see the shadows."

In December 2003, the San Simeon Earthquake seriously damaged the historic building. The force of the temblor was so great that the large pillars in the lower rotunda shuddered, cracked, and twisted on their bases. Amazingly, no one was injured in the building during the quake. The building was repaired in preparation for the colony's Centennial Celebration in 2013. The City of Atascadero enlisted the assistance of Pfeiffer Partners (a design firm of architects, interior designers, and planners with offices in Los Angeles and New York). Pfeiffer Partners has worked on such prestigious restoration projects as the Anaheim Muzeo, the Denver Museum of Nature and Science, the Los Angeles County Museum of Art, the Seattle King Street Station historic renovation, and the Griffith Park Observatory.

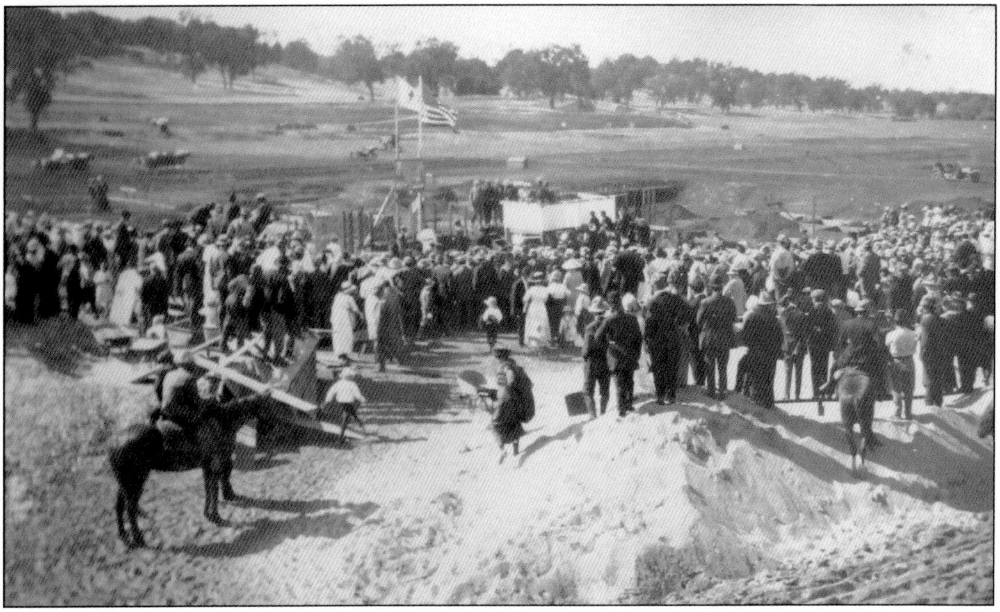

On June 12, 1914, the cornerstone for the great Atascadero Civic Center was laid. The four-story, double-domed building cost $458,000 to build. It was severely damaged in the 2003 San Simeon Earthquake. It will be repaired and opened for Atascadero's centennial in 2013. (Courtesy of Atascadero Historical Society.)

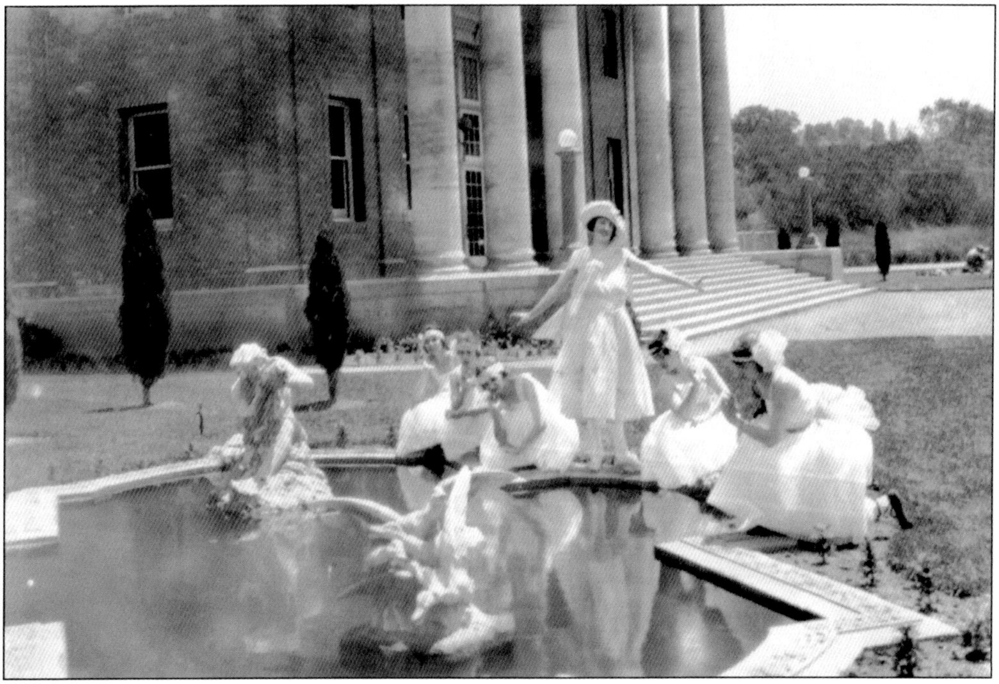

Life imitates art. Five local ladies pay homage to the fountain sculpture in front of the pillared Atascadero Civic Center. The fountains depict a woman blowing water through a conch shell and surrounded by swans. The sculptures, although damaged, remain today. The fountain no longer functions. (Courtesy of Kent Kenney Archives.)

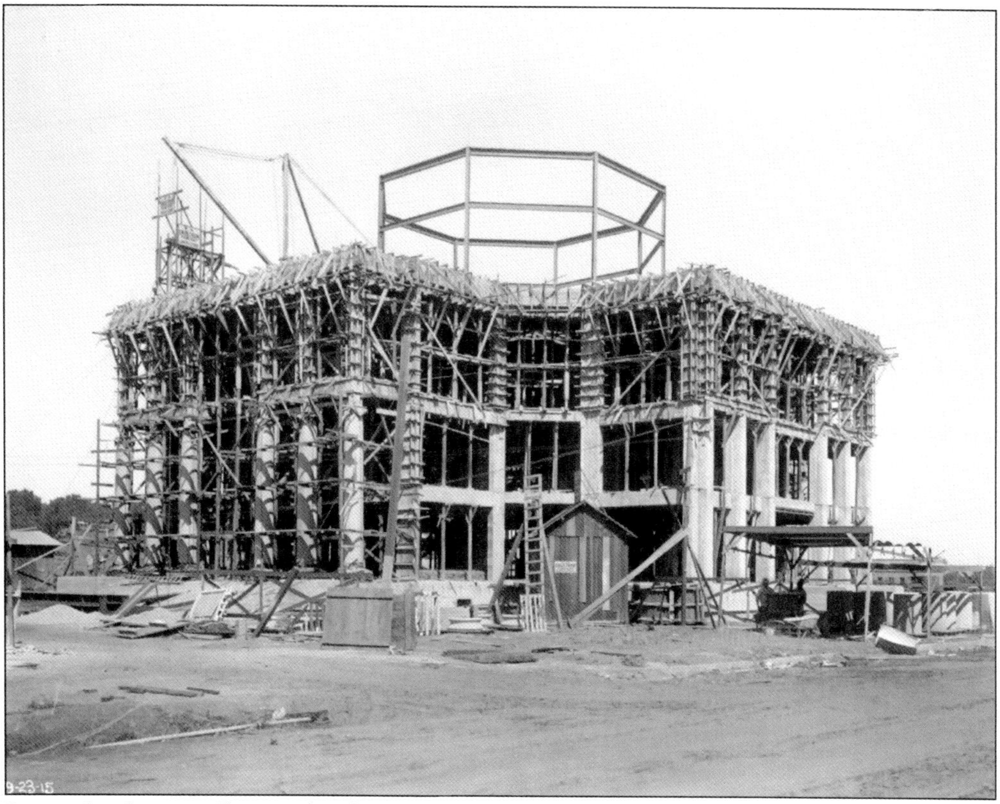

Pictured is the partially completed civic center building. The building contains more than 48,000 square feet of floor space and includes two domes, one over the other—a nearly unique design in the state of California. It has been said that, except for Hearst Castle, this structure is one of the most striking and memorable in the state. (Courtesy of Atascadero Historical Society.)

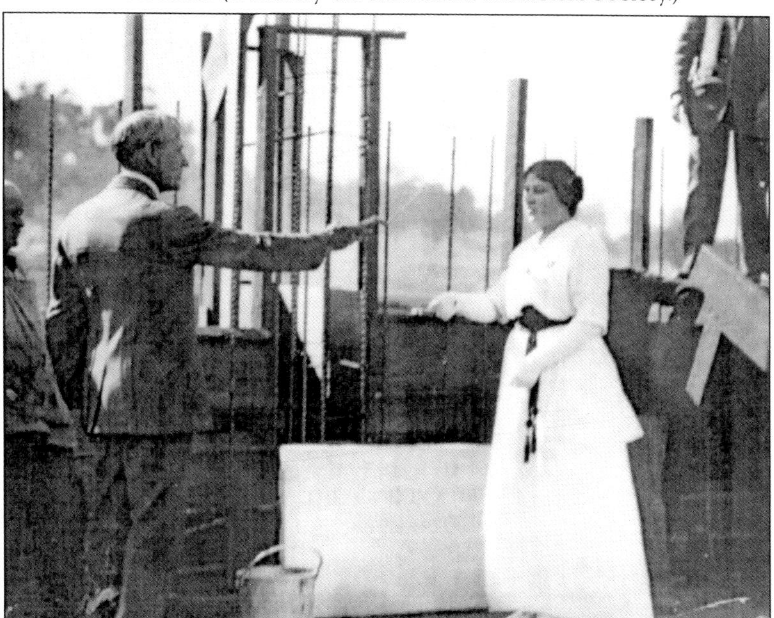

E.G. Lewis and wife Mabel salute each other with trowels as part of the cornerstone ceremony for the domed Atascadero Civic Center on June 12, 1914. Construction was complete in 1918. (Courtesy of Atascadero Historical Society.)

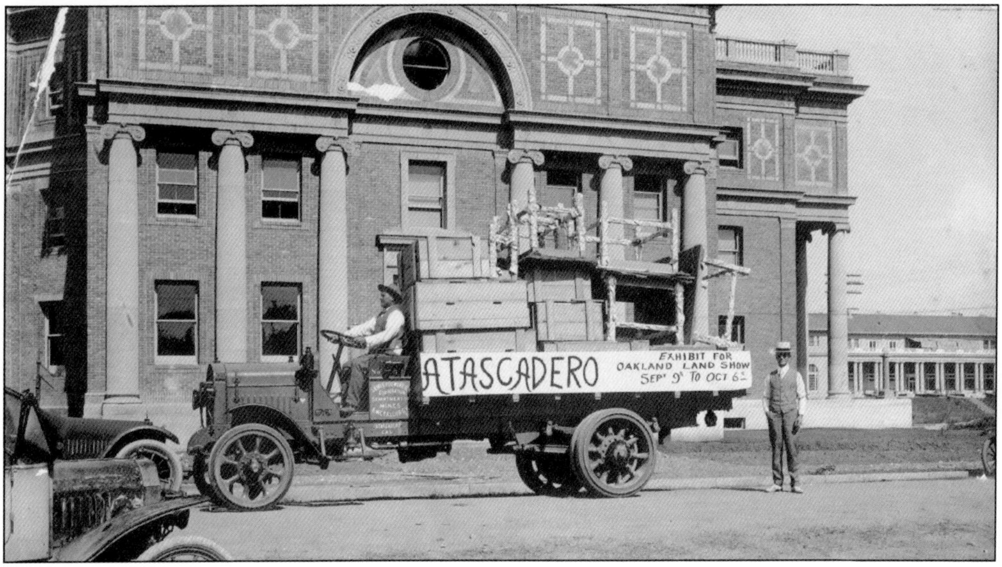

An exhibitor is headed to the Oakland Land Show outside the administration building. (Courtesy of Atascadero Historical Society.)

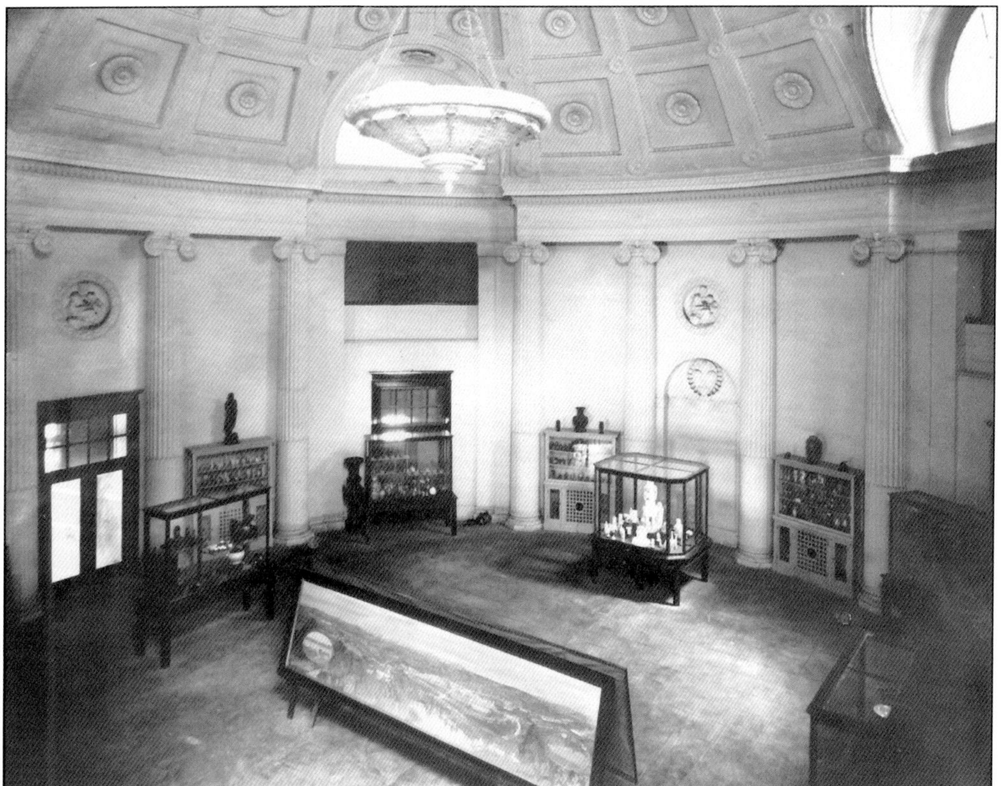

This image shows the first-floor rotunda of the administration building. Up until the San Simeon Earthquake struck in 2003, this area was used by the Atascadero Historical Society as a museum. Since that time, the society has put relics into storage and on display in the Colony House Museum across the street from the administration building. (Courtesy of Atascadero Historical Society.)

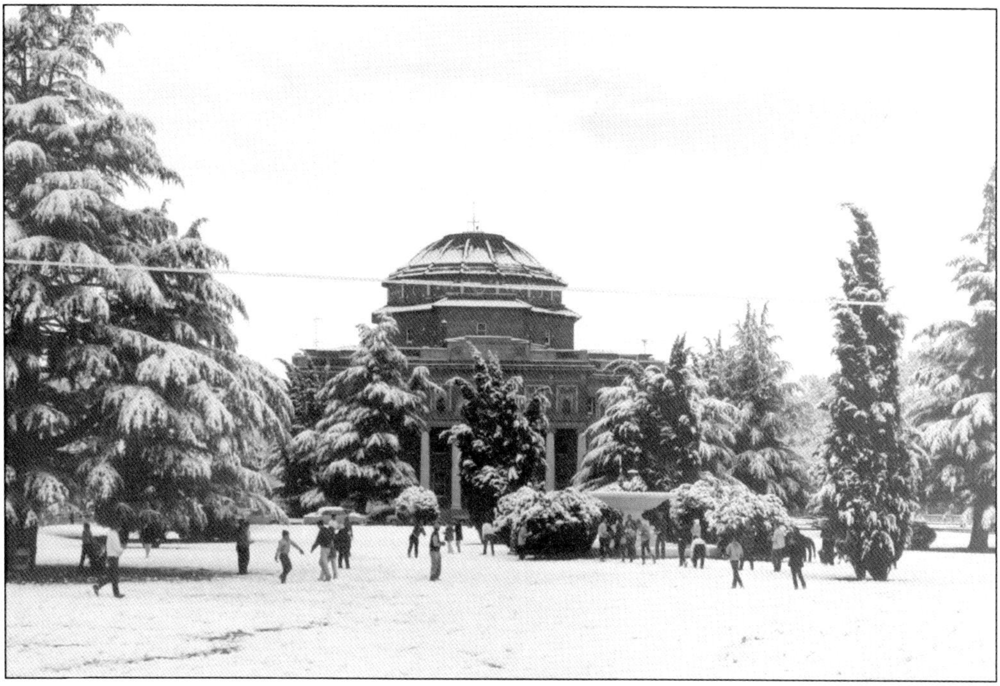

The historic city hall and veterans/administration building in the sunken gardens in downtown Atascadero is pictured after a rare snowfall. Snow comes to Atascadero about once every 10 years, but very rarely in amounts that last more than a few hours. This storm hit in the early 1960s. (Courtesy of Atascadero Historical Society.)

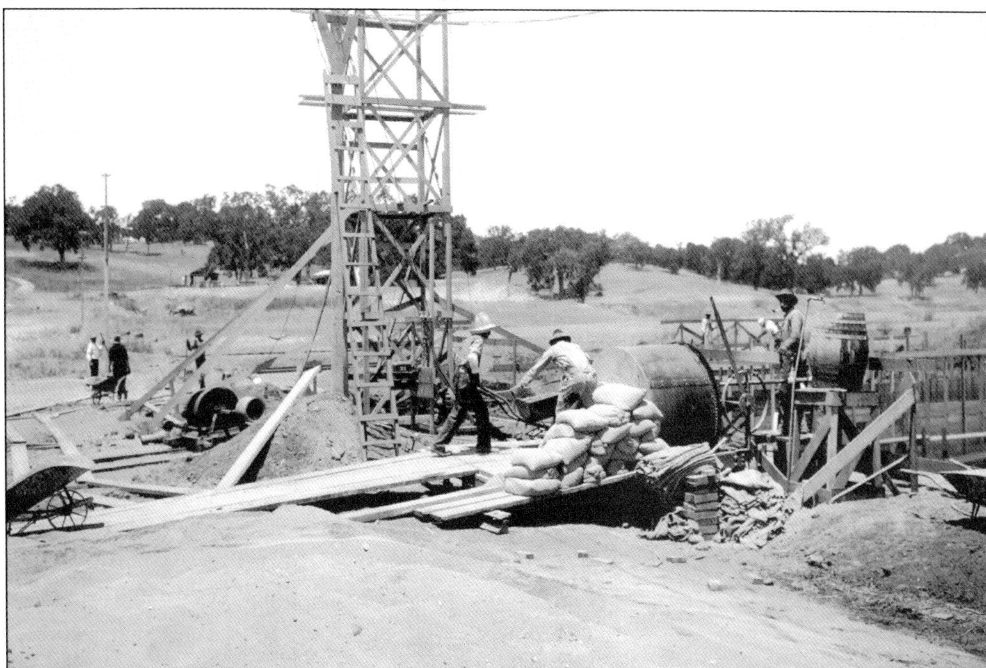

Pictured are the early stages during construction of the administration building. The process took three years. The building was complete in 1918. (Courtesy of Atascadero Historical Society.)

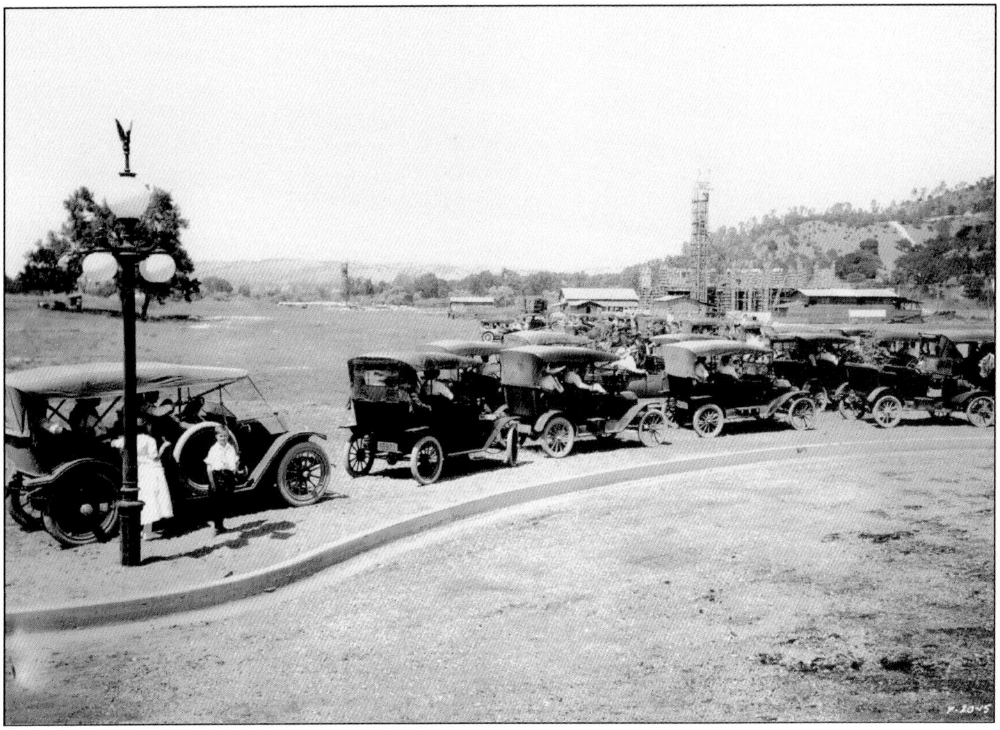

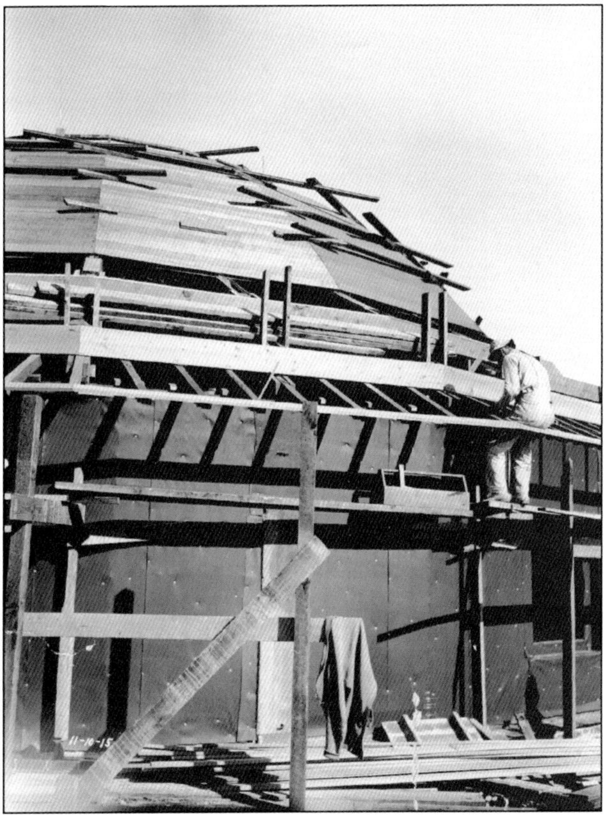

Cars, probably from the Colony Holding Corporation fleet, line up near the site of the new administration building. (Courtesy of Atascadero Historical Society.)

The administration building's dome was heavily damaged in the 2003 earthquake. A portion collapsed into the building, and restraints were installed to curtail further disintegration. (Courtesy of Atascadero Historical Society.)

This is a close-up of one of the two porticos that are part of the Atascadero Administration Building. (Courtesy of Atascadero Historical Society.)

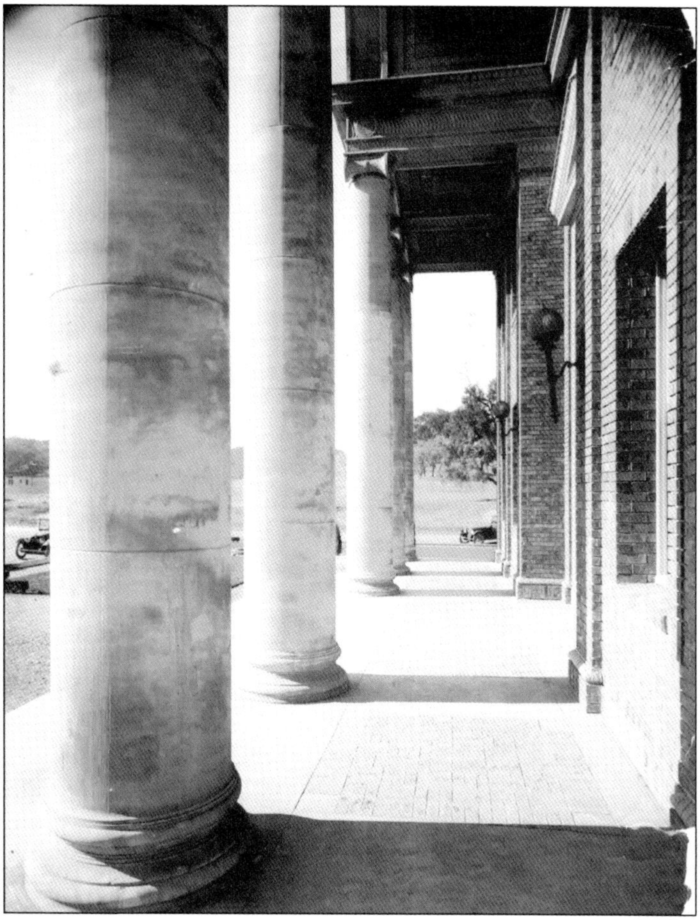

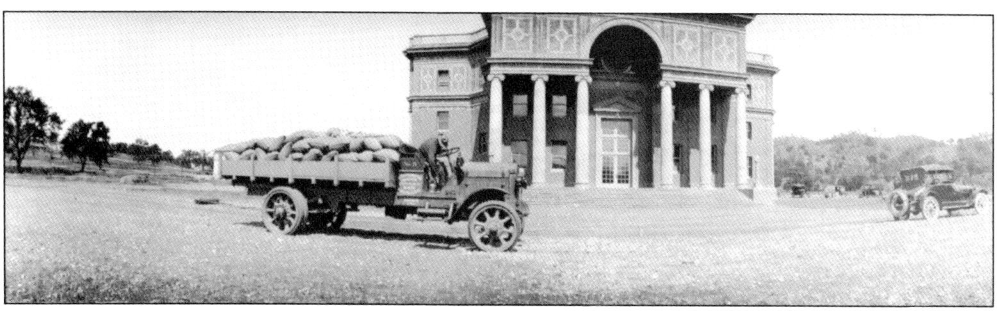

Although surrounded by trees and a park today, when the Atascadero Administration Building was complete in 1918, it stood alone. It must have appeared strange to travelers on nearby El Camino Real. The building must have seemed out of place, rising from the empty countryside. (Courtesy of Atascadero Historical Society.)

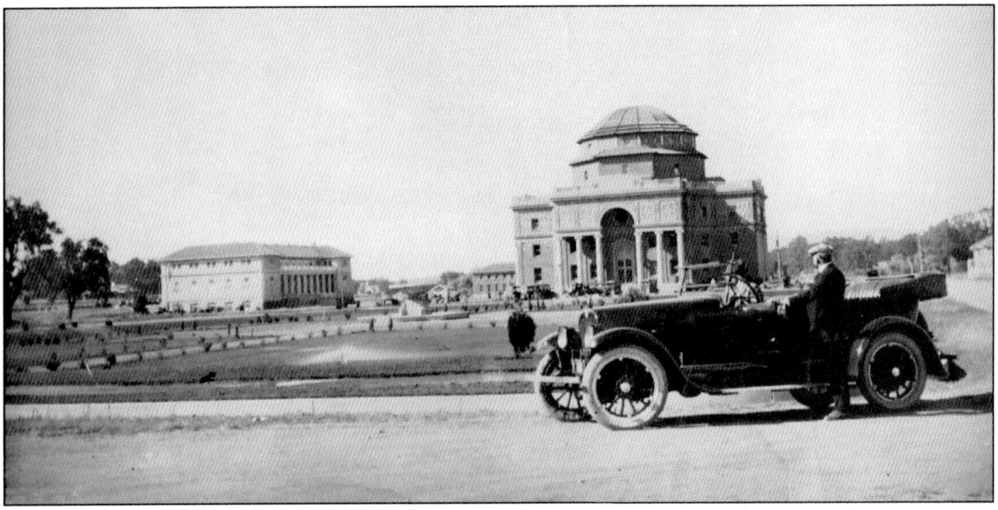

Here is another view of the iconic Atascadero Administration Building, also known as the Veterans Memorial Building. (Courtesy of Atascadero Historical Society.)

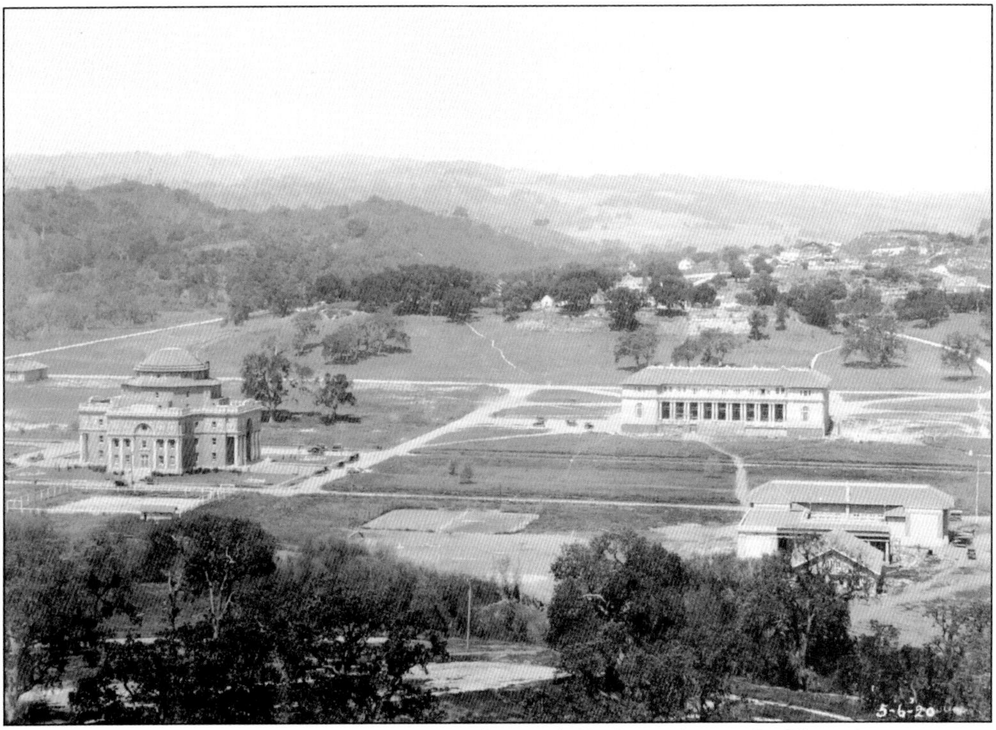

This panoramic view shows the civic center from a hillside to the south. The administration building is at left, and La Plaza is on the right. (Courtesy of Atascadero Historical Society.)

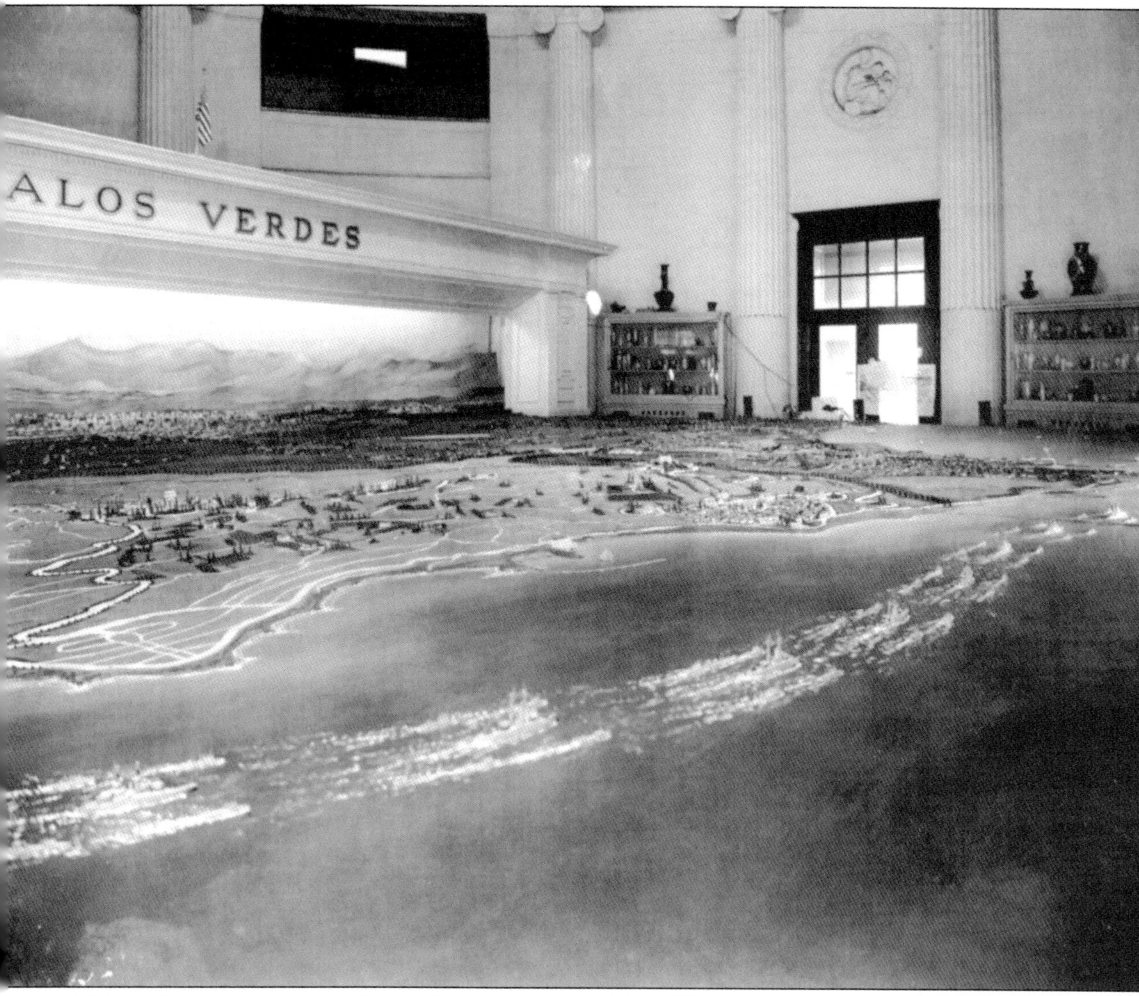

This is the lower rotunda of the administration building. This picture shows a tale of two cities. A miniature layout of Lewis's other California city, Palos Verdes, is set up in the room. Note the window above. This aperture opens into the circular hallway surrounding the rotunda. Skylights were installed in the other dome so that natural light could fill the interior of the building. These apertures were sealed up in a subsequent remodel. (Courtesy of Atascadero Historical Society.)

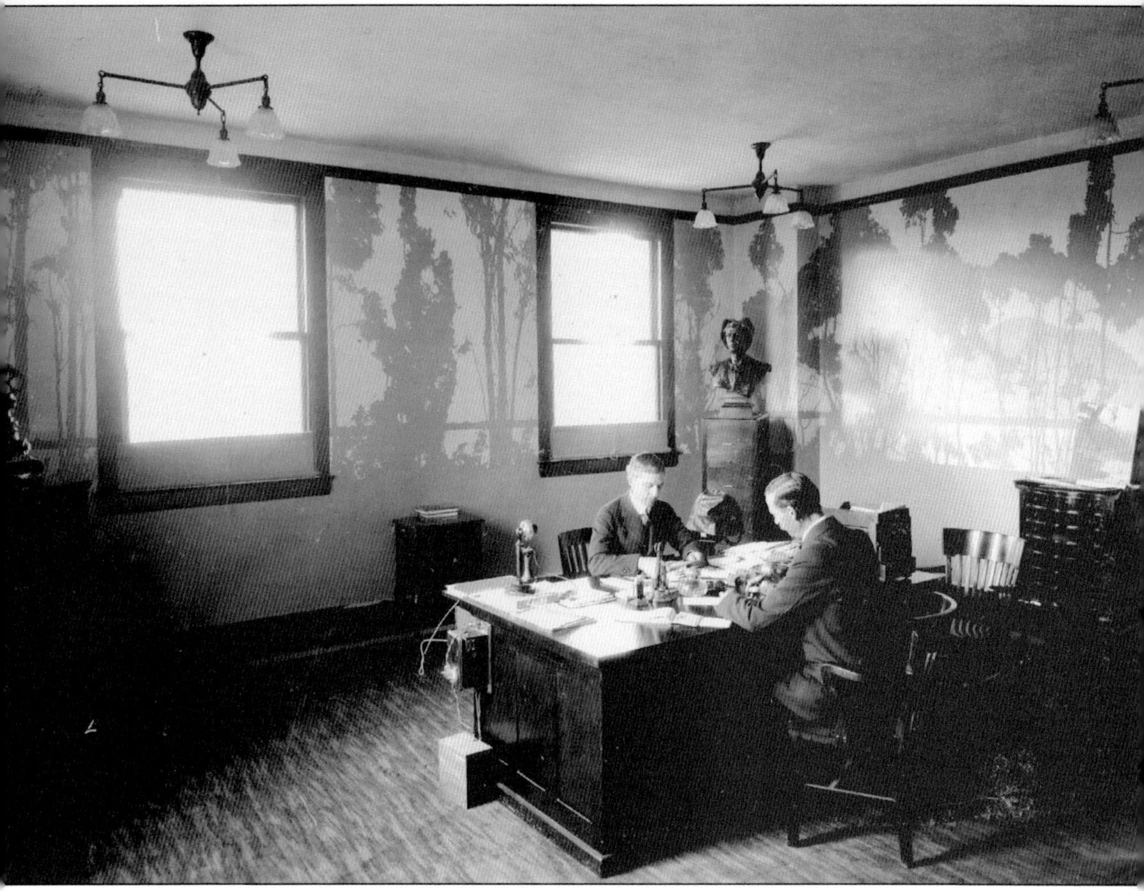

Wall murals were a recurring theme in early municipal structures. Notice the office decorations, including the statues and ornate lighting. Both men share a telephone. (Courtesy of Atascadero Historical Society.)

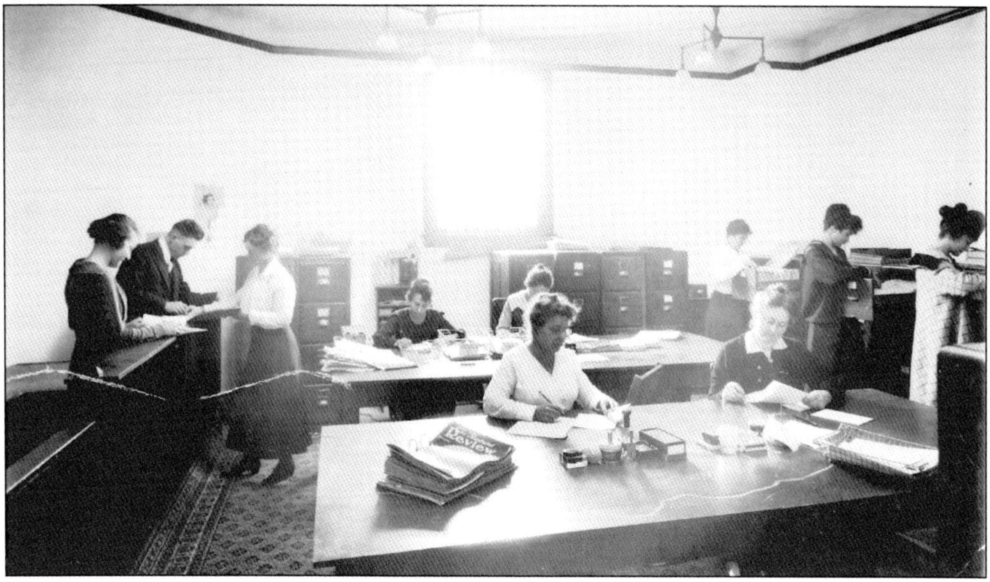

Women are at work in the early colony. Notice the stack of *Illustrated Review* magazines on the desk. E.G. Lewis printed this and other publications in the community's printery, the first building constructed in the community. (Courtesy of Atascadero Historical Society.)

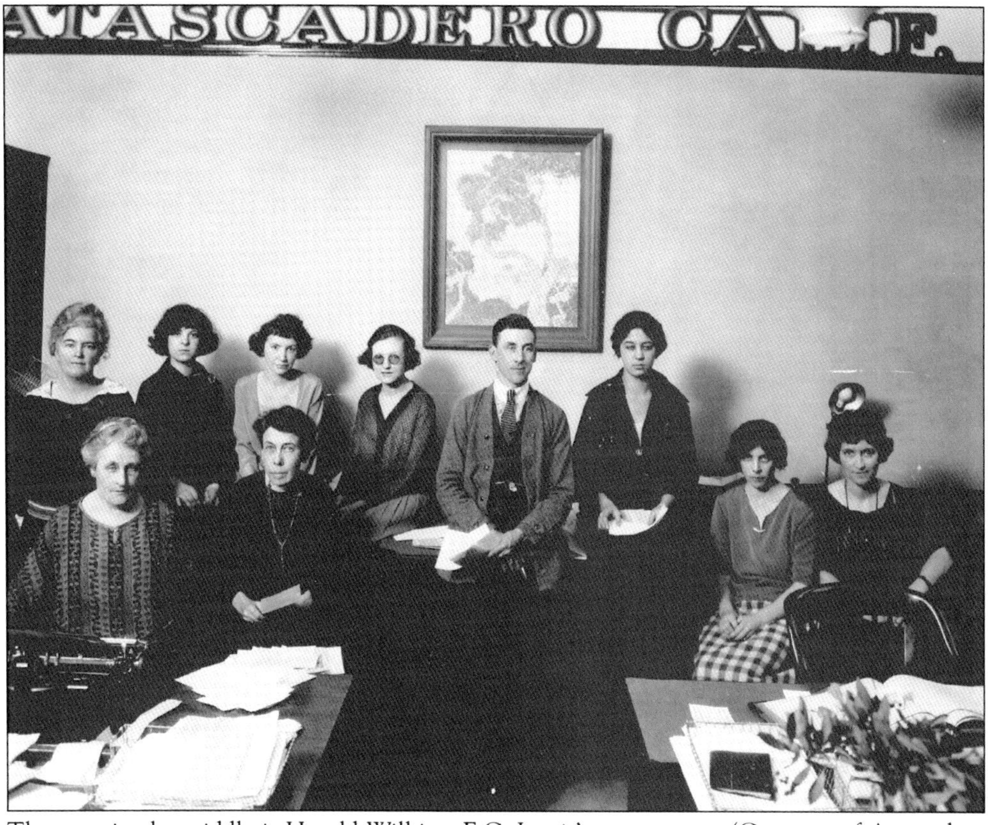

The man in the middle is Harold Wilkins, E.G. Lewis's accountant. (Courtesy of Atascadero Historical Society.)

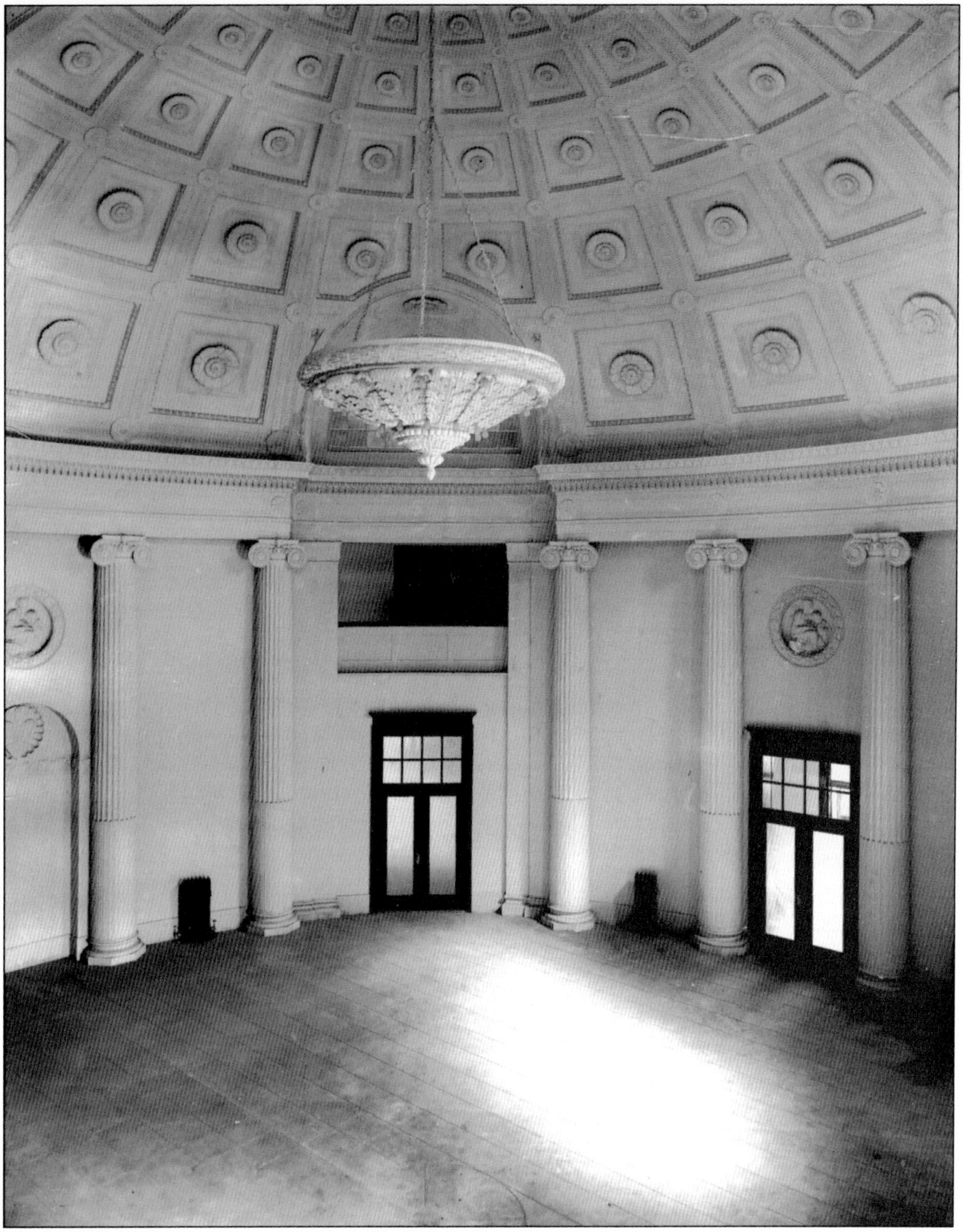

The empty lower rotunda room in the Atascadero Administration Building is pictured. Notice the decorative engravings, the ornate chandelier, and the patterned figures on the dome. (Courtesy of Atascadero Historical Society.)

Five

The Cloisters

Part and parcel of the incentives to colonize Atascadero was the promise of access to the Pacific Coast. There was just one problem: the range of coastal hills separating the colony of Atascadero from the beach. At that time, anyone in the Atascadero area would have to travel to San Luis Obispo to the south, over the steep Cuesta Grade, then westward to the coast from there.

To make the beach more accessible to Atascadero residents, work began in 1915 on a new 17-mile road (passable by automobiles) connecting the colony with Morro Bay. Building the road was a big challenge in the early part of the 20th century. Workers had to follow existing trails and creeks, using mules, steam shovels, and dynamite to smooth the way. Named the "Boulevard to the Sea" by Lewis, it is known today as California State Highway 41, or the E.G. Lewis Highway.

Residents brave enough to take their automobiles on the road spent a good two hours traveling in each direction. In stretches, the road was too narrow to allow two-way traffic, so visitors were advised to travel west during the early part of the day and east in the afternoon.

By 1919 at Atascadero Beach Estates, a beachfront complex called the Cloisters and consisting of 463 acres was developed by the Atascadero Beach Land and Improvement Company, a subsidiary of the Colony Holding Company. The Cloisters featured a comfortable hotel with accessory cabins, a golf course, and opportunities for swimming, fishing, and beach games. Beach cabins complete with private bathrooms were available for rent. Hundreds of small lots were created and offered for sale. To ensure the highest quality development, individuals who built bungalows were prohibited from spending less than $250 on the structures. Lewis tried to guarantee privacy for these bungalows by separating them from commercial development, a practice not common in community planning elsewhere for years to come.

The Cloisters boasted Spanish influence architecture, colonnades, and corridors. Lounge and dining rooms were well appointed and included murals by Ralph Holmes (the same artist who painted the murals in the printery and the civic center in Atascadero).

The Cloisters survived Lewis's financial difficulties for a while. After the stock market crash of 1929, many could not afford the cottages and bungalows. In 1941, the Cloisters served as barracks for servicemen guarding oil tanks on the coast. The complex was heavily damaged. No part of it exists today.

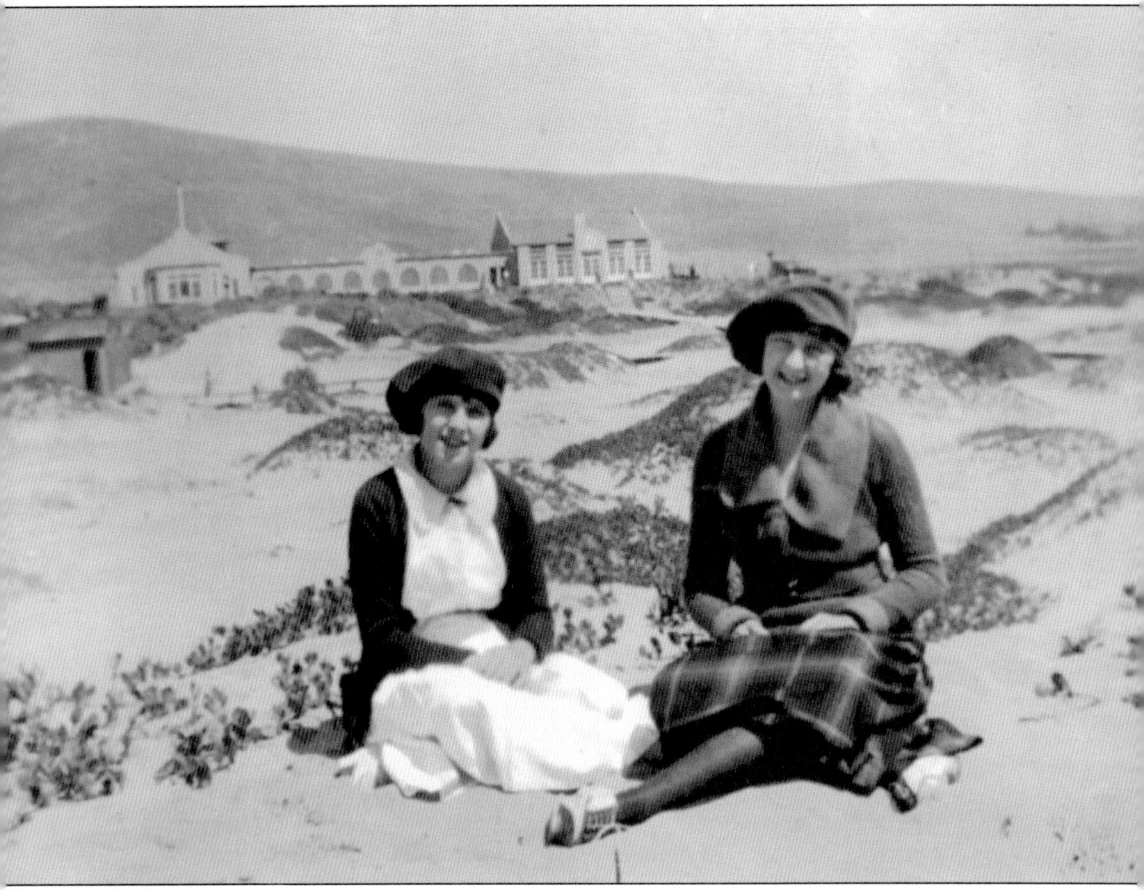

One of the major attractions of life in Atascadero was the promise of access to Atascadero Beach. The fact that the beach was located 17 miles away over the Santa Lucia Mountains was mitigated by the construction of a road for cars traveling back and forth to a complex called the Cloisters (seen in the background here). The two unidentified women are enjoying a day at the coast. They probably arrived before noon, as the road was so narrow cars were directed to drive west in the morning and return eastward in the afternoon to avoid conflict. Today, this road has been developed as a stretch of State Highway 41, dubbed the E.G. Lewis Highway. (Courtesy of Kent Kenney Archives.)

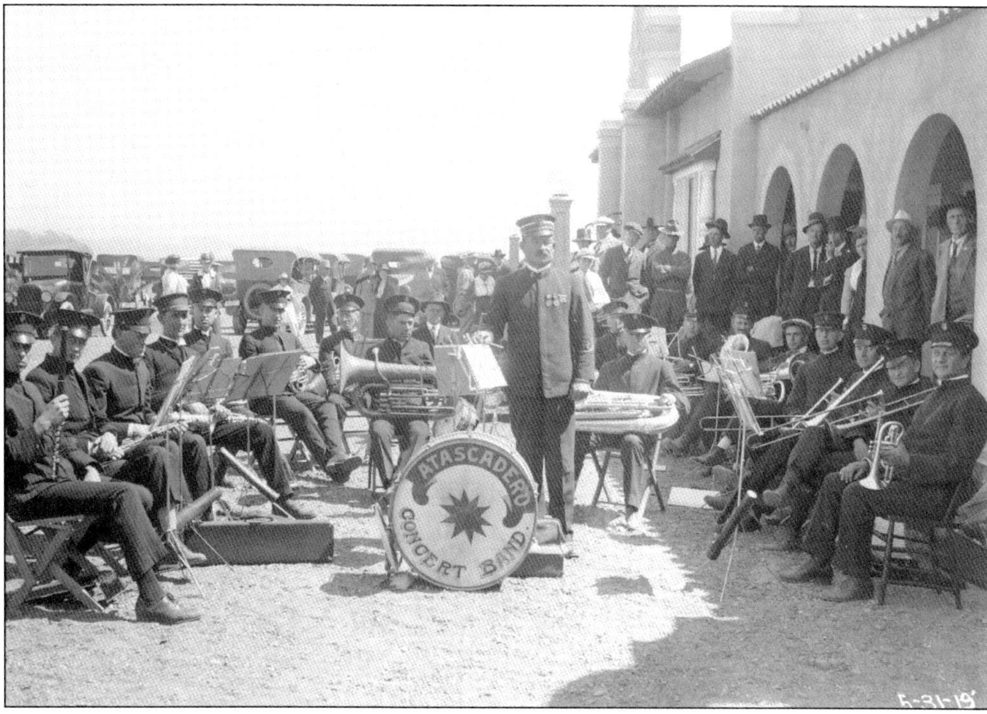

The Atascadero Concert Band assembles to entertain guests at the Cloisters, a recreational complex connected to Atascadero by what is now the 17-mile E.G. Lewis Highway (State Highway 41). Landowners in Atascadero received access to the Cloisters as part of their contract. Hundreds of small lots were marketed to visitors and residents on what was known as Atascadero Beach. (Courtesy of Kent Kenney Archives.)

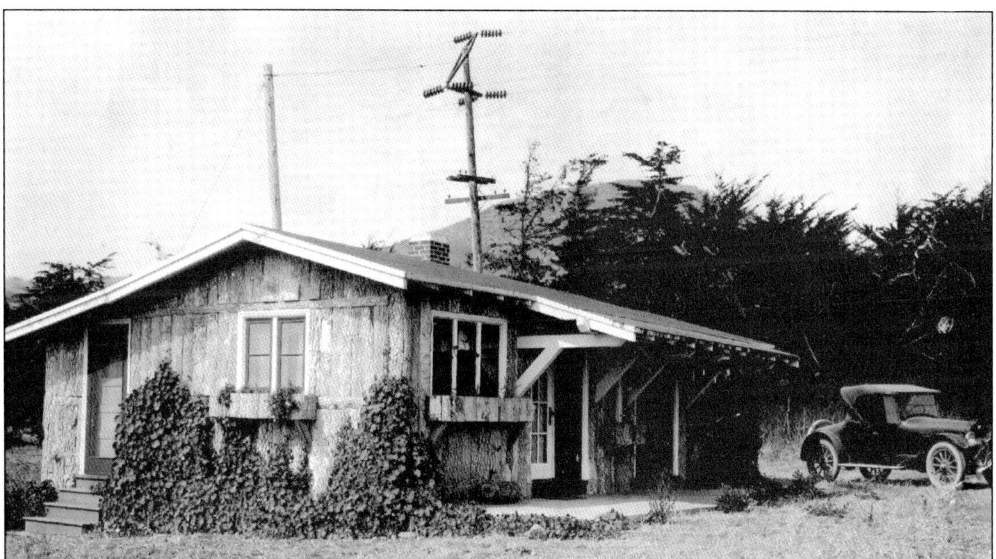

When E.G. Lewis tired of the administrative duties associated with the colony of Atascadero, he took his own prescription for relaxation—he retreated to the Pacific Coast and Atascadero Beach. This is a photograph of his beach bungalow. (Courtesy of Atascadero Historical Society.)

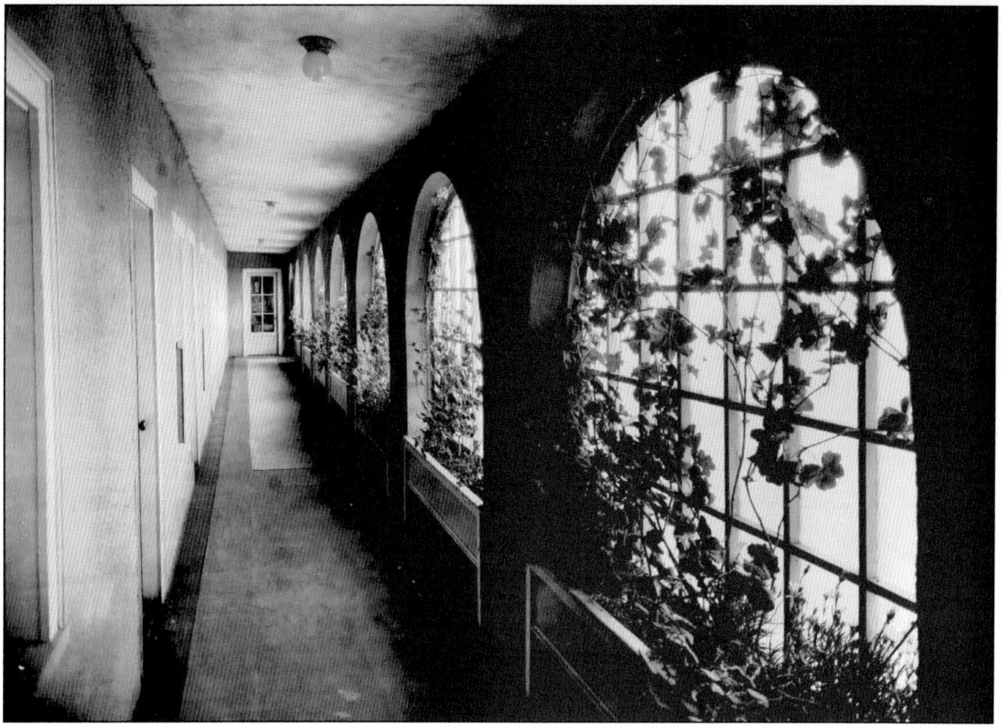

This photograph shows one of the long, cool walkways of the Cloisters on the coast. (Courtesy of Atascadero Historical Society.)

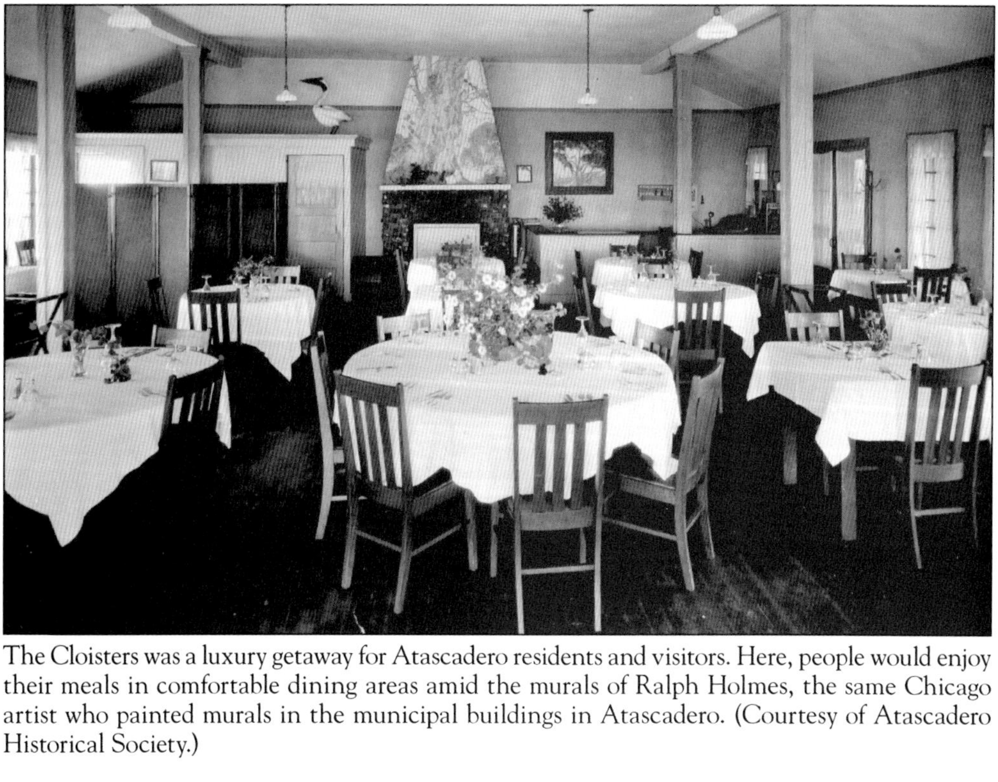

The Cloisters was a luxury getaway for Atascadero residents and visitors. Here, people would enjoy their meals in comfortable dining areas amid the murals of Ralph Holmes, the same Chicago artist who painted murals in the municipal buildings in Atascadero. (Courtesy of Atascadero Historical Society.)

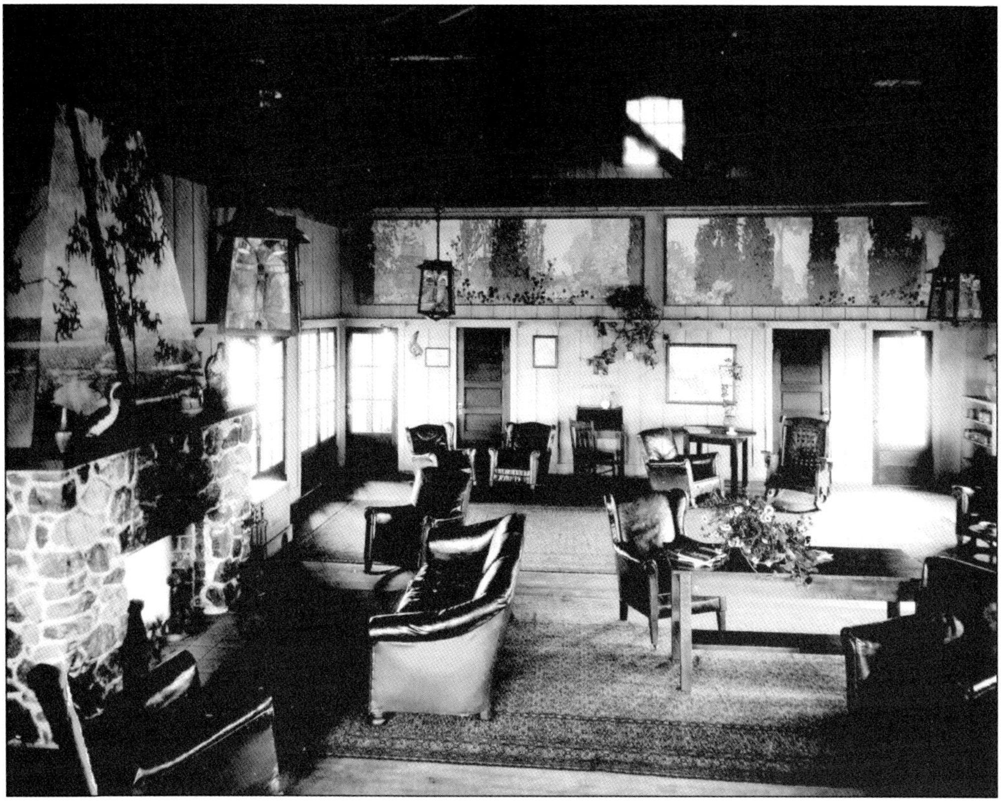

After recreation, guests would relax in the comfortable lounge at the Cloisters. (Courtesy of Atascadero Historical Society.)

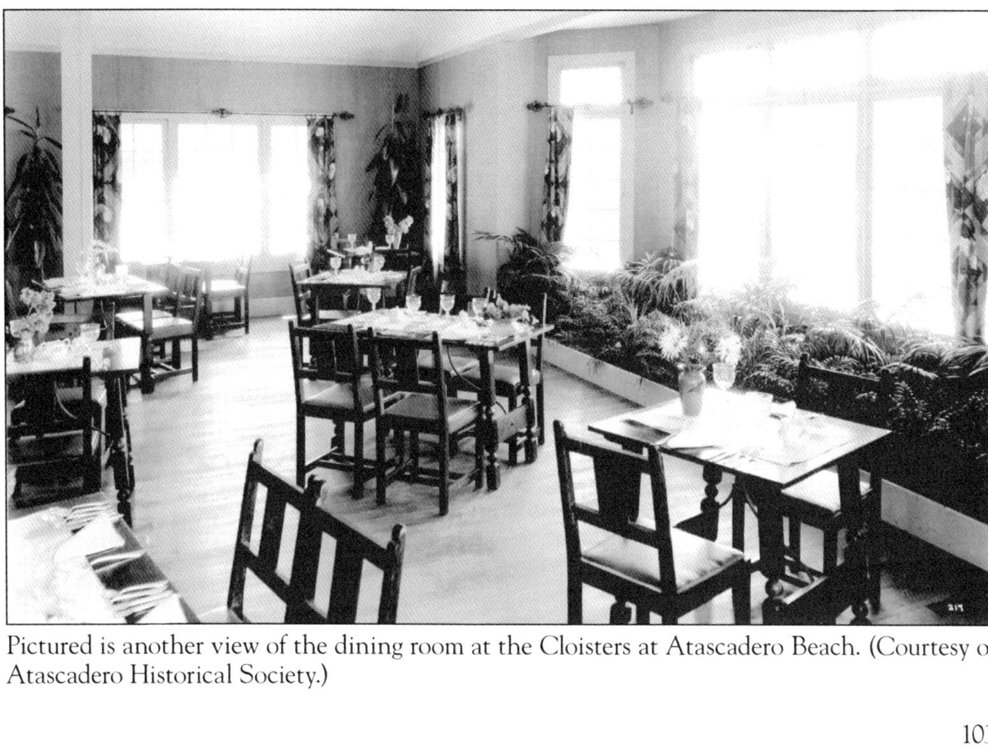

Pictured is another view of the dining room at the Cloisters at Atascadero Beach. (Courtesy of Atascadero Historical Society.)

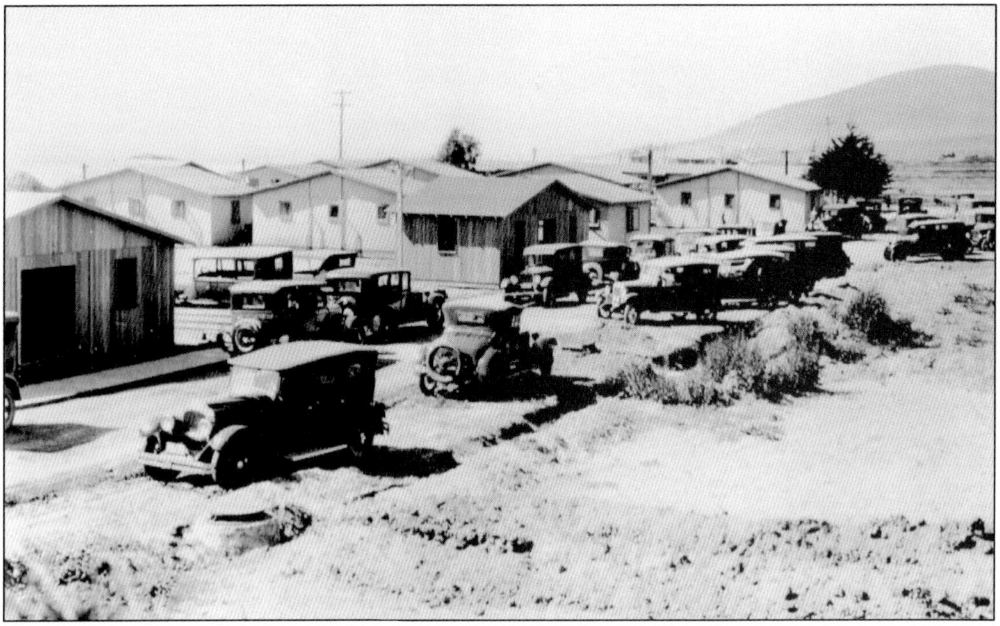

Beachside bungalows were situated on hundreds of small lots marketed by a subsidiary company of the Colony Holding Corporation. Design standards applied here, as well as in the colony. Parking was plentiful. Utilities were installed underground. (Courtesy of Atascadero Historical Society.)

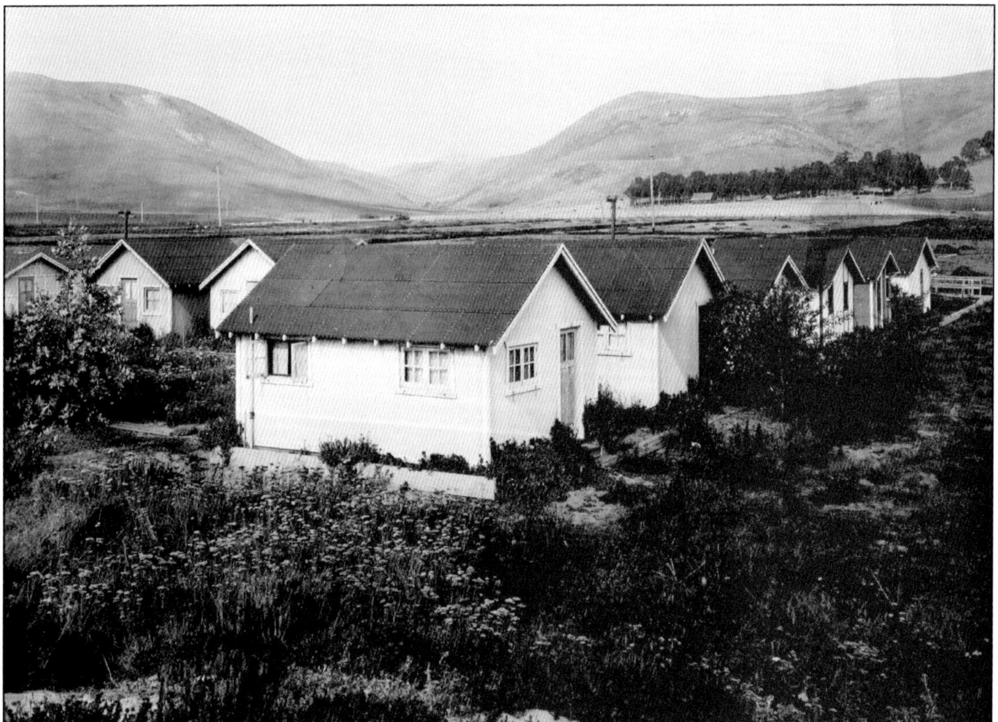

Those who purchased lots in the Atascadero Beach subdivision were encouraged to build upscale bungalows. Purchasers were required to spend no less than $250 on their residences. (Courtesy of Atascadero Historical Society.)

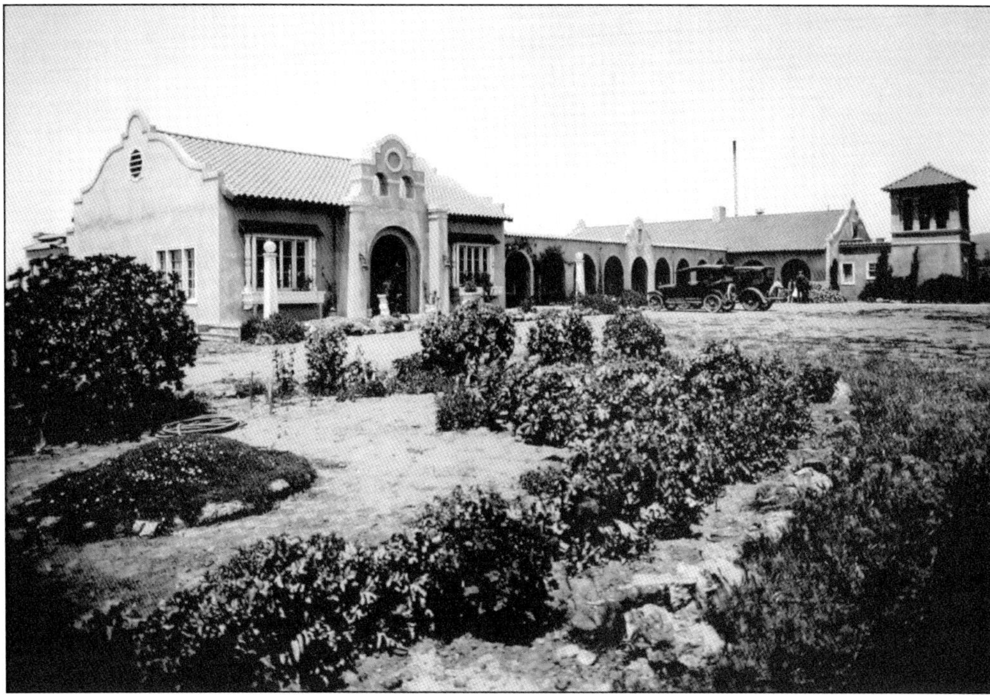

Perched on a sandy knoll, the Cloisters greeted westbound cars from Atascadero in the morning and bade them farewell in the afternoon. (Courtesy of Atascadero Historical Society.)

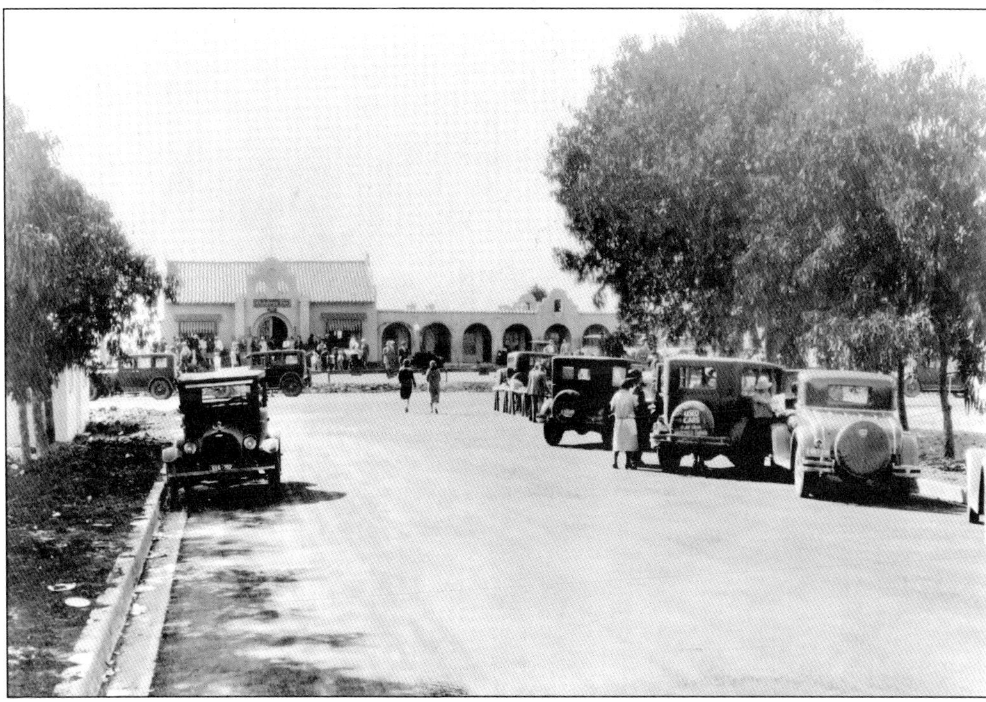

Wide boulevards seemed to be part of the psyche of Atascadero's founder. Here, at the Cloisters, automobile enthusiasts of the day surely felt comfortable and welcome. (Courtesy of Atascadero Historical Society.)

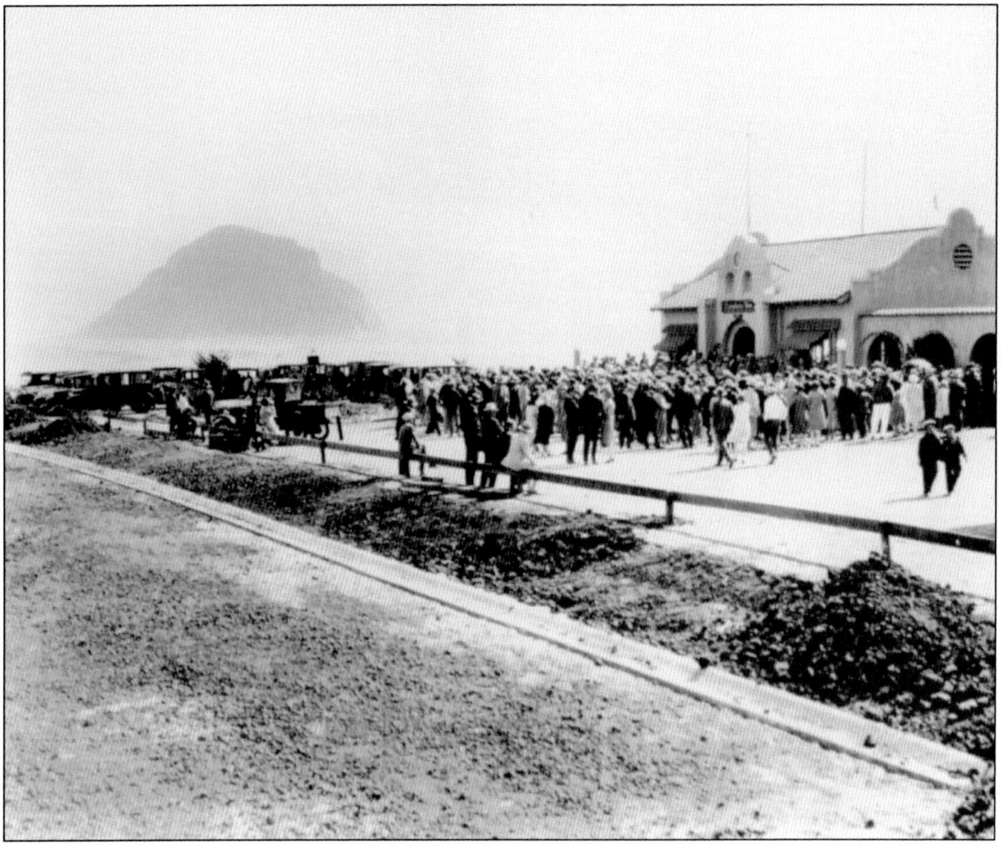

Morro Rock emerges from the mist in the background of this photograph of the Cloisters. Crowds of visitors stand outside the inn. (Courtesy of Atascadero Historical Society.)

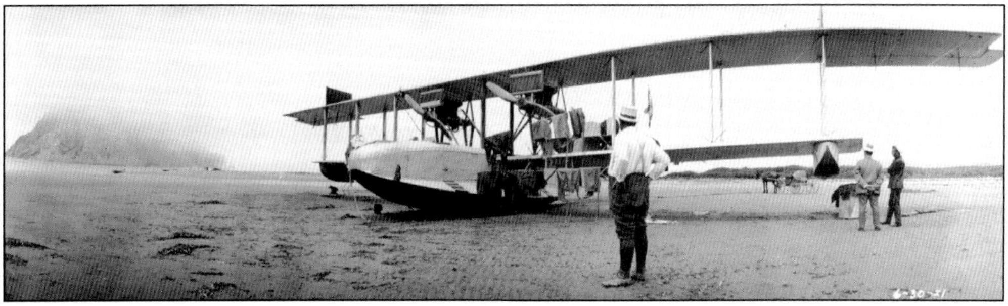

Apparently, wide-open beaches made the Cloisters accessible by aircraft. The pilot of this craft and his passengers obviously came to frolic. Note the towels and clothing drying on the plane's support wires. (Courtesy of Atascadero Historical Society.)

Six

The Bacchantes

One of the most visually striking and yet somewhat mysterious relics of the E.G. Lewis era in Atascadero weighs thousands of pounds and is made of solid carrera marble. It is a statue of three, seminude, wrestling women that has stood in various locations in the colony over the years. Known to residents as the *Bacchantes*, the *Three Graces*, the *Wood Nymphs*, the *Marble Maidens*, and *Three Girls Wrestling Over a Towel*, the sculpture is said to have been one of many pieces of Italian art on display during the World Exposition of 1904 in St. Louis, Missouri.

Investigations by local artists have turned up little detail about the statue. Apparently, Italy submitted so much artwork to the exposition that much of it was stored on-site. The Bacchantes' provenance as artwork from the 1904 exposition comes from John Lewis, brother of the founder of Atascadero, who claimed the statue was purchased at the end of the exposition around 1906. It is believed the name of the artist was A. Petrilla or A. Petrilli.

Through the decades, weather, wear and tear, and vandals caused significant damage to the statue. Chips appeared. Fingers and toes went missing. At one time, an entire leg became detached. Local residents did their best to repair the damage with paint and other simple remedies, but it was not until 1983 that the City of Atascadero hired an expert to do more extensive repairs. In 2001, the City of Atascadero authorized the removal of the statue for professional restoration. The cost of the repairs was estimated at $215,000. Today, that work is nearing completion, and the statue is expected to return to Atascadero in time for the Centennial Celebration in 2013.

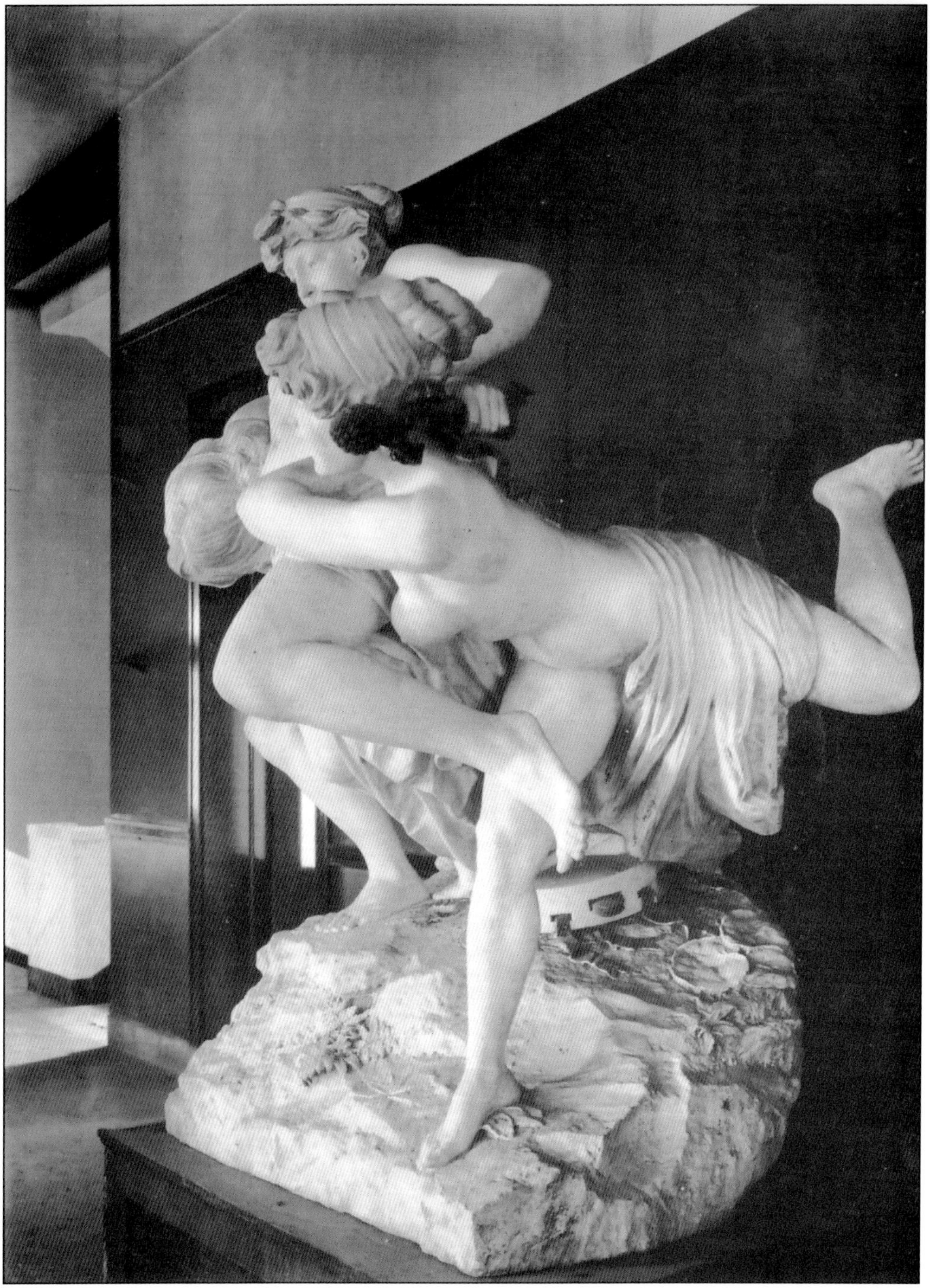

The *Bacchantes* statue was also known as the *Water Nymphs*, *Wood Nymphs*, *Marble Maidens*, and *Three Girls Wrestling Over a Towel*. This statue carved from carrera marble is thought to have been created by Italian artist A. Petrilli (or Petrilla) for the 1904 World's Fair in St. Louis. E.G. Lewis purchased it and transported it to Atascadero. (Courtesy of Kent Kenney Archives.)

Seven

Atascadero Lake Park and Zoo

Located on the E.G. Lewis Highway (State Highway 41) just east of the intersection with US Highway 101, Atascadero Lake has existed since before the beginning of the colony, formed on a hardpan depression and filled with runoff from the nearby Santa Lucia Mountains and an inlet from nearby Atascadero Creek. An earthen dam constructed by the US Army holds back the runoff to form the lake. That dam still exists today. A mile-long road encircles the lake, and a small, man-made island sits in its western end.

E.G. Lewis used the natural community swimming hole to promote the sale of colony lots. He deepened the lake a bit and added a small bandstand. For decades, families have gathered at the lake to picnic, sail, fish, and even water-ski. Today, motorized craft and even swimming are prohibited. For nearly 30 years, the lake was home to a spectacular Fourth of July fireworks presentation. That was terminated by the city in the 1980s.

In 1917, the lake was the location for a performance of Gilbert and Sullivan's *HMS Pinafore*. A large replica of a sailing ship was constructed as the stage. In the 1920s, a wooden stage was placed by the water's edge. In 1930, walls and a roof were added to form the first lakeside pavilion. A new pavilion was built and opened in 1992.

The Charles Paddock Zoo is located adjacent to Atascadero Lake. It began in 1955 as a collection of wire cages housing sick or injured animals, as well as cast-offs from other facilities. The man responsible for collecting this ragtag menagerie was a San Luis Obispo County Park Ranger and local Boy Scout leader, Charles "Chuck" Paddock. In 1962, Paddock used $750 of his own money to acquire animals from a zoo in Southern California. It would set the stage for his involvement for nearly a quarter of a century.

Today, the Charles Paddock Zoo is the only zoo accredited by the Association of Zoos and Aquariums between San Jose and Santa Barbara. It offers a beautiful shaded park with a wide variety of exotic animals and birds, educational and social programs, and many other features. It meets the highest standards of care for all of its animals, and it attracts thousands of visitors each year. Other more recent features at Atascadero Lake include Alvord Baseball Field and the impressive Veterans Memorial Complex.

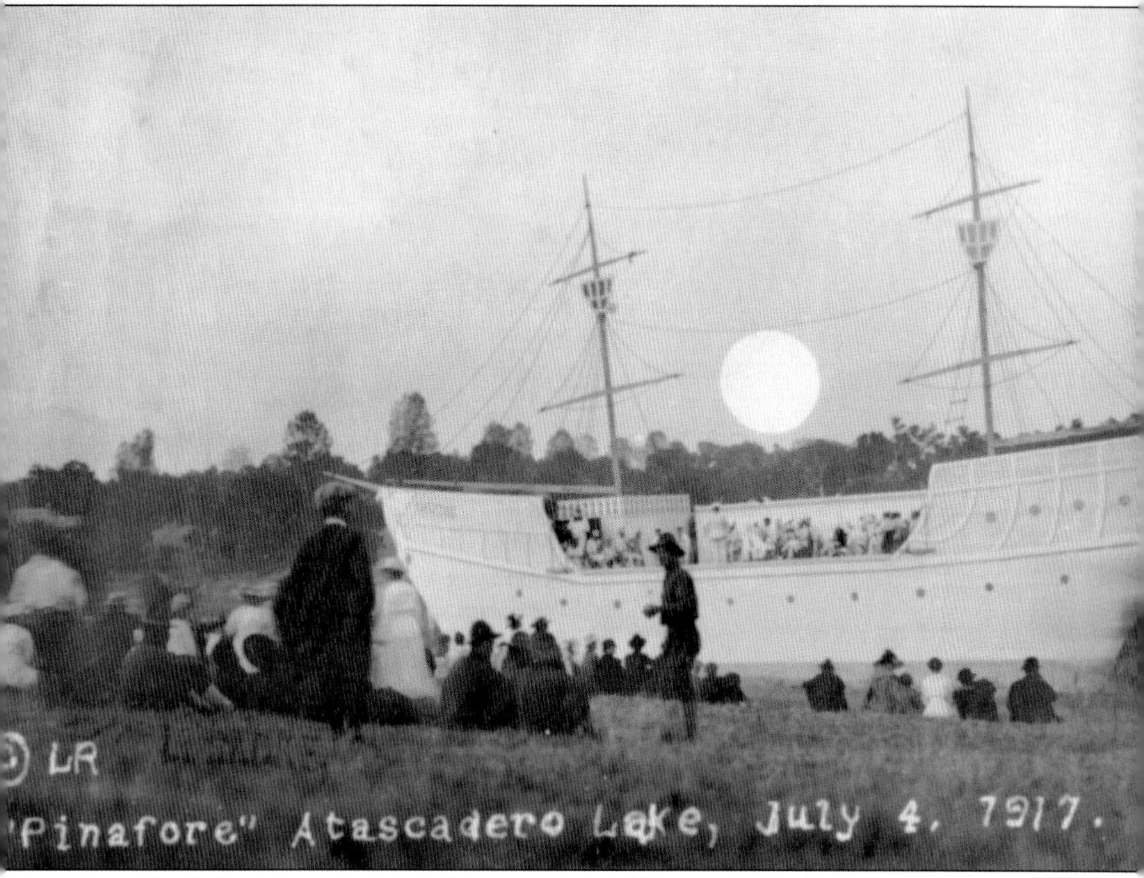

Atascadero Lake was an early draw to the community and became a center for entertainment. Pictured here is a local production of *HMS Pinafore* in 1917. (Courtesy of Kent Kenney Archives.)

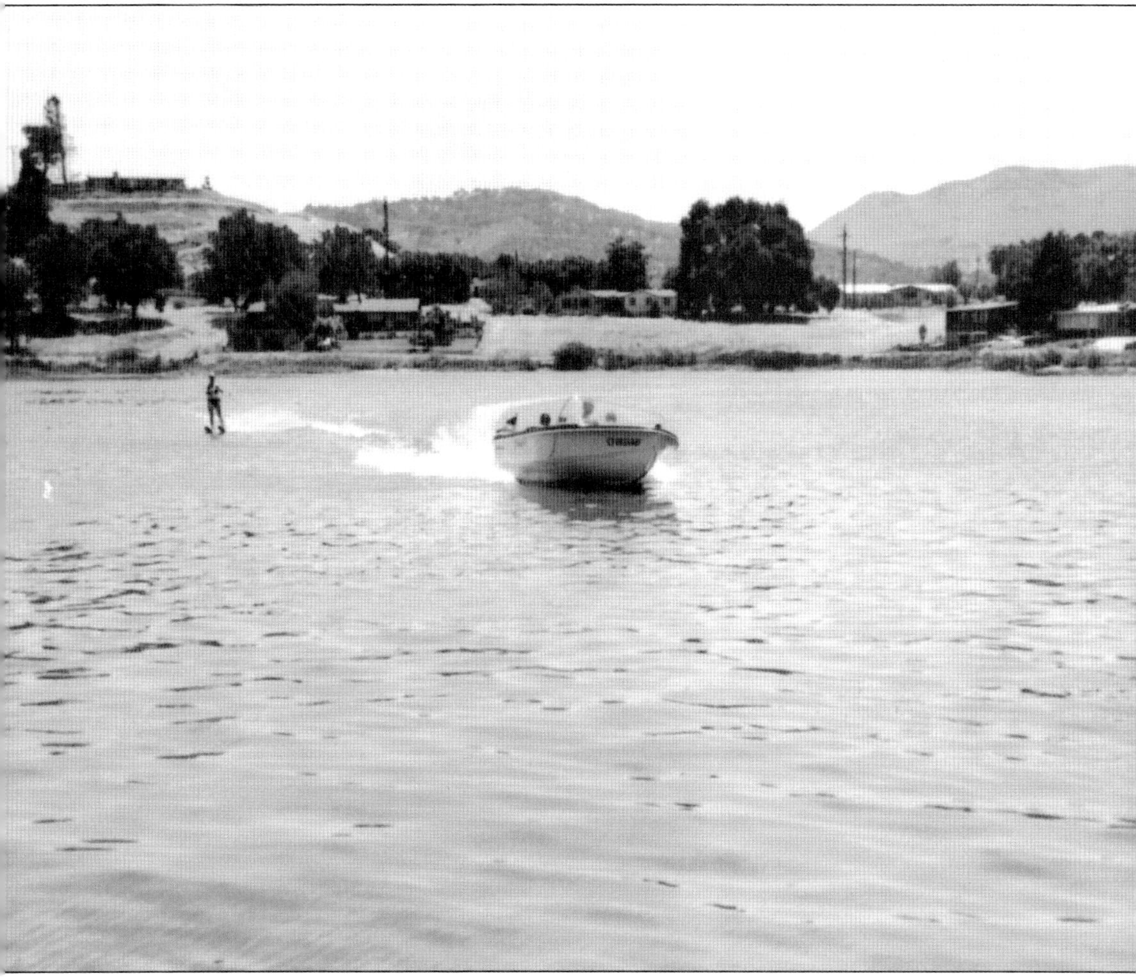

Small and shallow, it seems unlikely to newcomers that Atascadero Lake was ever the site of extensive water sports. Home photographs tell a different story. Water-skiing was a popular activity on the lake in the 1950s and 1960s. (Courtesy of Kent Kenney Archives.)

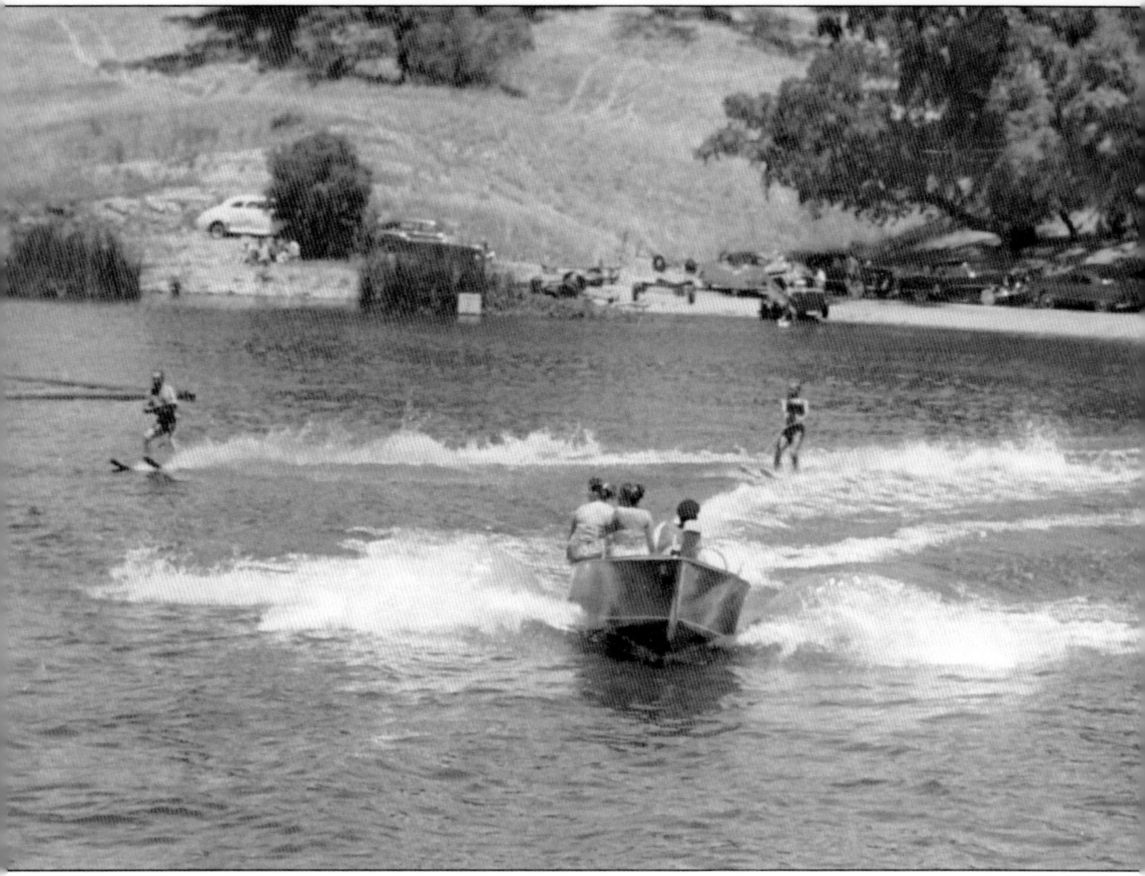

More proof that, yes, there was water-skiing on Atascadero Lake. (Courtesy of Kent Kenney Archives.)

Eight

Highway 101

It is ironic that the colony of Atascadero, a city planned with automobiles in mind from its very inception in the early 1900s, has often suffered from the impacts of the automobile. The Mercantile slowly declined due, in part, to increasing business competition along the busy El Camino Real through the center of the city. The Doble Steam Car Company, touted as an economic boon, went belly-up before one vehicle could be built in Atascadero. Then, in the 1950s, the needs of the automobile would once again backfire in Atascadero's face. US Highway 101 arrived in the city, dividing the downtown and severely limiting crosstown traffic circulation.

Prior to 1948, El Camino Real (the King's Highway) carried the bulk of north–south traffic up and down the Salinas Valley. El Camino Real ran through the center of downtown Atascadero, causing congestion but assuring local businesses exposure to thousands of travelers. That would have to change, according to CalTrans, owing to the increasing amount of traffic on the road. The plan called for a new highway paralleling El Camino Real between San Francisco and Los Angeles. The plan improved north–south traffic flow but, in Atascadero, severely diminished east–west cross-traffic.

Some Atascadero residents wanted the new highway to be routed along the Southern Pacific railway on the east side of the city. Others argued business would suffer and property values would drop if that should happen. In the end, the highway was placed just 300 feet away from El Camino Real, behind existing businesses.

Extensive grading and terracing were required to prepare for the new highway. When it was finished, a number of businesses reported significant drops in sales. Over the years, the hope of developing a traditional downtown faded as retail development spread up and down El Camino Real with nodes where off-ramps and overpasses provided access to and from the highway. In the historic downtown area, pedestrian traffic from one side of the highway to the other is accommodated primarily by a pedestrian underpass. To this day, traffic circulation and parking issues resulting from the placement of US Highway 101 still vex local planners.

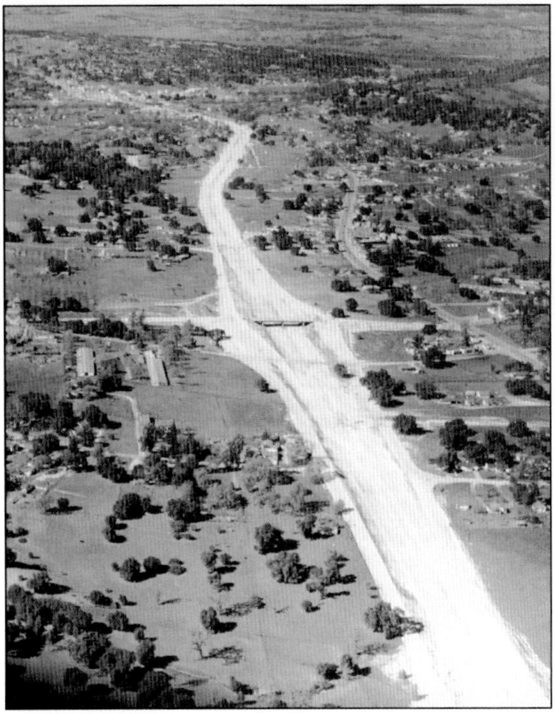

In the late 1950s, US Highway 101 was constructed parallel to El Camino Real. The highway cut downtown in half. (Courtesy of Kent Kenney Archives.)

Extensive terracing and grading were required to create US Highway 101 through the city of Atascadero. (Courtesy of Kent Kenney Archives.)

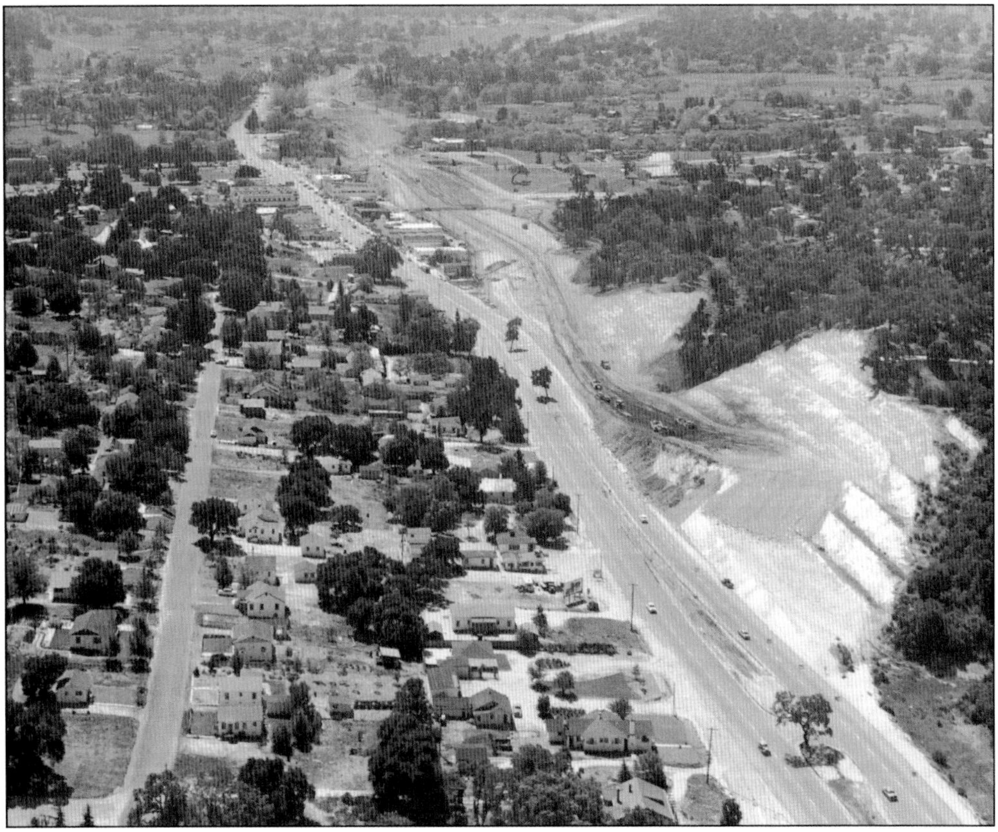

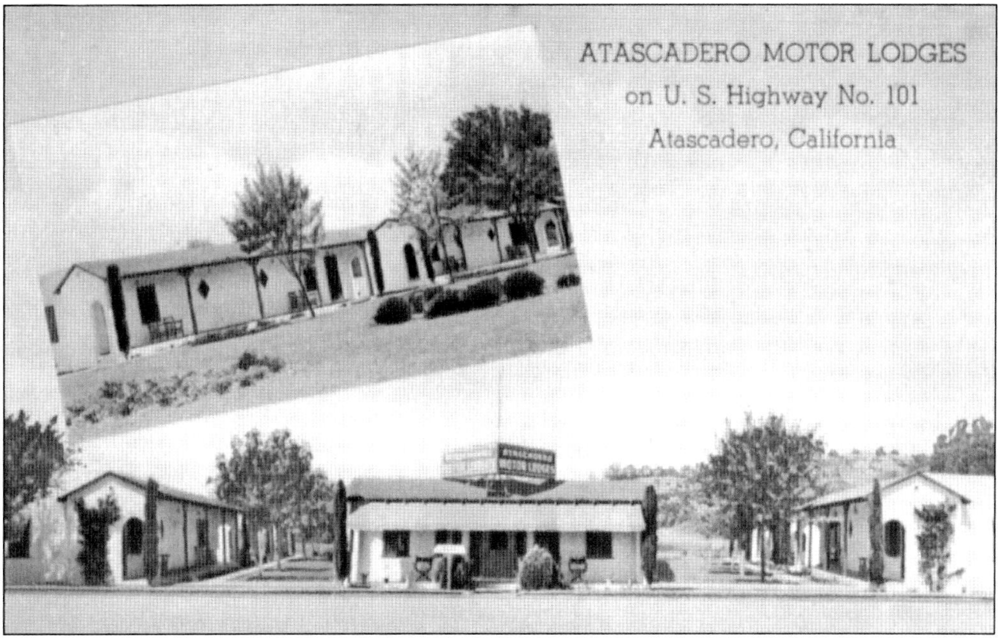

Always associated with El Camino Real and the automobile, Atascadero was touted on postcards as the ideal place to stop and stay on a motoring trip. (Both, courtesy of Kent Kenney Archives.)

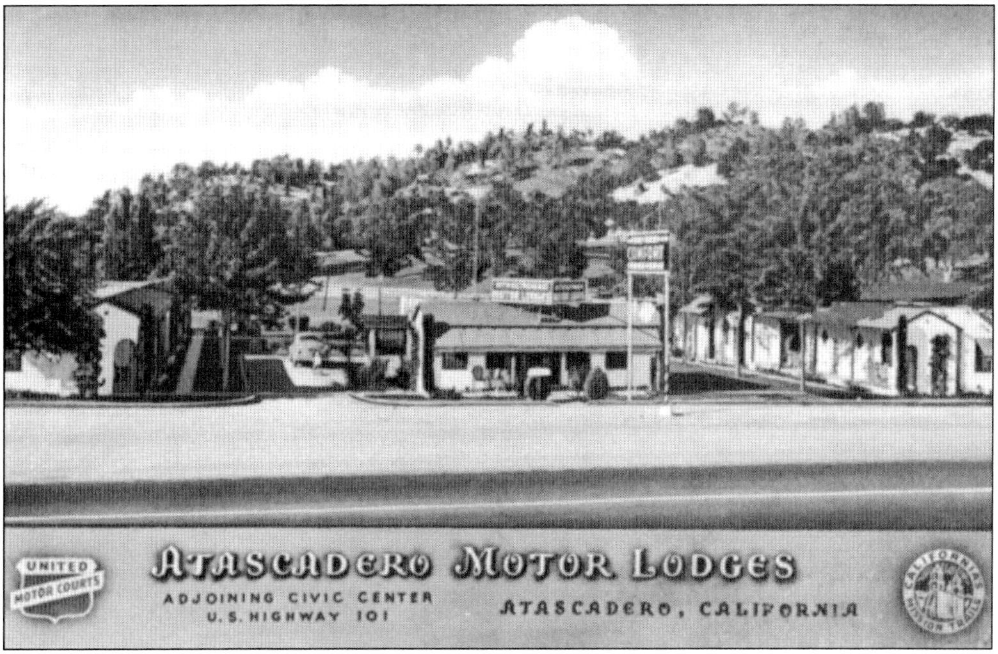

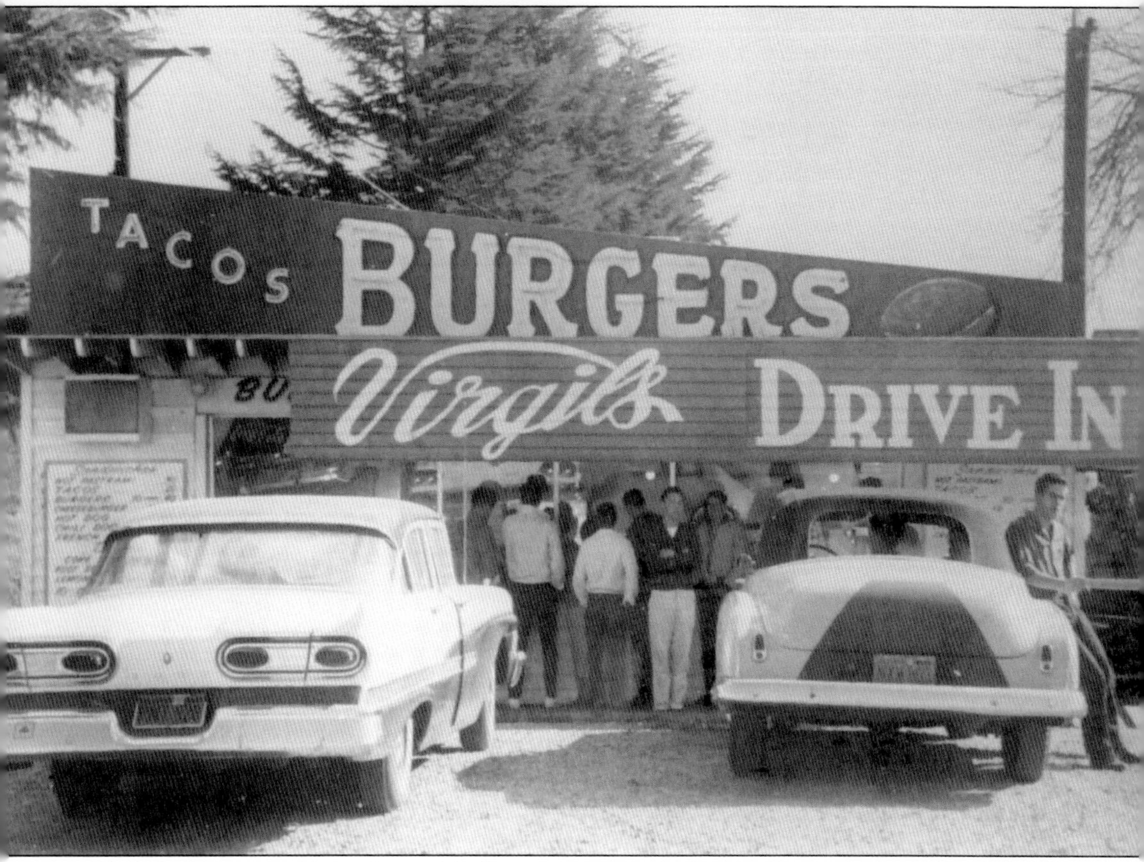

Of all the burger stands in the world, there was only one Virgil's. This was the gathering place for high school students and highway travelers. The secret Virgil's hamburger recipe is said to be in the possession of another restaurant now, but only those who have tasted the original can judge the accuracy of that claim. Today, where Virgil's once stood is a bank. Burger lovers weep. (Courtesy of Kent Kenney Archives.)

Nine

Atascadero Speedway

For 20 years, race enthusiasts from all over flocked to Atascadero Speedway on the south end of Atascadero to sit on backless wooden benches behind chain-link fencing and watch local racing heroes fly around the track, sometimes ending up off the track or upside down. The roar was deafening as car after car sprinted down the straightaways and up and around the turns. At the checkered flag, the winner would cruise in front of the crowd, engine roaring, and then step out to receive his trophy and a kiss from a pretty girl.

Atascadero Speedway, a quarter-mile oval track, was built by a group of local racing enthusiasts and opened in September 1953. At first there were no lights, and races were held on Sunday afternoons. Over the years, that changed to Friday nights, then Saturday nights. An evening's program was usually composed of four heat races, a trophy dash, and a main event. Sometimes special 50- and 150-lap races were also held. Crowds loved the demolition derbies. Cars crashing into cars—the kids loved it. (OK, the adults too.)

Back in those days, one did not need big-name sponsors and hundreds of thousands of dollars to race on a Saturday night. According to speedway veterans, one could get a hot car running for about $300. "All you really had to do to race was get an old car and weld a roll-bar on it," said driver Russ Mattice. According to him, there were two classes of cars racing in those days: jalopies and hardtops. Jalopies were generally cars from before 1936. Hardtops were vehicles with metal tops from the 1939–1946 era.

The speedway closed in 1973, and today, not much remains but the terraced hillside where the spectator benches stood. There's still racing in the blood of many of the people who were involved in the speedway, however, and enthusiasts keep the memory of the good old days alive. Today's cars may be faster and more high-tech, say the old-timers, but there is still nostalgia for the simpler days when a fellow could climb into his $300 race car and hit the track at the old Atascadero Speedway.

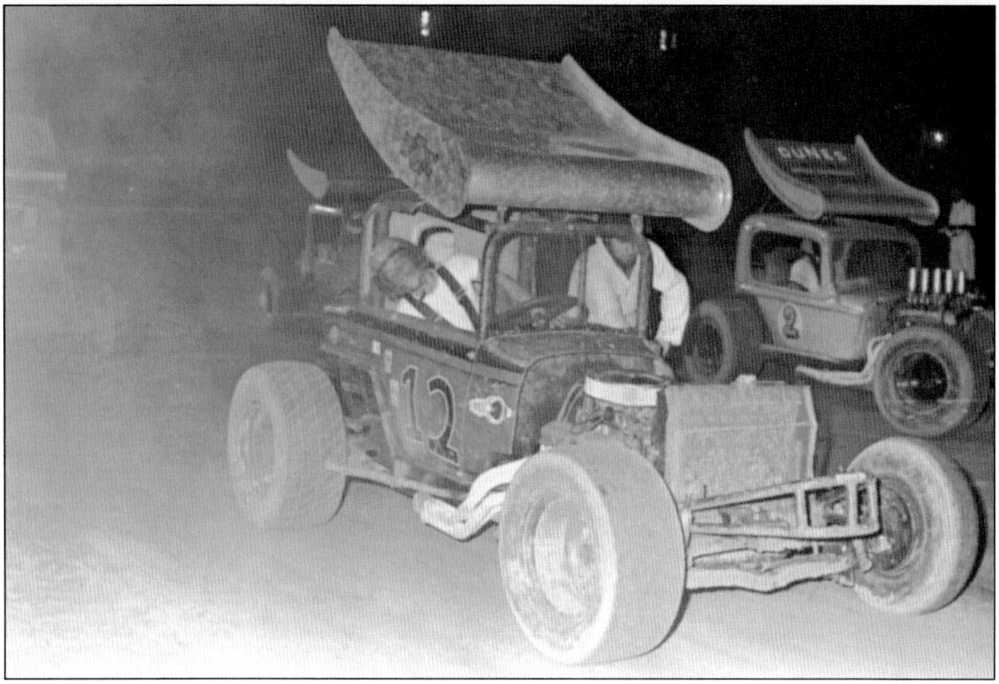

From 1953 to 1973, the Atascadero Speedway, a quarter-mile clay track on the south side of the city, provided thrills and chills for locals and drivers from near and far. Jalopies, hardtops, midgets, and destruction derby cars vied for lots of fame, little money, and an occasional kiss from the trophy girl. Local racing legends could bring just about anything with a roll bar to the races and give it a whirl. Spectators watched from wooden bleachers set into a hillside. (Both, courtesy of Joyce Rabellino.)

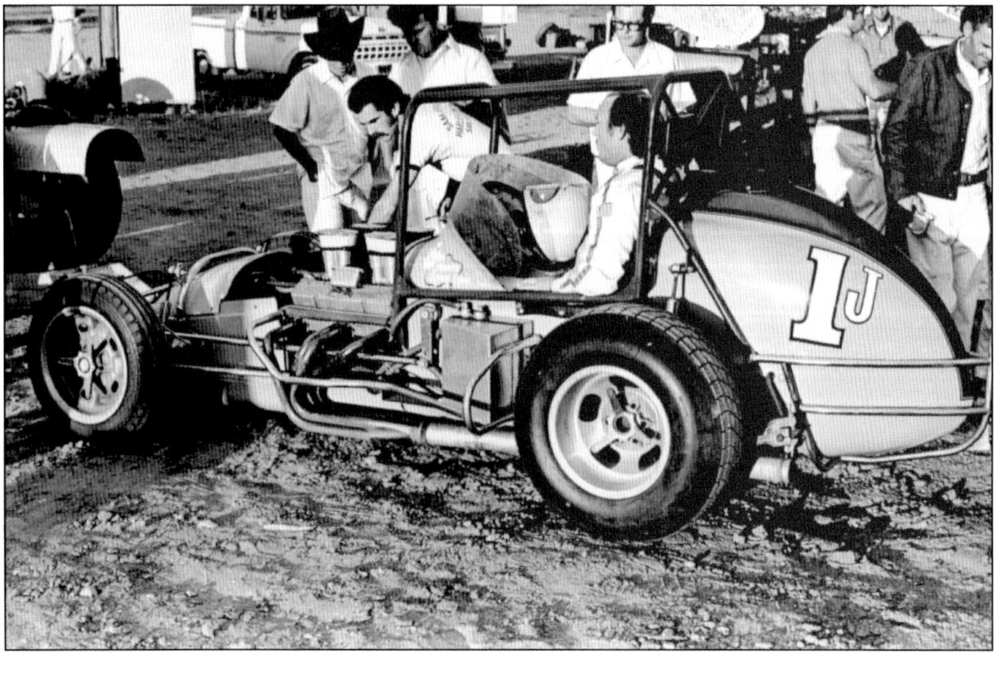

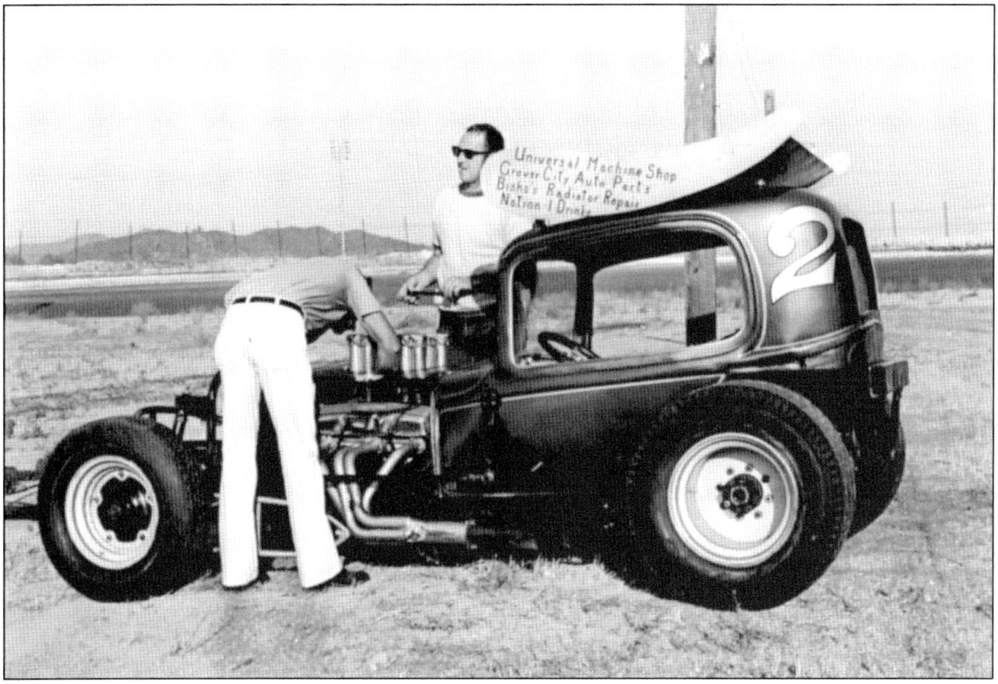

Local race car drivers would encourage sponsors to pay for their need for speed. Note the sponsor names handwritten on the airfoil of this car. (Courtesy of Joyce Rabellino.)

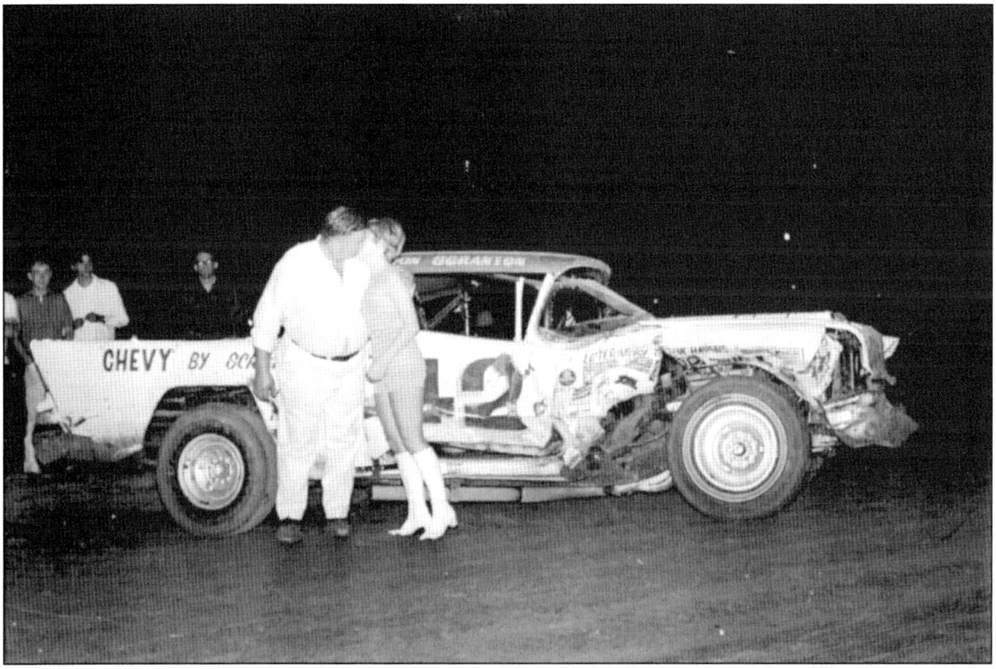

The crowd oohed and aahed as victorious road warriors claimed their prize: a kiss from the trophy girl. (Courtesy of Joyce Rabellino.)

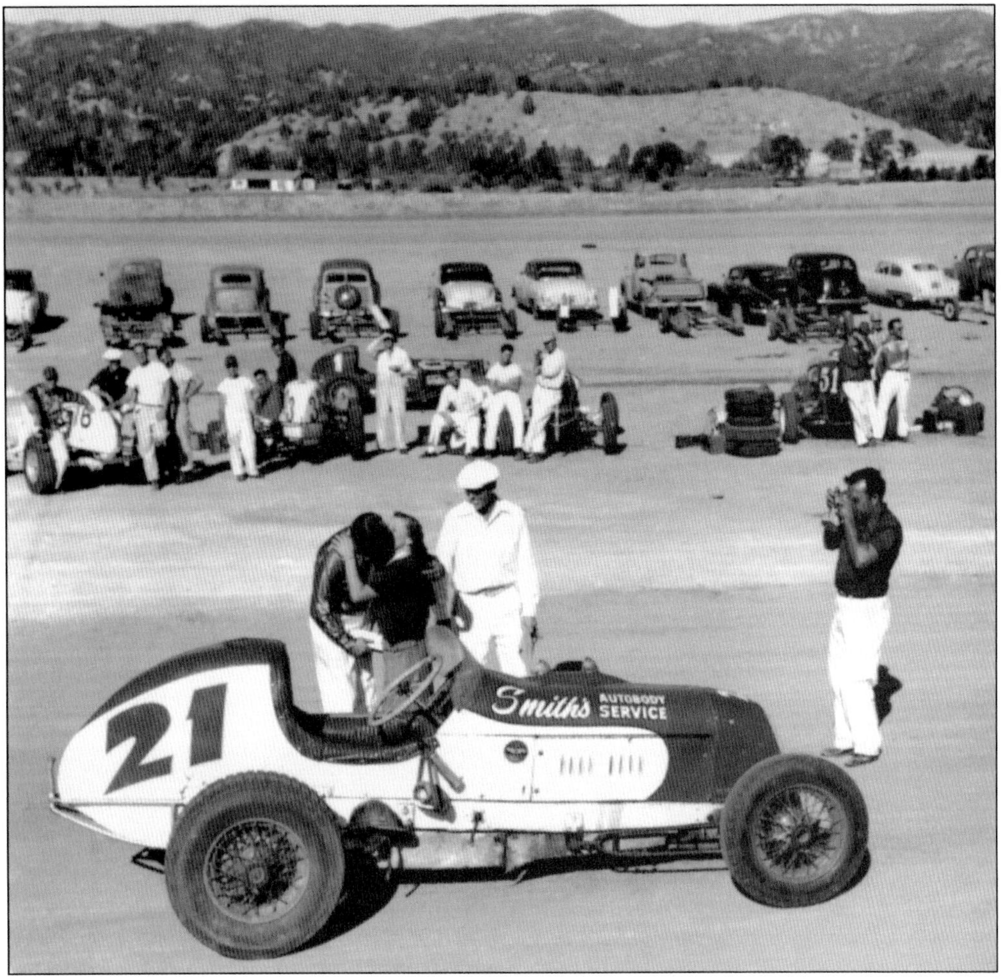

Obviously, Smith's Autobody was the bigger winner in this race, as was the driver who received the traditional reward. (Courtesy of Joyce Rabellino.)

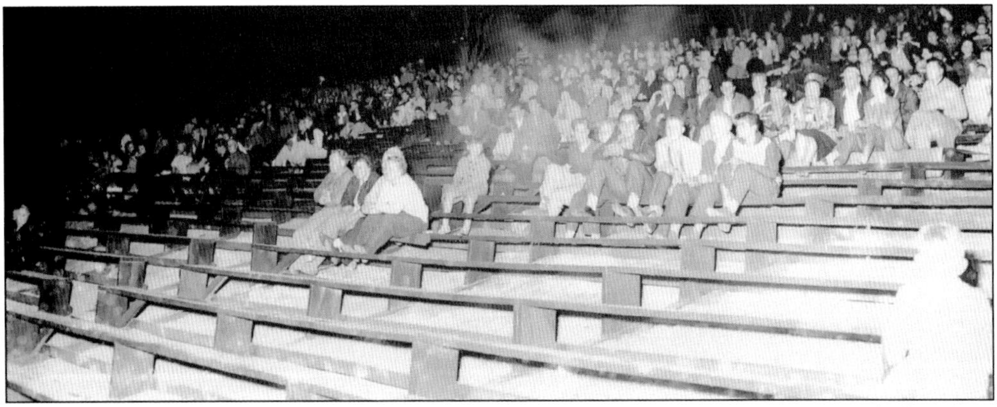

Spectators watched from wooden bleachers set into a hillside. (Courtesy of Joyce Rabellino.)

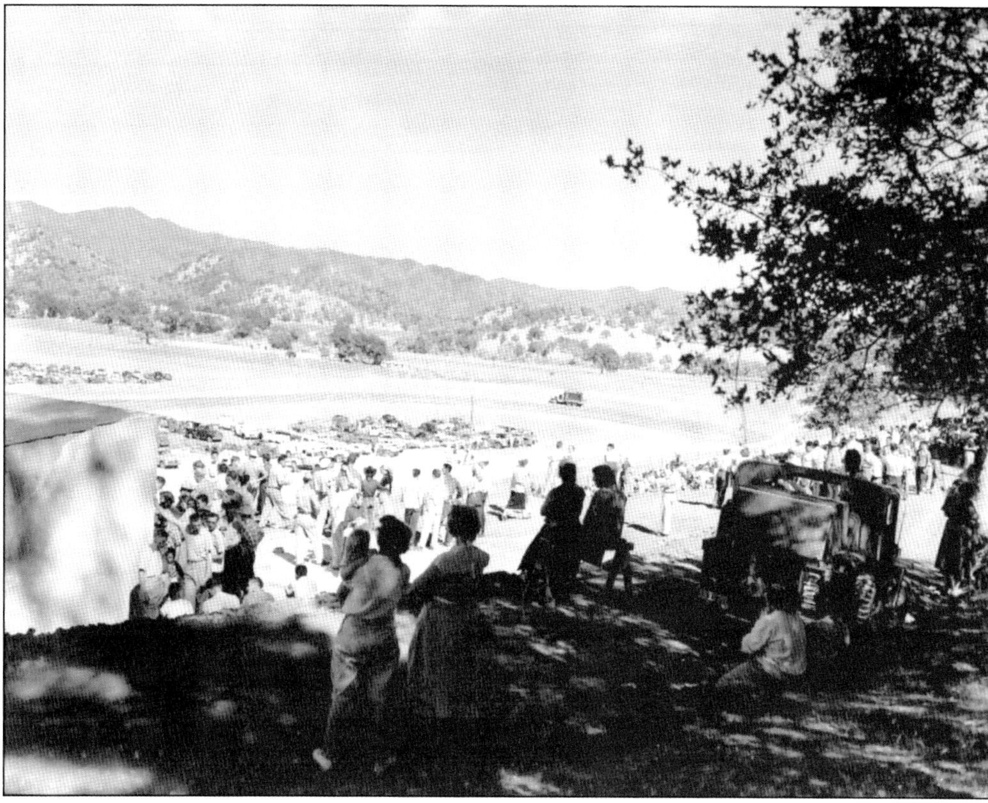

Race fans assembled in the afternoon as the quarter-mile track was prepared for the festivities. (Courtesy of Joyce Rabellino.)

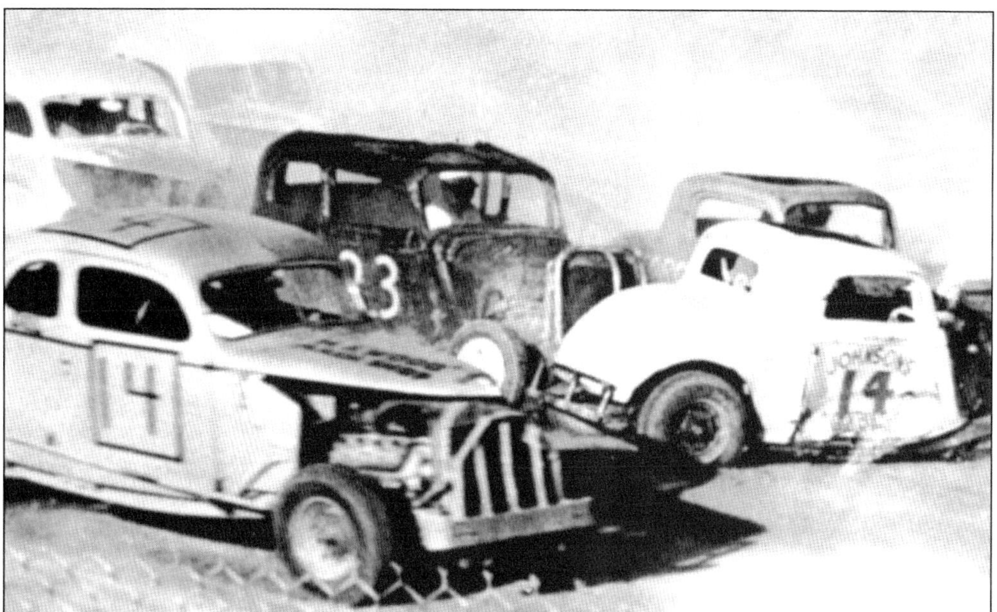

It was not always about speed. Demolition derbies called for steely nerves and durable cars. (Courtesy of Joyce Rabellino.)

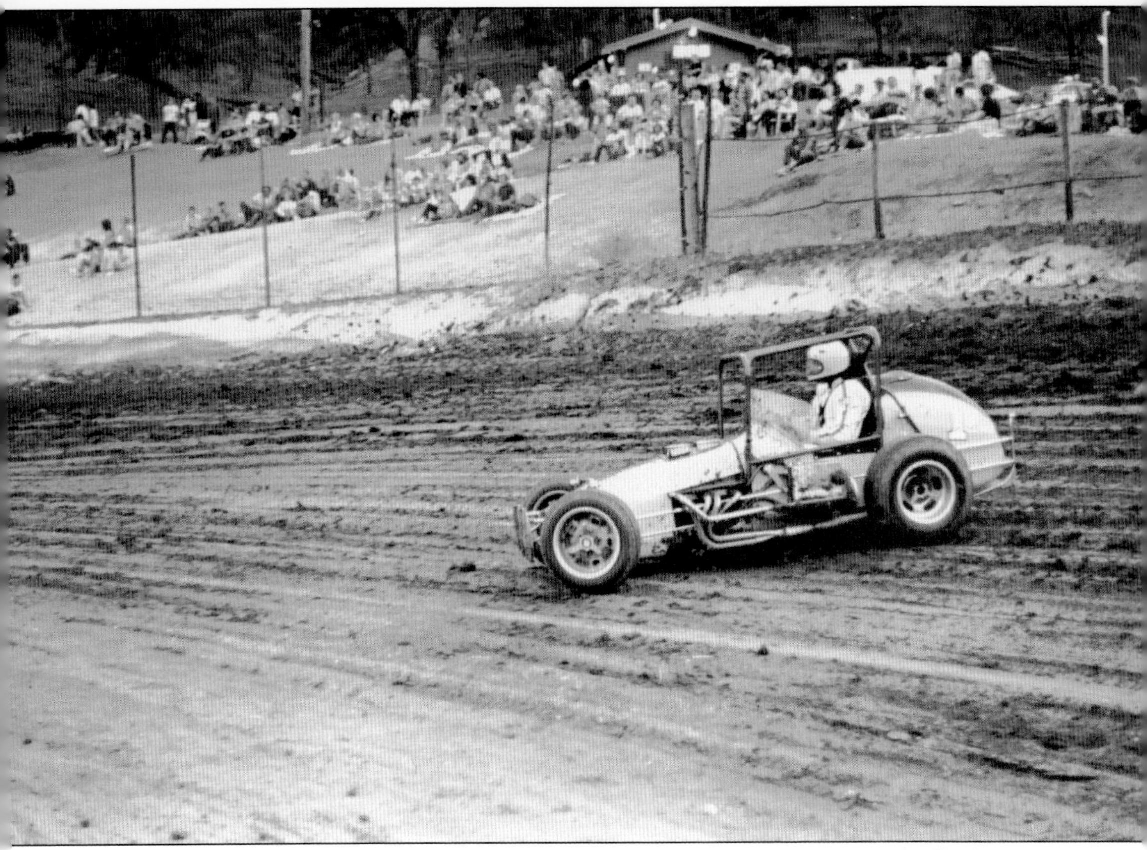

Seating for the speedway races was far from luxurious. Need shade? Bring an umbrella. (Courtesy of Joyce Rabellino.)

Ten

The Man, the Colony, the Vision

It becomes obvious when collecting and arranging materials for a book such as this that, in the end, only a taste of the community can be offered. Every page researched and every picture located screams out to be included. That, of course, is impossible. Therefore, the vision of Atascadero's history presented here is narrow at best, but several themes deserving recognition emerge.

First, it is impossible to tell the story of Atascadero without telling the story of its founder, E.G. Lewis. Lewis obviously was a man of immense energy and creativity. He was also incredibly optimistic and charismatic. He made and lost fortunes built on the trust and money of investors large and small from all over the country. And, while his many schemes and public relations strategies may paint him as a con man, in his passing, he left a record of grand achievements that include the development of a major publishing business, banking by mail, the founding of three cities, the construction of beautiful municipal buildings, and the forging of a road that would become a major state highway. He was an early supporter of women's rights. He was a man of soaring vision and spectacular failures, but he always picked himself up and started over again.

Second, the story of Atascadero is that of a city that was well planned before it was built. Designed for the automobile and with power, water, and sewer systems created by experts in every field, Atascadero was no Potemkin village designed to dupe potential landowners.

Third, the story of Atascadero is inextricably linked to the automobile, a fact that has sometimes profited and other times impeded the community's development. From the earliest tin lizzies that chugged into town on El Camino Real, to the failure of the Doble Steam Car Company, to the division of the city by US Highway 101, to the roaring of the engines at the old Atascadero Speedway, Atascadero and automobiles have had a love affair for nearly a century.

The city of Atascadero is again blossoming in the 21st century, and citizens work to remain true to E.G. Lewis's vision while addressing the unique challenges ahead. They will do well to remember Lewis's example of vision, persistence, and optimism: "Let us keep our faces to the sunshine and we will not see the shadows."

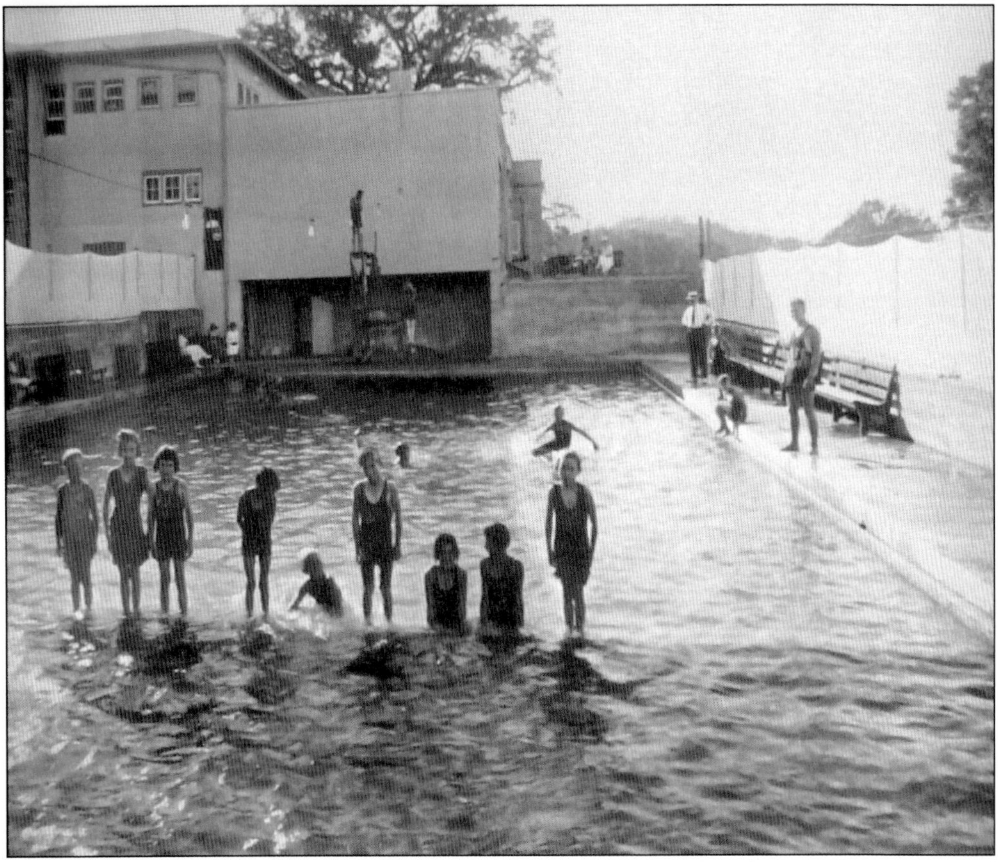

Over the years, thousands of Atascadero kids learned to swim in the Plunge, a swimming pool behind what would become the ABC Church. The pool has long since been filled in, but just about everyone who lived in that era will share stories about summers at the Plunge. (Courtesy of Atascadero Historical Society.)

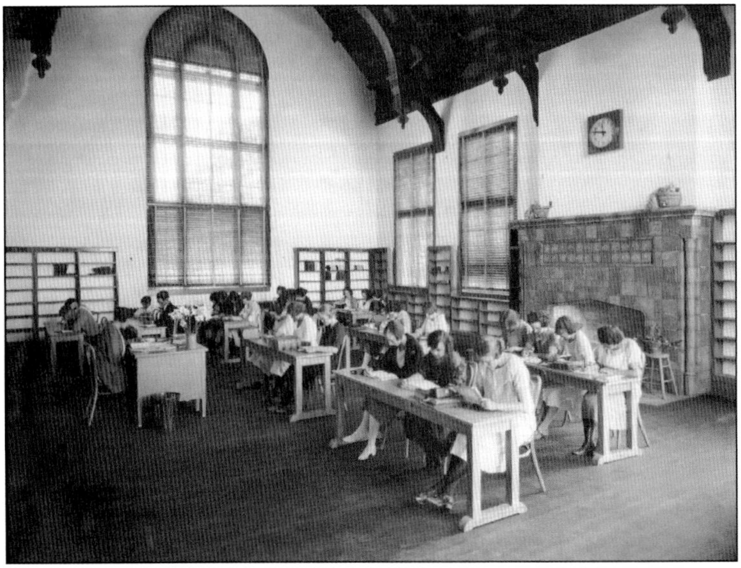

Atascadero High School, originally Margarita Black Union High School, is set on a hill to the west of downtown Atascadero. This is a photograph of the school's library. (Courtesy of Atascadero Historical Society.)

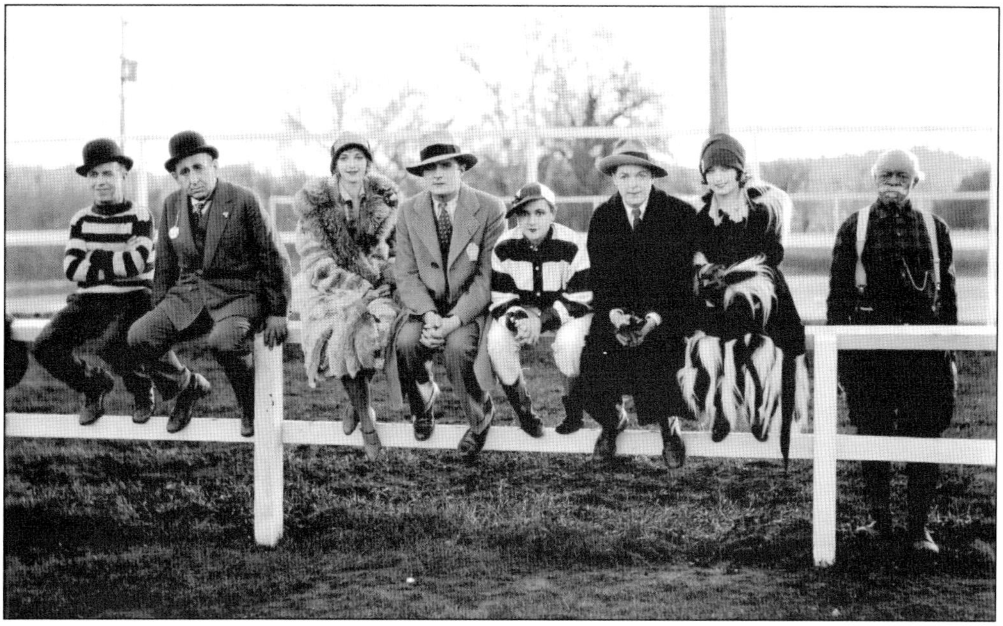

These are cast members of the silent film *Better Days*, which was filmed in and around Atascadero. The *Cinema News and Property Gazette* describes the story as "a prodigal son's descent down the easy path of show life, living on unredeemed pledges and the occasional grants from his impoverished mother, who is finally forced into the workhouse. In the palmy days, the family owned a racehorse whose name gives the title to the picture, and they run [sic] it with happy results in a race for old timers. Meanwhile, a girl who is in the mother's ward enters into a romance with the son's friend, a better specimen than the son himself." The film starred Dorothy Devore, Mary Carr, Gareth Hughes, Gaston Glass, Jay Hunt, Reata Hoyt, Jimmy Aubrey, Sidney M. Goldin, George Ovey, Arthur Hotaling, Bill Bletcher, and Sam Sidman. The film was produced by Pacific Pictures and distributed by First Division Pictures, Inc. (Both, courtesy of Kent Kenney Archives.)

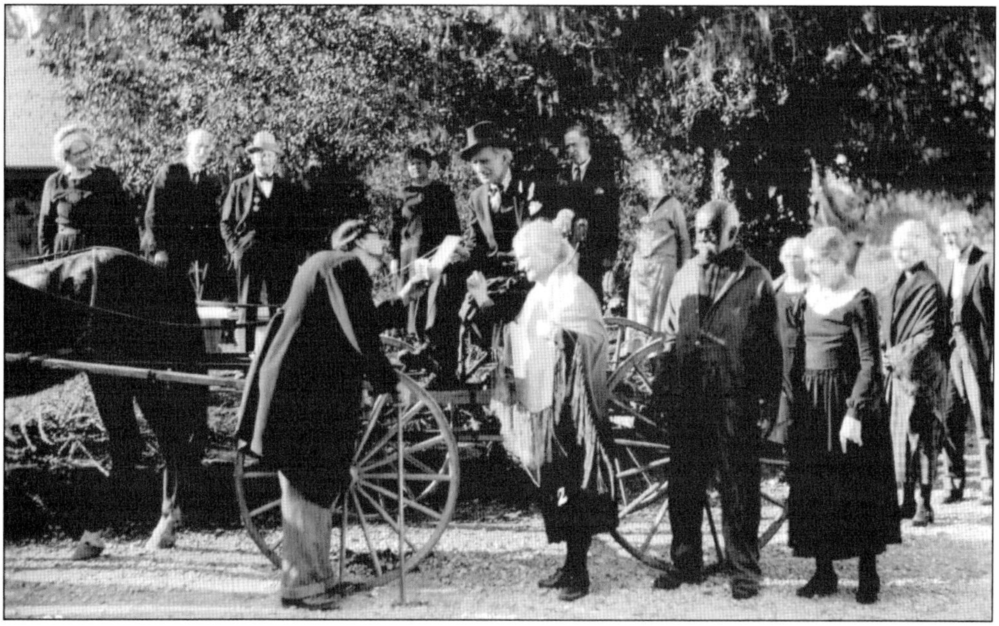

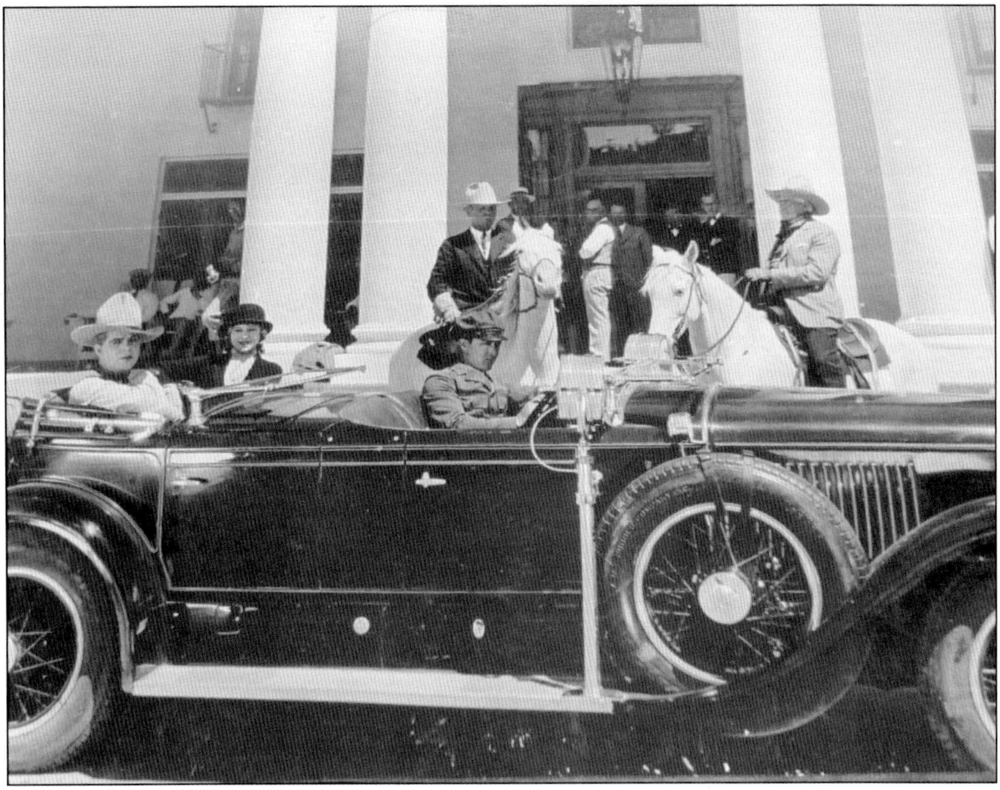

Famous movie star Hoot Gibson (seated in the rear) visits the Atascadero Inn. His father is riding the white horse on the right in the background. (Courtesy of Atascadero Historical Society.)

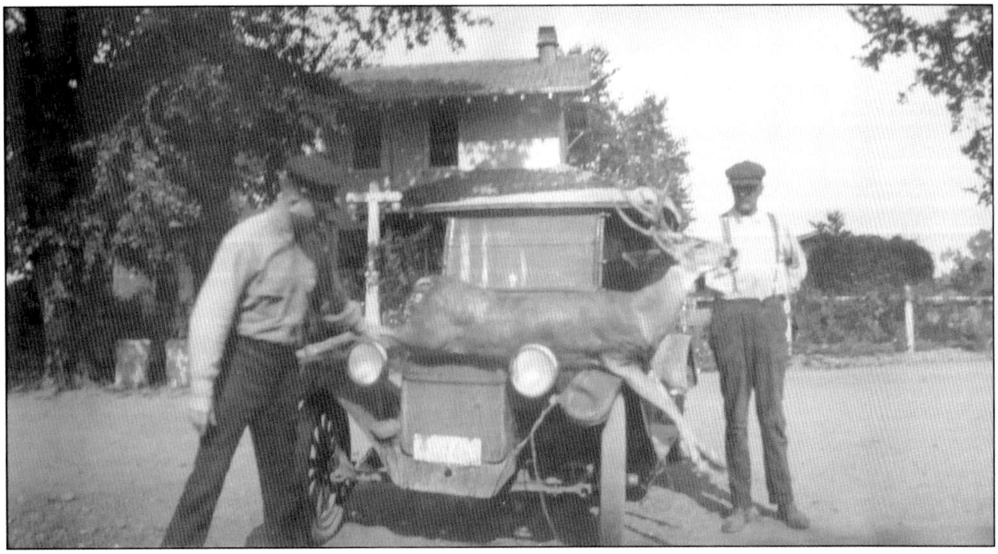

Urban amenities may have been part of the promise of Atascadero, but the community was essentially rural in nature. Wild game was plentiful. Even today, one of the joys of living in Atascadero is watching deer and wild turkeys wander down from the hillsides. (Courtesy of Kent Kenney Archives.)

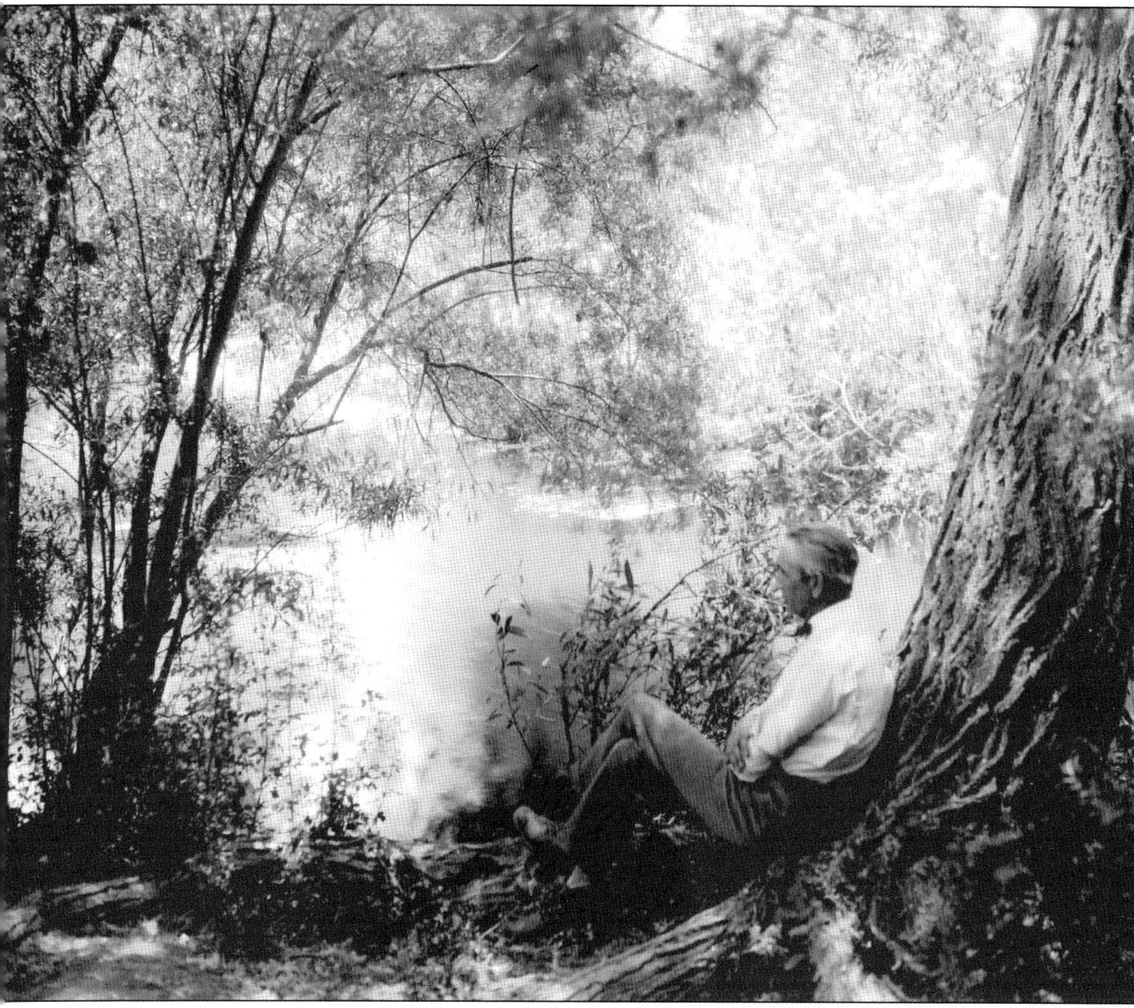

An Atascadero resident enjoys the cool stillness of Atascadero Creek. (Courtesy of Kent Kenney Archives.)